ぴよ

pyo

Other titles available from Broccoli Books

Di Gi Charat Theater – Dejiko's Summer Vacation
Join Dejiko and the gang as they hit the beach, switch bodies, blow up the Black Gema Gema Gang, and discover the secret of Hokke Mirin and her cat corp!
Story & Art by Koge-Donbo and others
Suggested Retail Price: $9.99

Di Gi Charat Theater – Dejiko's Adventure (Spring 2004)
Dejiko's done it again. With her Laser Eye Beam, Dejiko destroys the Gamers store! Now it's up to Dejiko, Puchiko, and Rabi~en~Rose to find the "secret treasure" that will bring prosperity to Gamers and rebuild the store!!
Story & Art by Yuki Kiriga
Suggested Retail Price: $9.99
Volumes 1-3 Coming Soon!

Di Gi Charat Theater – Leave it to Piyoko! (Summer 2004)
Follow the daily adventures of the Black Gema Gema Gang, as they continue their road to evil.
Story & Art by Hina.
Suggested Retail Price: $9.99
Volumes 1-2 Coming Soon!

Galaxy Angel (Spring 2004)
It's up to five female pilots, each possessing a unique talent, to protect young Prince Shiva and save the universe!
Story & Art by Kanan
Suggested Retail Price: $9.99

Aquarian Age – Juvenile Orion (January 2004)
Sixteen-year-old Mana returns to her hometown and reunites with her childhood friend after 7 years. But Kaname seems to have changed during their years apart. They soon discover that they are part of the Aquarian Age—a secret war raging for thousands of years—and Mana just might hold the key to end it!
Story & Art by Sakurako Gokurakuin
Suggested Retail Price: $9.99

Piyoko is Number One!

by Koge-Donbo and others

brought to you by
BROCCOLI BOOKS
A DIVISION OF BROCCOLI INTERNATIONAL USA

Di Gi Charat™ Theater - Piyoko is Number One!

English Adaptation Staff
Translation: Ken "KJ1980" Wakita
English Adaptation: Stephanie Sheh
Touch-Up, Lettering, and Graphic Design: Fawn "tails" Lau
Cover & Design Supervision: Chris McDougall

Editor: Satsuki Yamashita
Sales Manager: Ardith D. Santiago
Managing Editor: Shizuki Yamashita
Publisher: Hideki Uchino

Email: editor@broccolibooks.com
Website: www.broccolibooks.com

All illustrations by Koge-Donbo with the exception of:
pg. 15, 102 Majin Gappa by Clim; pg 103 Takaaki Kidani by Miki Yokoyama

A BROCCOLI BOOKS Manga
Broccoli Books is a division of Broccoli International USA, Inc.
12211 W. Washington Blvd, Suite 110, Los Angeles CA 90066

Japanese Edition Staff
Editor: Hitomi Koshiki, Iwao Yanagisawa, Yuki Mikawa, Takuto Hanai
Publisher: Takaaki Kidani

ISBN: 1-932480-08-0

Published by Broccoli International USA, Inc.
First printing, November 2003

ANIME GAMERS
www.animegamers.com

BROCCOLI INTERNATIONAL USA

10 9 8 7 6 5 4 3 2 1
Printed in the United States

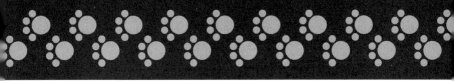

Table of Contents

DI GI CHARAT
T H E A T E R
Piyoko is Number One!

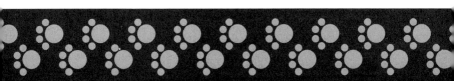

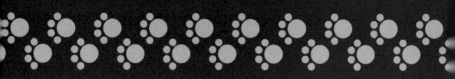

Table of Contents

Synopsis

The Black Gema Gema Gang are from Planet Analogue, and due to their poor resources they have been trying to conquer Planet Di Gi Charat for years. Finding out that the princess of Planet Di Gi Charat, Dejiko, went to Earth, they quickly follow suit to kidnap her and hold her for ransom to support their home planet. Piyoko is the leader of the Black Gema Gema Gang, and Rik, Ky, and Coo work under her loyally and lovingly. However, Piyoko's plans always seem to backfire, and the goal of a prosperous planet is far away…

About Di Gi Charat

Dejiko was created in 1998 as the official mascot character for the popular anime/game store Gamers in Japan. When Gamers decided to create a commercial featuring Dejiko and her friends, a television network producer saw it and suggested that they make an anime out of it. And thus, the TV anime series *Di Gi Charat* was created. The popularity of the show then led to creating a whole line of merchandise, including figures, trading cards, books, and CDs.

Pyocola (Piyoko)

Piyoko is the head of the evil organization known as the Black Gema Gema Gang. She came after Dejiko to kidnap and hold her ransom to raise money for Planet Analogue. But her gullible personality allows Dejiko to trick her one way or the other, and she never succeeds in capturing Dejiko. Piyoko pursues a road of evil, but she is actually kind-hearted and loving toward her subjects. Her dialect back at home makes her end her sentences with a "pyo."

Real name: Pyocola Analogue III
Alias: Piyoko
Hometown: Planet Analogue
Height: 4' 6"
Weight: Secret
Birthday: October 23 (Libra)
Age: 8
Blood type: AB
Favorite food: Crème-filled cookies
Special move: Upchuck Bazooka
Remarks: Calls Dejiko "Oneechan," which means "big sister," but no relation

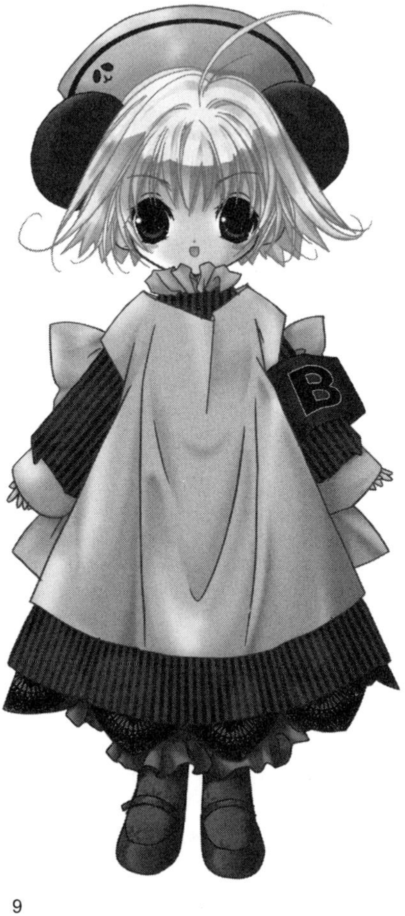
B

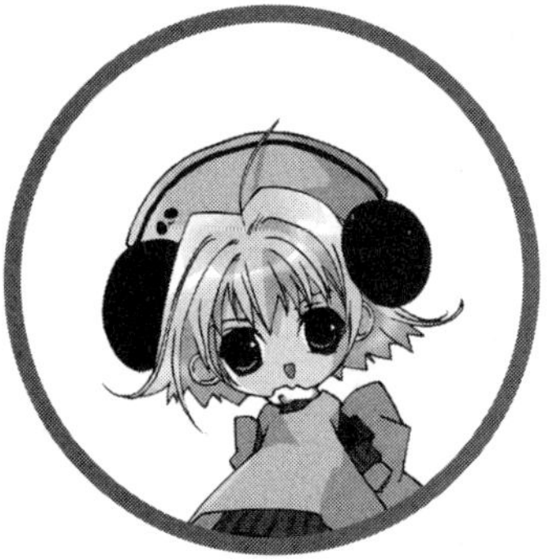

Coo Erhard

Coo is the Major of the Black Gema Gema Gang. He is part of the Pyocola Keeping Operations, also known as PKO. He knows Piyoko from childhood, and thinks of her like a little sister. Thus, he is closest to Piyoko among the PKO. He treasures a stuffed panda. He is Piyoko's personal doctor.

Real Name: Coo Erhard
Height: 5' 1"
Weight: 110 lbs.
Birthday: May 5 (Taurus)
Age: 13
Blood type: O
Favorite food: Mochi (rice cake), Natto (fermented soy beans)
Remarks: Physician

Ky Schweitzer

Ky is the Lieutenant General of the Black Gema Gema Gang, and also part of PKO. He has a strong sense of responsibility. He is Piyoko's personal dentist, and is in charge of checking Piyoko's dental hygiene everyday.

Real name: Ky Schweitzer
Height: 5' 6"
Weight: 123 lbs.
Birthday: March 3 (Pisces)
Age: 17
Blood type: A
Favorite food: Mild curry rice
Remarks: Dentist

Rik Heisenberg

Rik is the General of the Black Gema Gema Gang, and also part of PKO. He is calm and blunt; he easily comes up with cruel things to say. He is a Veterinarian, and thus loves animals of all kinds.

Real Name: Rik Heisenberg
Height: 6' 3"
Weight: 187 lbs.
Birthday: April 4 (Aries)
Age: 26
Blood type: AB
Favorite food: Sushi, fried noodles
Remarks: Veterinarian

Name: Black Gema Gema
Gang Member
Age: Various
Birthday: Various
Blood Type: Various
Favorite Food: Piyoko's
Black Beans
Special Skills: Cheering for
Piyoko
Personality: Noisy
Remarks: They add "geba"
to the end of their sentences.

Name: Nazo Gema
Age: ?
Birthday: ?
Blood Type: ?
Favorite Food: ?
Special Skills: ?
Personality: Quiet

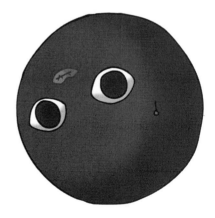

Di Gi Charat (Dejiko)

Dejiko is the princess of Planet Di Gi Charat, and comes to Earth to study and become a star. Contrary to her cute appearance, she is self-centered and evil, and often plots against Rabi~en~Rose and Piyoko. Her dialect back at home makes her sentences end with a "nyo."

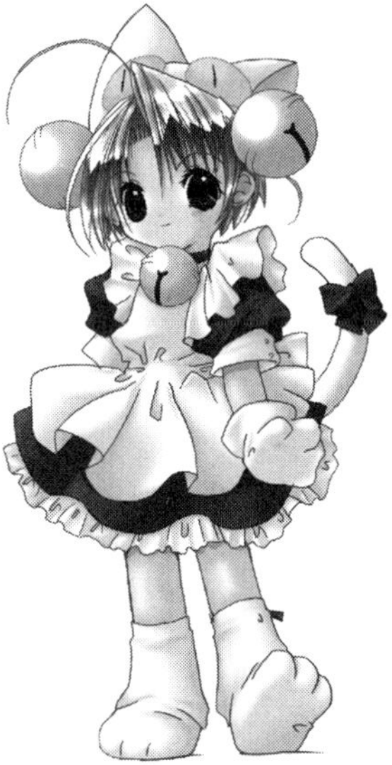

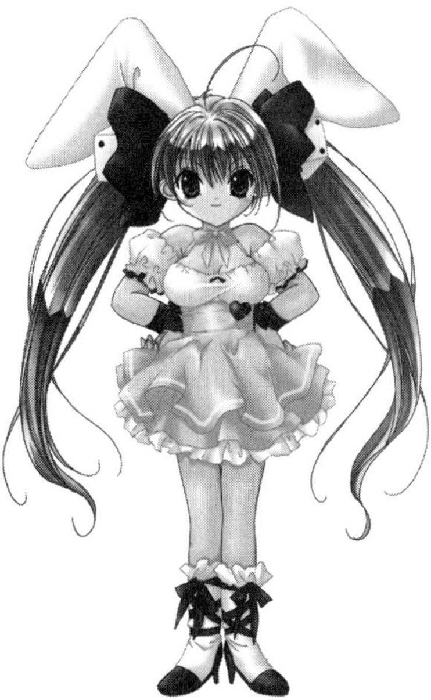

Rabi~en~Rose (Usada)

Rabi~en~Rose is a normal human being, and has been working for Gamers before Dejiko joined. She often competes with Dejiko for the number one clerk position. Her real name is Hikaru Usada, but hates it when people refer to her as Usada.

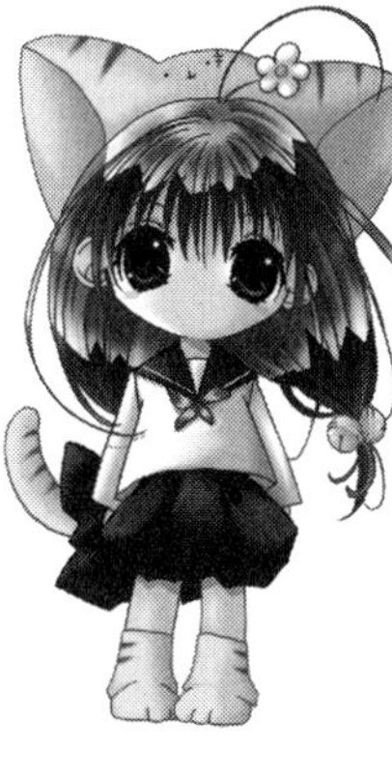

Petit Charat (Puchiko)

Puchiko has been with Dejiko ever since Dejiko saved her when she was stuck down a hole. Although she is quiet for most of the time, when she speaks she is really sharp-tongued. She ends her sentences with a "nyu."

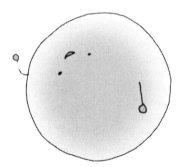

Gema

Gema is Dejiko's unidentified flying caretaker. His duty is to stop Dejiko's reckless behavior, but for a lack of any special moves, he gets beaten up in return. He has a habit of adding "gema" to the end of his sentences.

Hokke Mirin

Hokke Mirin has been with Puchiko ever since she was found abandoned on a rainy day. She is very good at walking sideways. She recently gave birth to five kittens "Sa," "Shi," "Su," "Se," and "So."

Majin Gappa

Majin Gappa is Rabi~en~Rose's secret weapon against Dejiko. But actually, he is just a kappa. Sometimes appears in multiple quantities to support Usada.

PYOCOLA-SAMA IS NUMBER ONE!!

Koge-Donbo

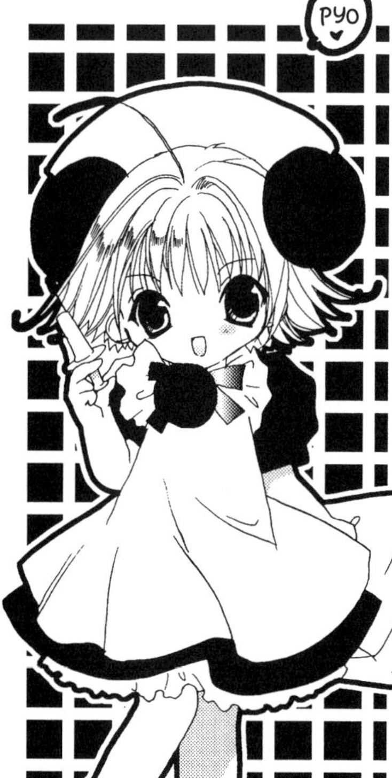
PYO

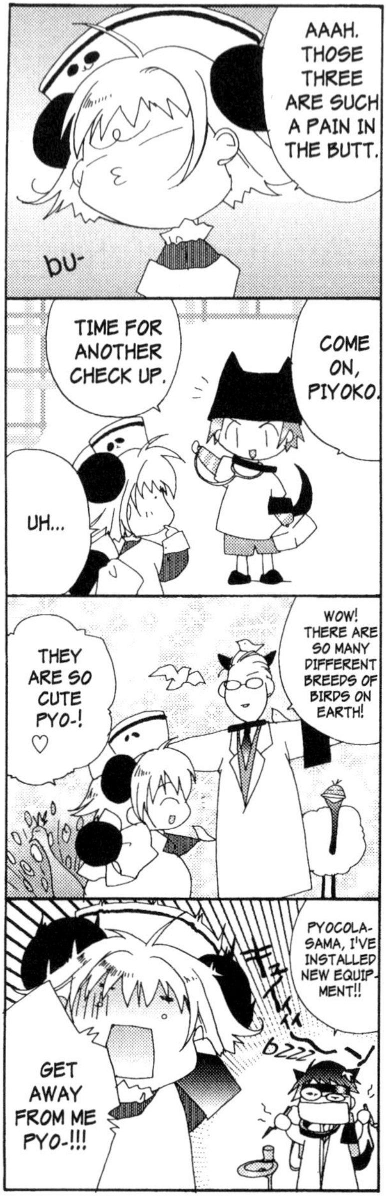
AAAH. THOSE THREE ARE SUCH A PAIN IN THE BUTT.
BU-
COME ON, PIYOKO.
TIME FOR ANOTHER CHECK UP.
UH...
WOW! THERE ARE SO MANY DIFFERENT BREEDS OF BIRDS ON EARTH!
THEY ARE SO CUTE PYO-! ♡
PYOCOLA-SAMA, I'VE INSTALLED NEW EQUIPMENT!!
BZZZ
GET AWAY FROM ME PYO-!!!

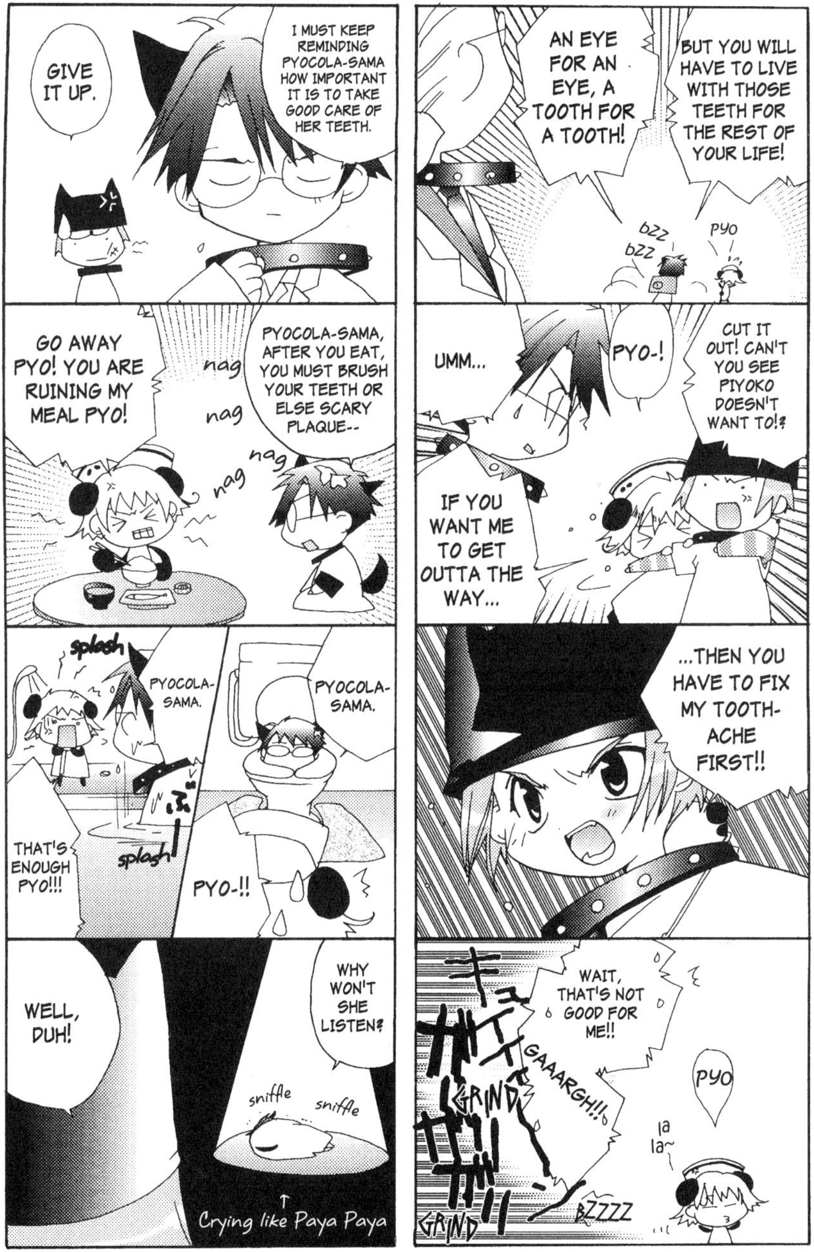
BUT YOU WILL HAVE TO LIVE WITH THOSE TEETH FOR THE REST OF YOUR LIFE!
AN EYE FOR AN EYE, A TOOTH FOR A TOOTH!
PYO
bzz bzz
CUT IT OUT! CAN'T YOU SEE PIYOKO DOESN'T WANT TO!?
PYO-!
UMM...
IF YOU WANT ME TO GET OUTTA THE WAY...
...THEN YOU HAVE TO FIX MY TOOTH-ACHE FIRST!!
PYO
WAIT, THAT'S NOT GOOD FOR ME!!
la la~
GAAARGH!!!
GRIND
BZZZZ
GRIND
I MUST KEEP REMINDING PYOCOLA-SAMA HOW IMPORTANT IT IS TO TAKE GOOD CARE OF HER TEETH.
GIVE IT UP.
PYOCOLA-SAMA, AFTER YOU EAT, YOU MUST BRUSH YOUR TEETH OR ELSE SCARY PLAQUE--
nag nag nag nag
GO AWAY PYO! YOU ARE RUINING MY MEAL PYO!
PYOCOLA-SAMA.
PYO-!!
splash
PYOCOLA-SAMA.
THAT'S ENOUGH PYO!!!
splash
WHY WON'T SHE LISTEN?
WELL, DUH!
sniffle sniffle
Crying like Paya Paya

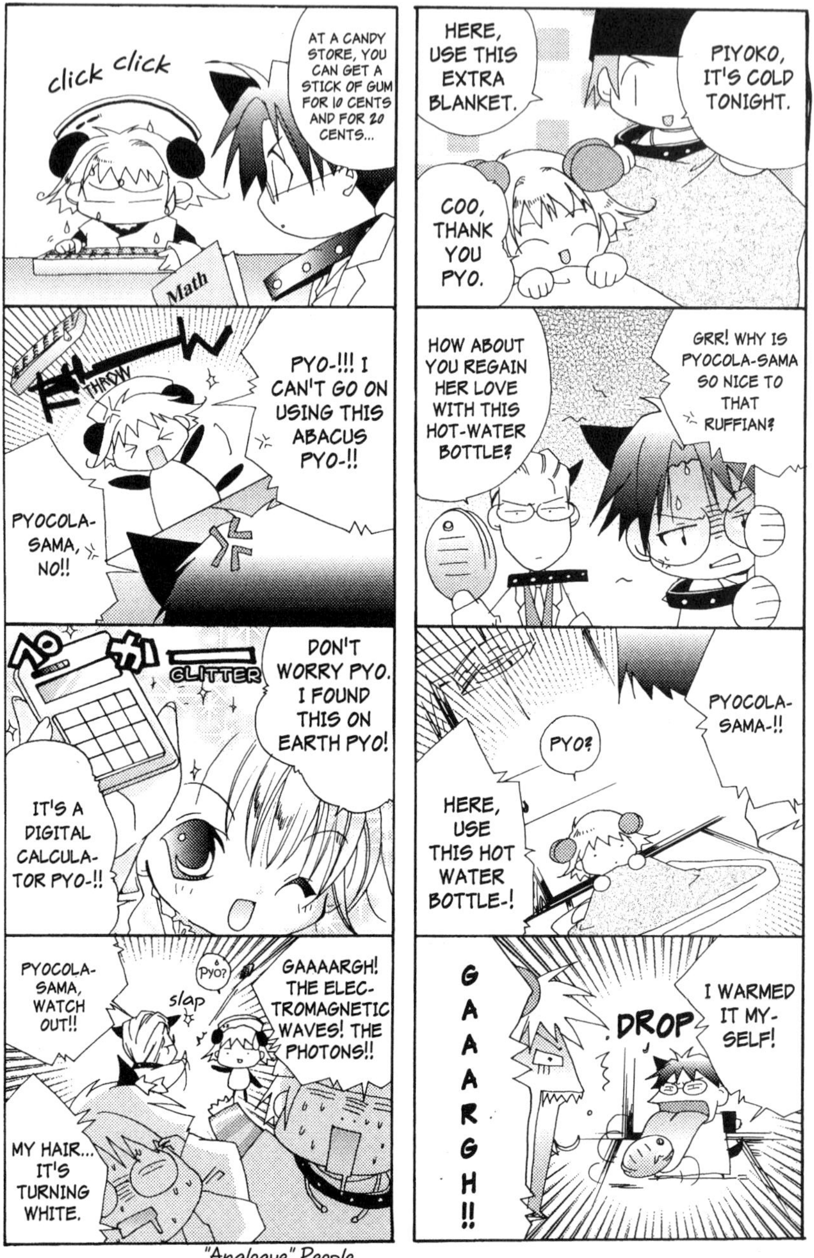
PIYOKO, IT'S COLD TONIGHT.
HERE, USE THIS EXTRA BLANKET.
COO, THANK YOU PYO.
GRR! WHY IS PYOCOLA-SAMA SO NICE TO THAT RUFFIAN?
HOW ABOUT YOU REGAIN HER LOVE WITH THIS HOT-WATER BOTTLE?
PYOCOLA-SAMA-!!
PYO?
HERE, USE THIS HOT WATER BOTTLE-!
I WARMED IT MY-SELF!
DROP
GAAARGH!!
AT A CANDY STORE, YOU CAN GET A STICK OF GUM FOR 10 CENTS AND FOR 20 CENTS...
click click
Math
PYO-!!! I CAN'T GO ON USING THIS ABACUS PYO-!!
THROW
PYOCOLA-SAMA, NO!!
DON'T WORRY PYO. I FOUND THIS ON EARTH PYO!
GLITTER
IT'S A DIGITAL CALCULATOR PYO-!!
GAAAARGH! THE ELEC-TROMAGNETIC WAVES! THE PHOTONS!!
Pyo?
slap
PYOCOLA-SAMA, WATCH OUT!!
MY HAIR... IT'S TURNING WHITE.
"Analogue" People

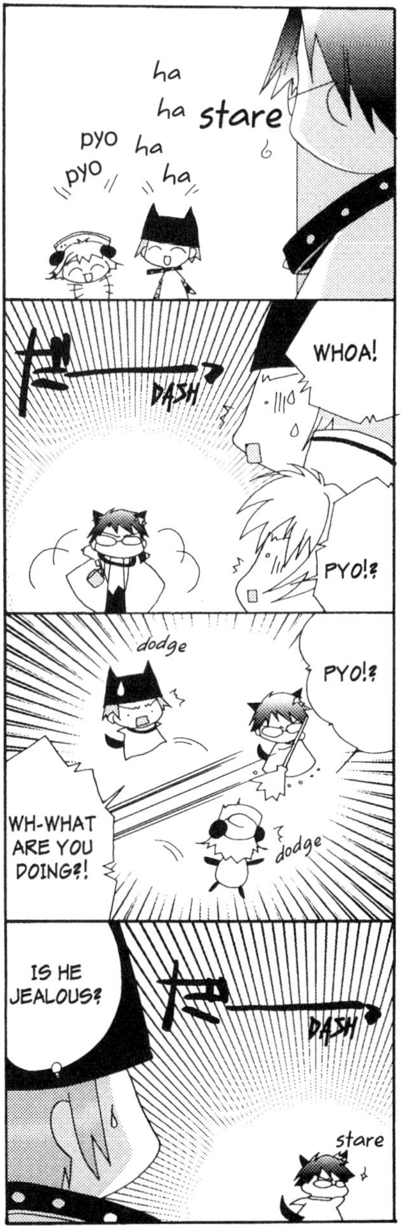
ha
ha
stare
pyo
ha
pyo
ha
WHOA!
DASH
PYO!?
dodge
PYO!?
WH-WHAT ARE YOU DOING?!
dodge
IS HE JEALOUS?
DASH
stare

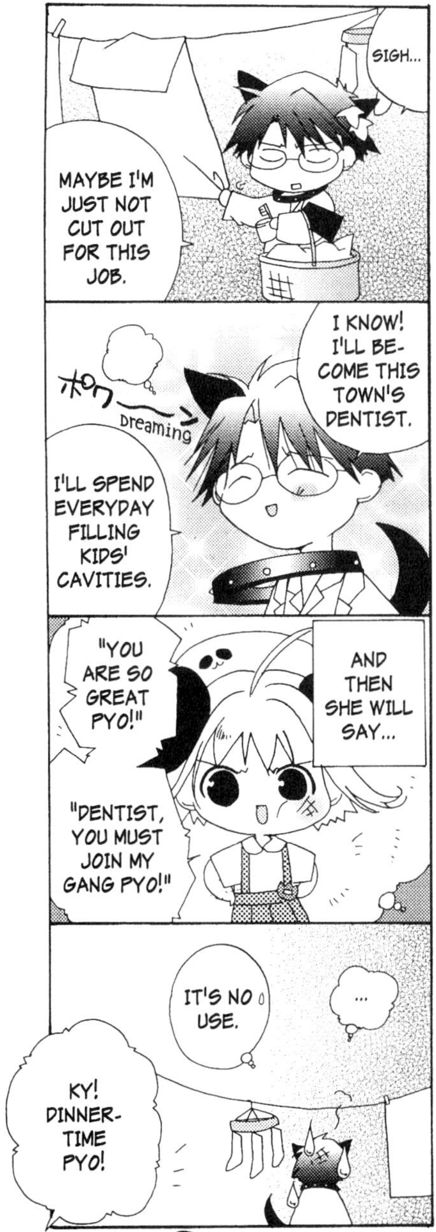
SIGH...
MAYBE I'M JUST NOT CUT OUT FOR THIS JOB.
I KNOW! I'LL BE-COME THIS TOWN'S DENTIST.
Dreaming
I'LL SPEND EVERYDAY FILLING KIDS' CAVITIES.
AND THEN SHE WILL SAY...
"YOU ARE SO GREAT PYO!"
"DENTIST, YOU MUST JOIN MY GANG PYO!"
...
IT'S NO USE.
KY! DINNER-TIME PYO!

The End

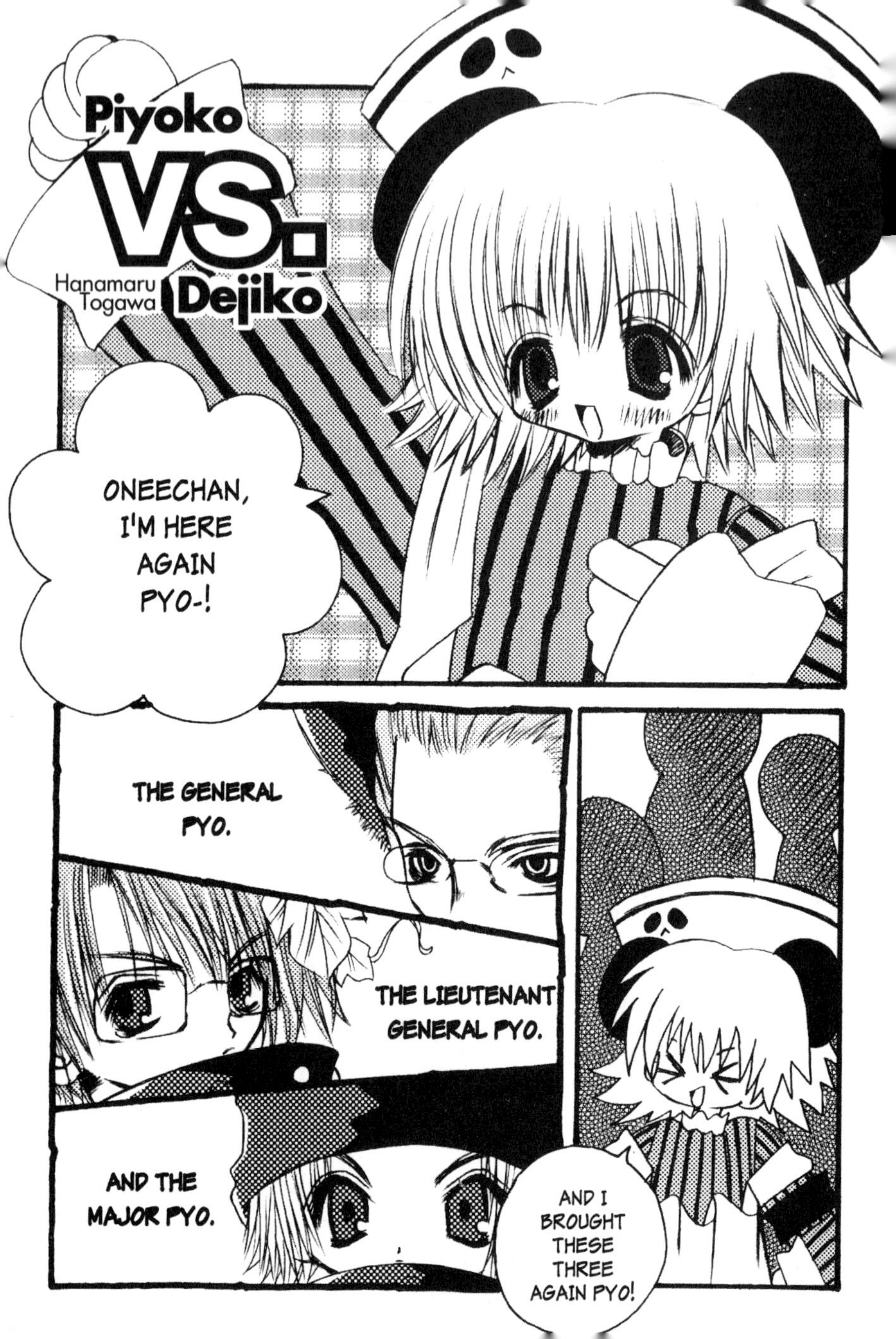
Piyoko VS. Dejiko
Hanamaru Togawa
ONEECHAN, I'M HERE AGAIN PYO-!
AND I BROUGHT THESE THREE AGAIN PYO!
THE GENERAL PYO.
THE LIEUTENANT GENERAL PYO.
AND THE MAJOR PYO.

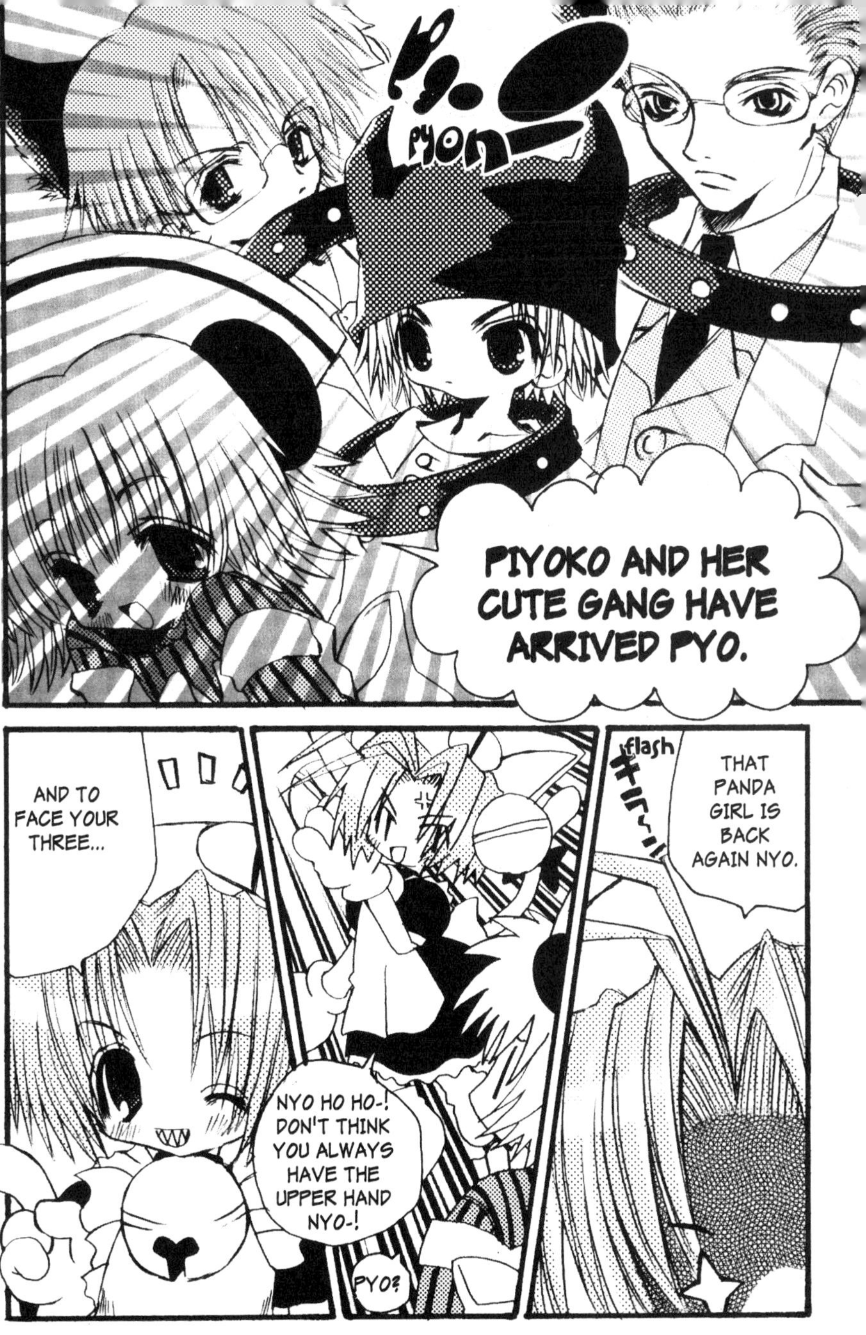
pyon
PIYOKO AND HER CUTE GANG HAVE ARRIVED PYO.
flash
THAT PANDA GIRL IS BACK AGAIN NYO.
NYO HO HO-! DON'T THINK YOU ALWAYS HAVE THE UPPER HAND NYO-!
PYO?
AND TO FACE YOUR THREE...

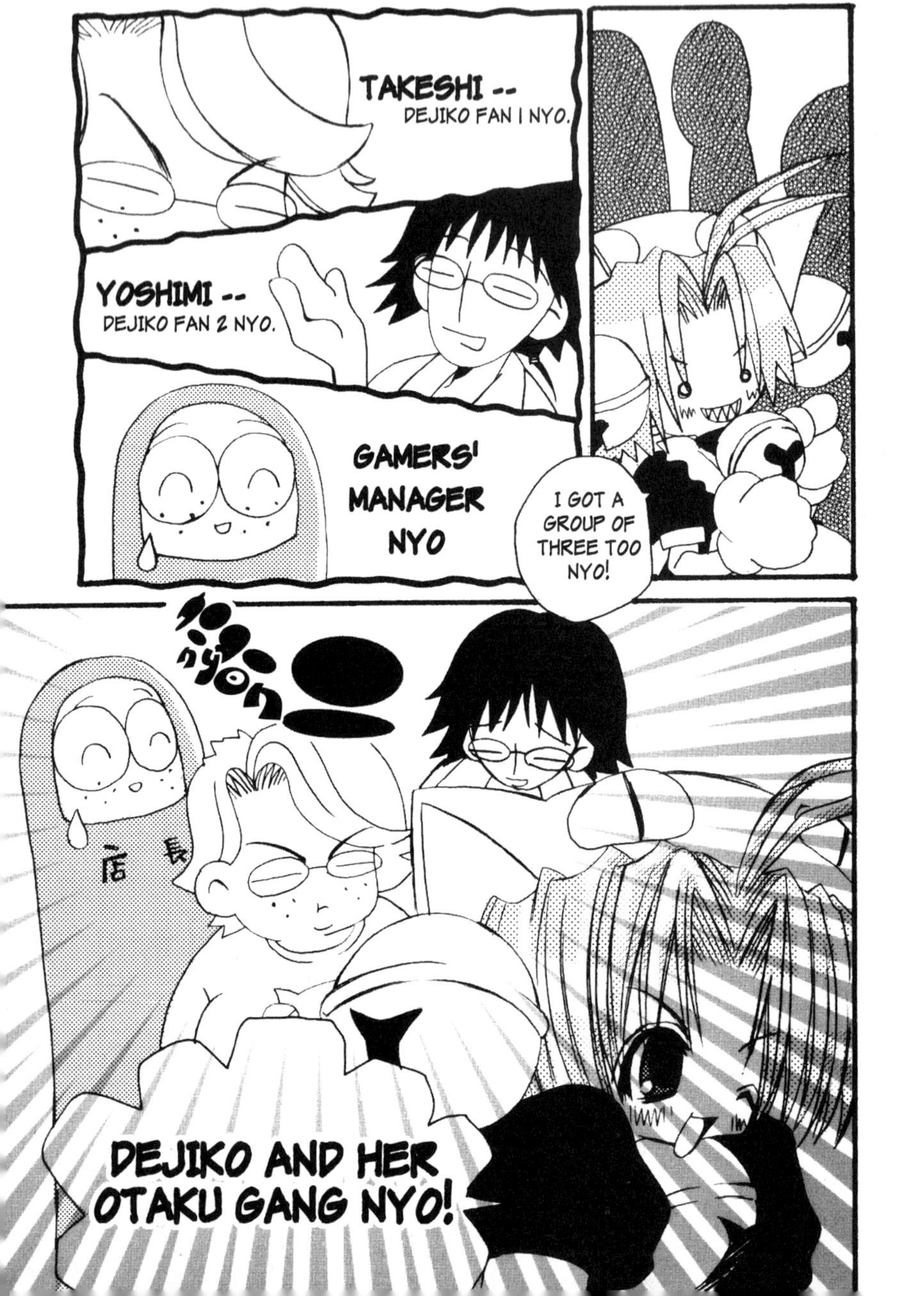
I GOT A GROUP OF THREE TOO NYO!
TAKESHI -- DEJIKO FAN 1 NYO.
YOSHIMI -- DEJIKO FAN 2 NYO.
GAMERS' MANAGER NYO
店長
DEJIKO AND HER OTAKU GANG NYO!

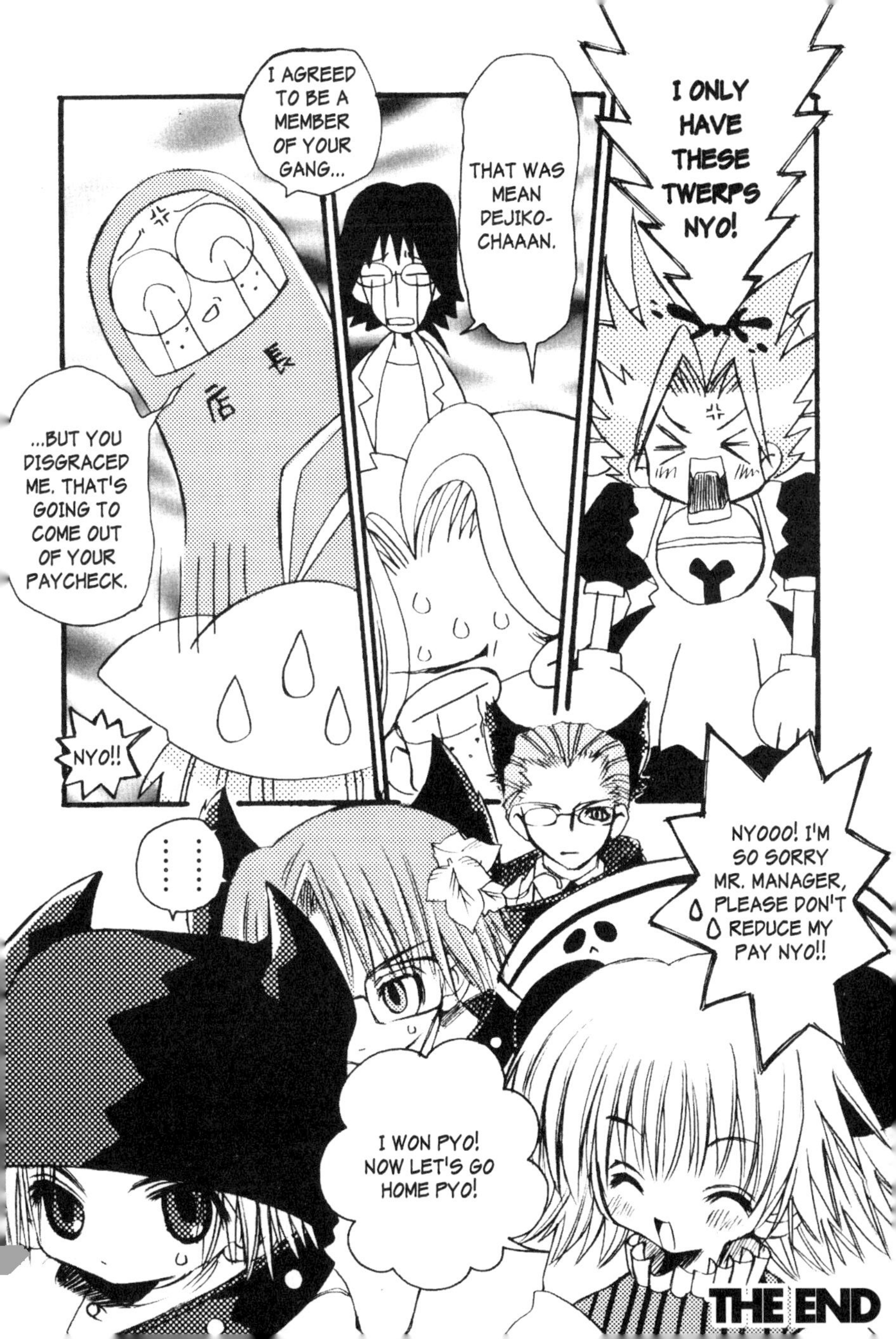
I ONLY HAVE THESE TWERPS NYO!
THAT WAS MEAN DEJIKO-CHAAAN.
I AGREED TO BE A MEMBER OF YOUR GANG...
...BUT YOU DISGRACED ME. THAT'S GOING TO COME OUT OF YOUR PAYCHECK.
NYO!!
NYOOO! I'M SO SORRY MR. MANAGER, PLEASE DON'T REDUCE MY PAY NYO!!
......
I WON PYO! NOW LET'S GO HOME PYO!
THE END

A Message to Piyoko-sama!

YOU'RE SO YOUNG, AND YET YOUR LIFE IS SO TOUGH...

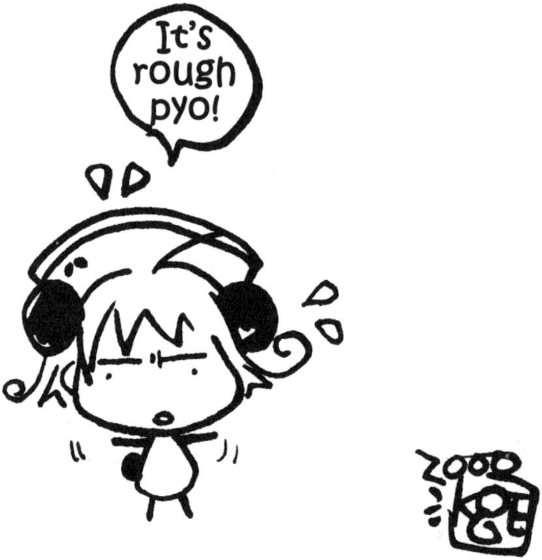
It's rough pyo!

Koge-Donbo

A Message to Piyoko-sama!

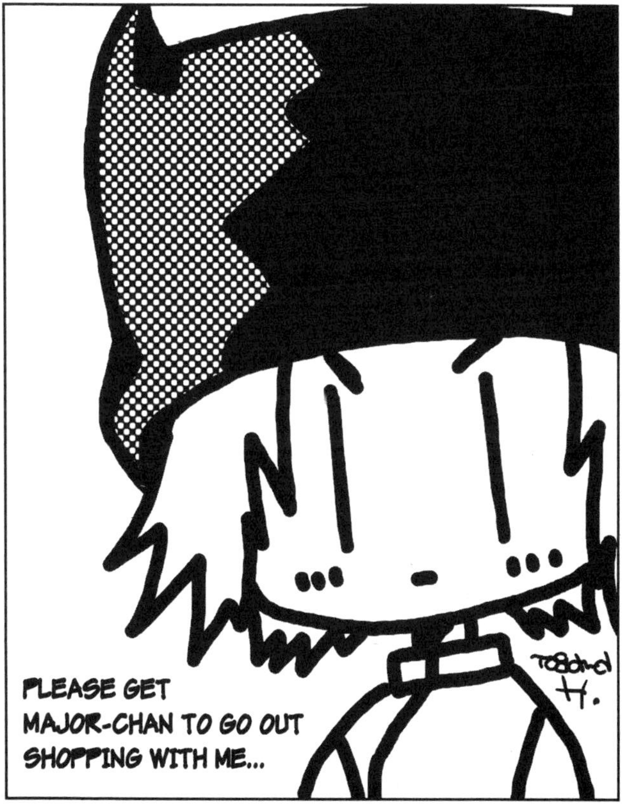
PLEASE GET MAJOR-CHAN TO GO OUT SHOPPING WITH ME...
TOGAWA H.

B Hanamaru Togawa

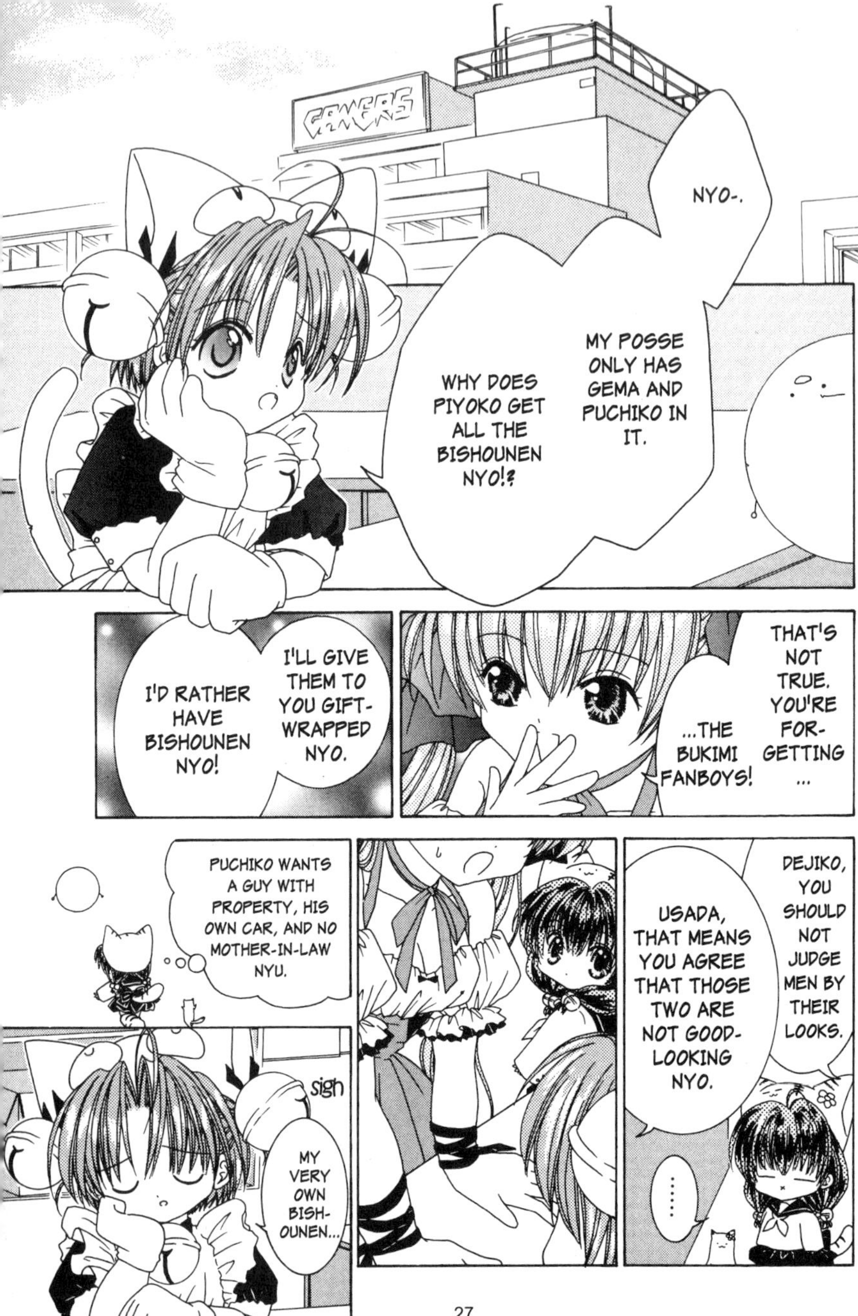

NYO-.
MY POSSE ONLY HAS GEMA AND PUCHIKO IN IT.
WHY DOES PIYOKO GET ALL THE BISHOUNEN NYO!?
THAT'S NOT TRUE. YOU'RE FOR-GETTING ...
...THE BUKIMI FANBOYS!
I'LL GIVE THEM TO YOU GIFT-WRAPPED NYO.
I'D RATHER HAVE BISHOUNEN NYO!
DEJIKO, YOU SHOULD NOT JUDGE MEN BY THEIR LOOKS.
USADA, THAT MEANS YOU AGREE THAT THOSE TWO ARE NOT GOOD-LOOKING NYO.
......
PUCHIKO WANTS A GUY WITH PROPERTY, HIS OWN CAR, AND NO MOTHER-IN-LAW NYU.
sigh
MY VERY OWN BISH-OUNEN...

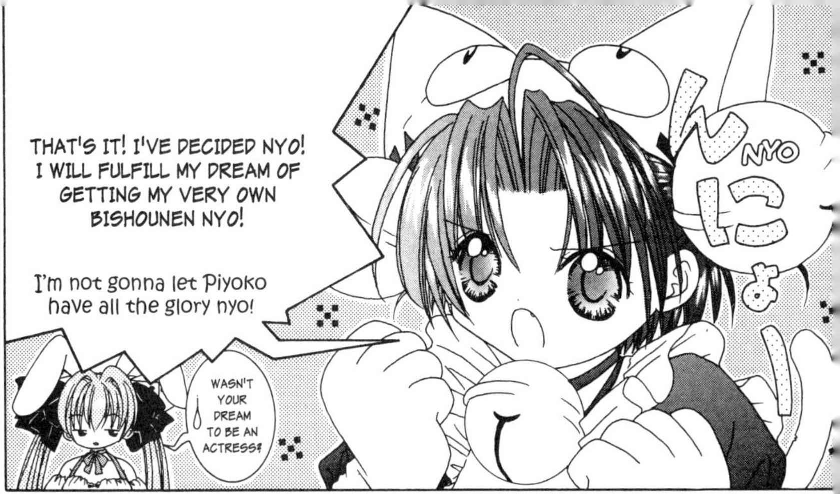
NYO
にょ
THAT'S IT! I'VE DECIDED NYO! I WILL FULFILL MY DREAM OF GETTING MY VERY OWN BISHOUNEN NYO!
I'm not gonna let Piyoko have all the glory nyo!
WASN'T YOUR DREAM TO BE AN ACTRESS?

Happy Sisters

Seara

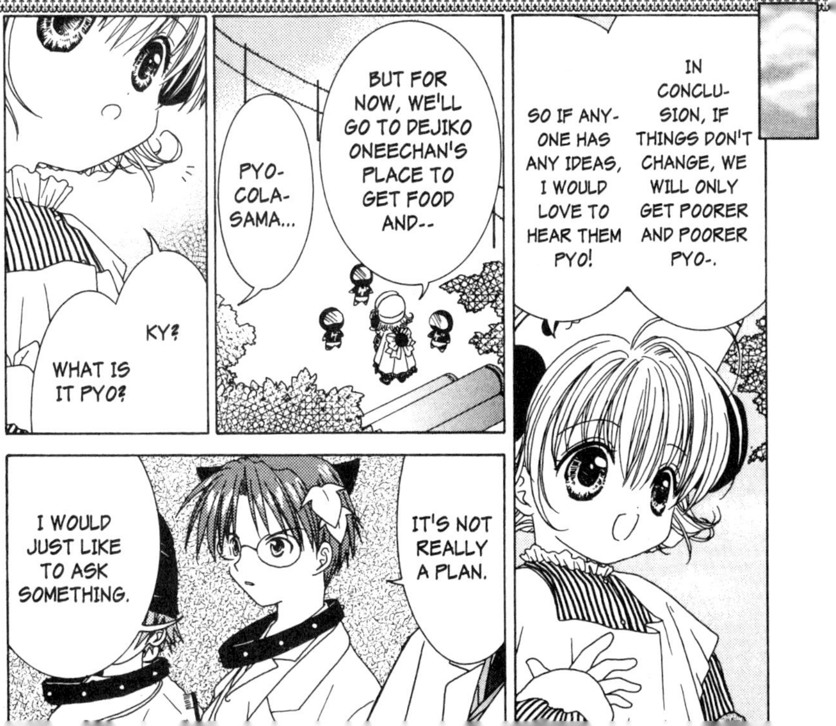
IN CONCLUSION, IF THINGS DON'T CHANGE, WE WILL ONLY GET POORER AND POORER PYO-.
SO IF ANYONE HAS ANY IDEAS, I WOULD LOVE TO HEAR THEM PYO!
BUT FOR NOW, WE'LL GO TO DEJIKO ONEECHAN'S PLACE TO GET FOOD AND--
PYO-COLA-SAMA...
KY?
WHAT IS IT PYO?
IT'S NOT REALLY A PLAN.
I WOULD JUST LIKE TO ASK SOMETHING.

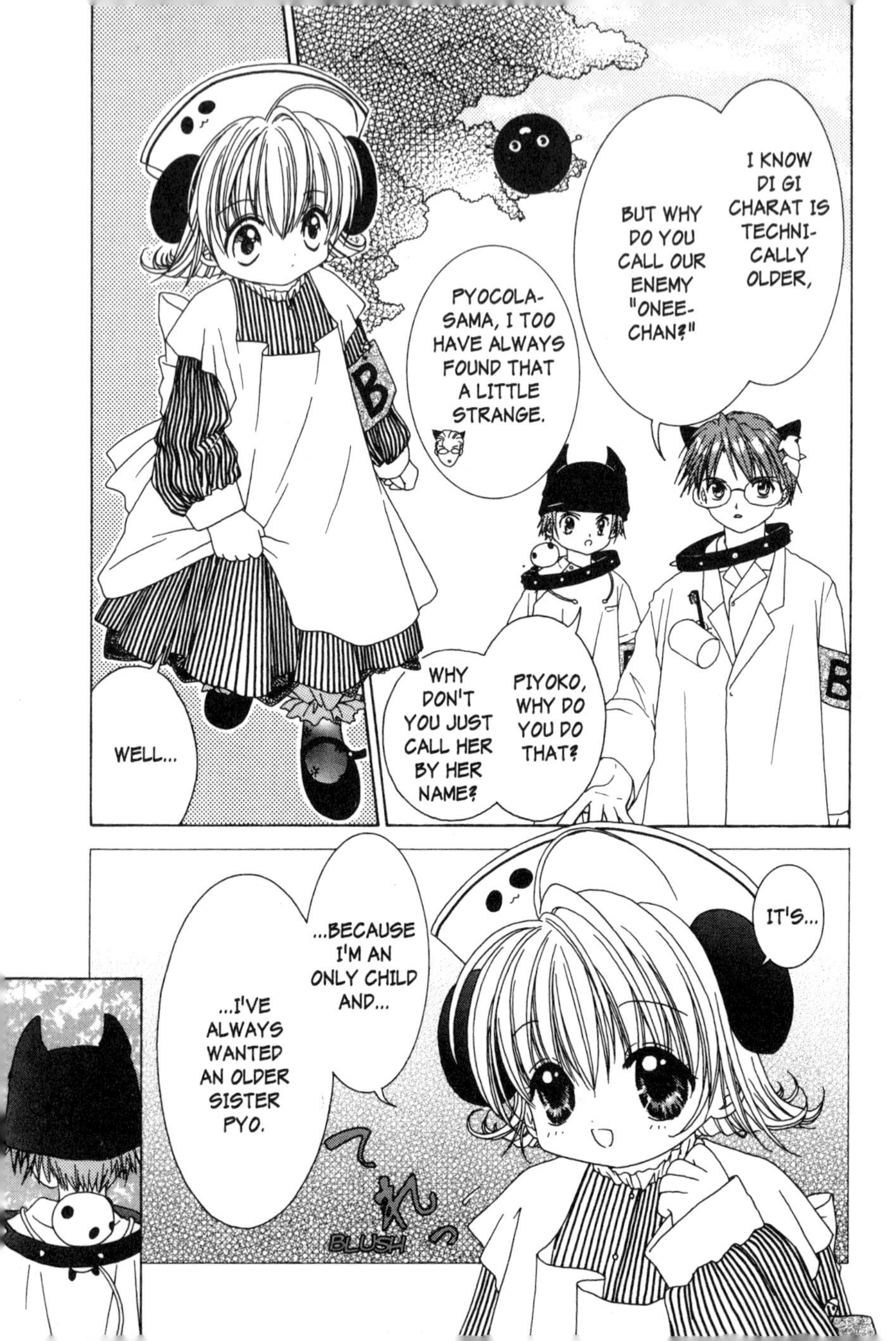
I KNOW DI GI CHARAT IS TECHNICALLY OLDER,
BUT WHY DO YOU CALL OUR ENEMY "ONEE-CHAN?"
PYOCOLA-SAMA, I TOO HAVE ALWAYS FOUND THAT A LITTLE STRANGE.
PIYOKO, WHY DO YOU DO THAT?
WHY DON'T YOU JUST CALL HER BY HER NAME?
WELL...
IT'S...
...BECAUSE I'M AN ONLY CHILD AND...
...I'VE ALWAYS WANTED AN OLDER SISTER PYO.
BLUSH

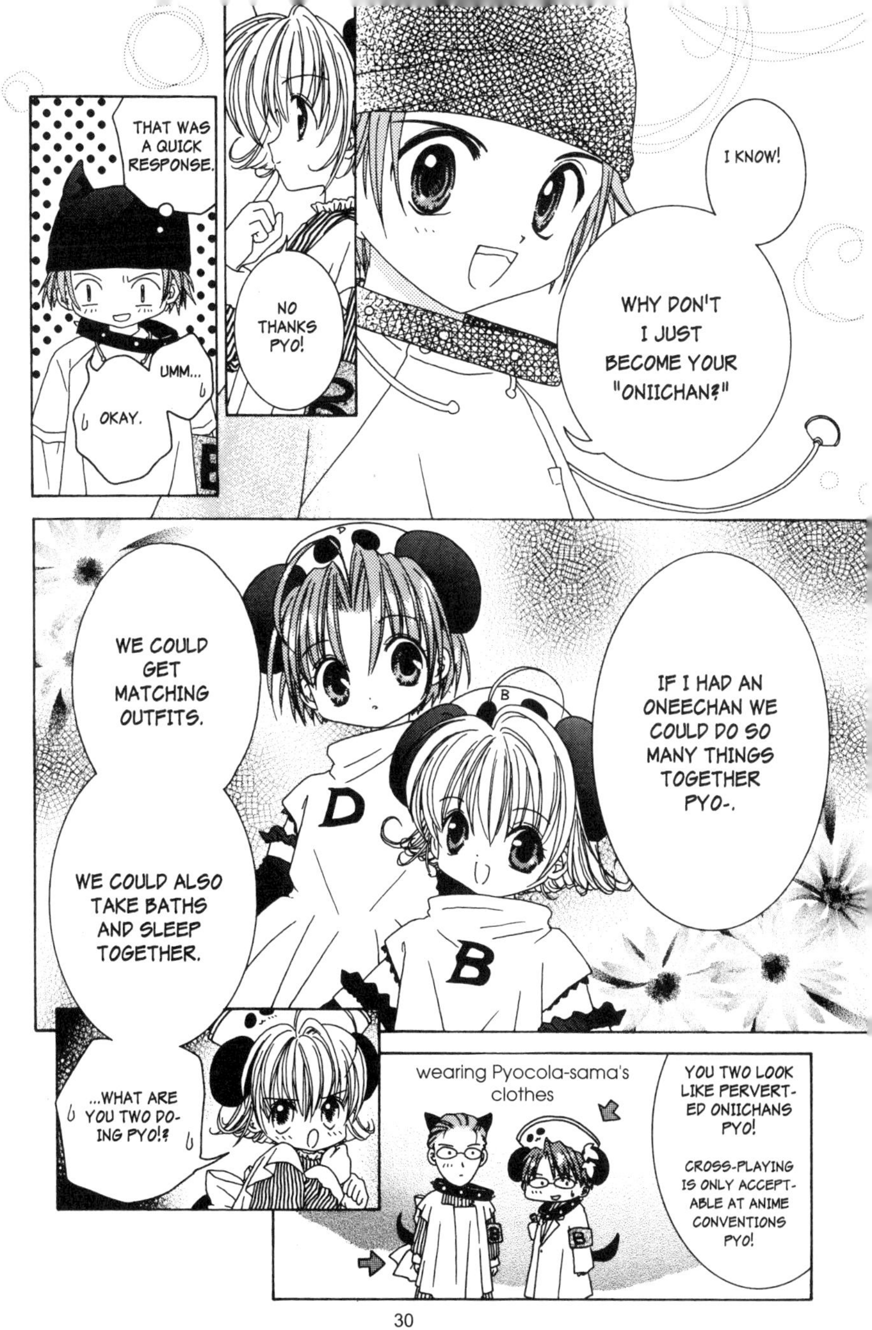

I KNOW!
WHY DON'T I JUST BECOME YOUR "ONIICHAN?"
NO THANKS PYO!
THAT WAS A QUICK RESPONSE.
UMM...
OKAY.
IF I HAD AN ONEECHAN WE COULD DO SO MANY THINGS TOGETHER PYO-.
WE COULD GET MATCHING OUTFITS.
WE COULD ALSO TAKE BATHS AND SLEEP TOGETHER.
YOU TWO LOOK LIKE PERVERTED ONIICHANS PYO!
wearing Pyocola-sama's clothes
CROSS-PLAYING IS ONLY ACCEPTABLE AT ANIME CONVENTIONS PYO!
...WHAT ARE YOU TWO DOING PYO!?

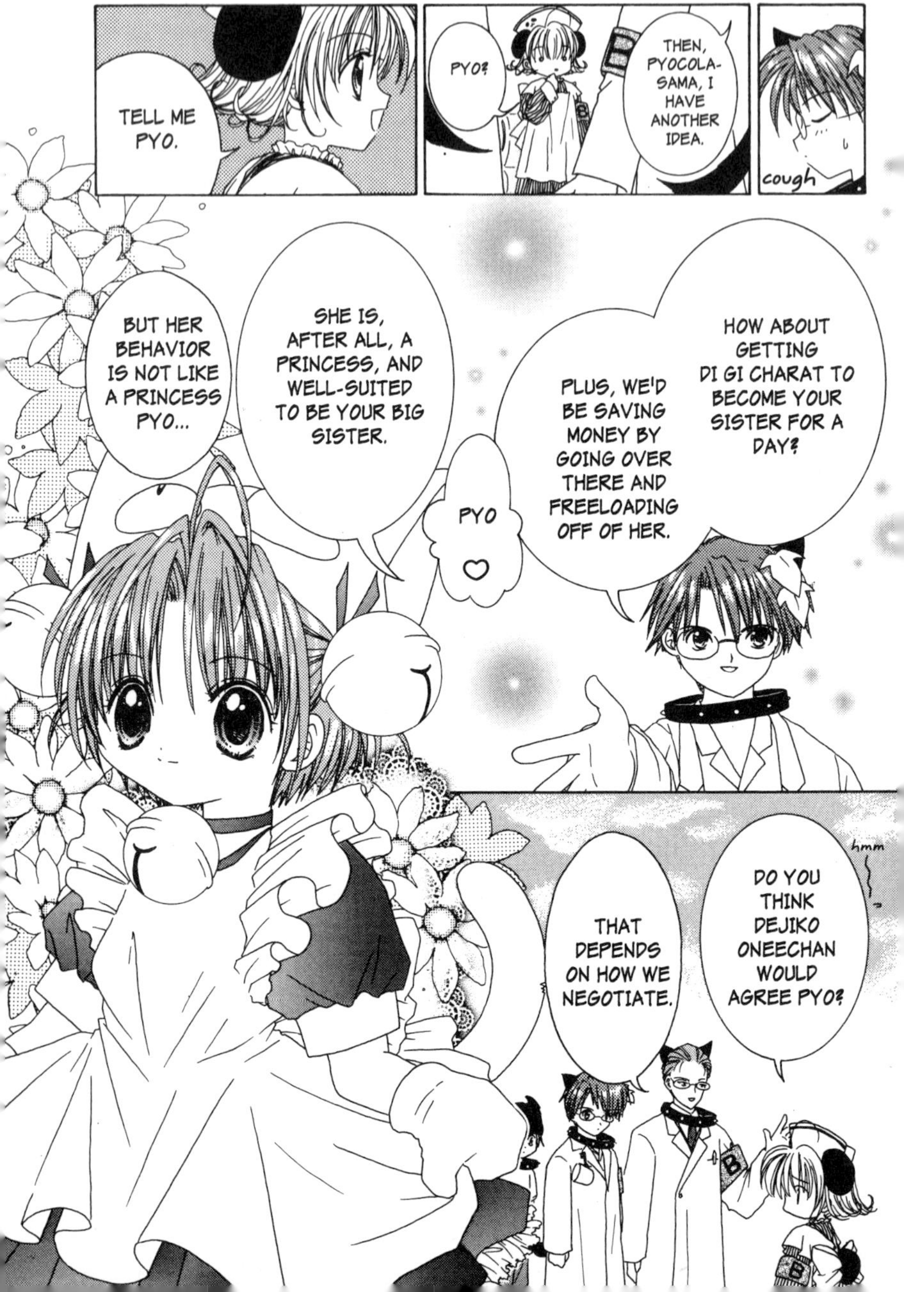
cough
THEN, PYOCOLA-SAMA, I HAVE ANOTHER IDEA.
PYO?
TELL ME PYO.
HOW ABOUT GETTING DI GI CHARAT TO BECOME YOUR SISTER FOR A DAY?
PLUS, WE'D BE SAVING MONEY BY GOING OVER THERE AND FREELOADING OFF OF HER.
PYO ♡
SHE IS, AFTER ALL, A PRINCESS, AND WELL-SUITED TO BE YOUR BIG SISTER.
BUT HER BEHAVIOR IS NOT LIKE A PRINCESS PYO...
hmm
DO YOU THINK DEJIKO ONEECHAN WOULD AGREE PYO?
THAT DEPENDS ON HOW WE NEGOTIATE.

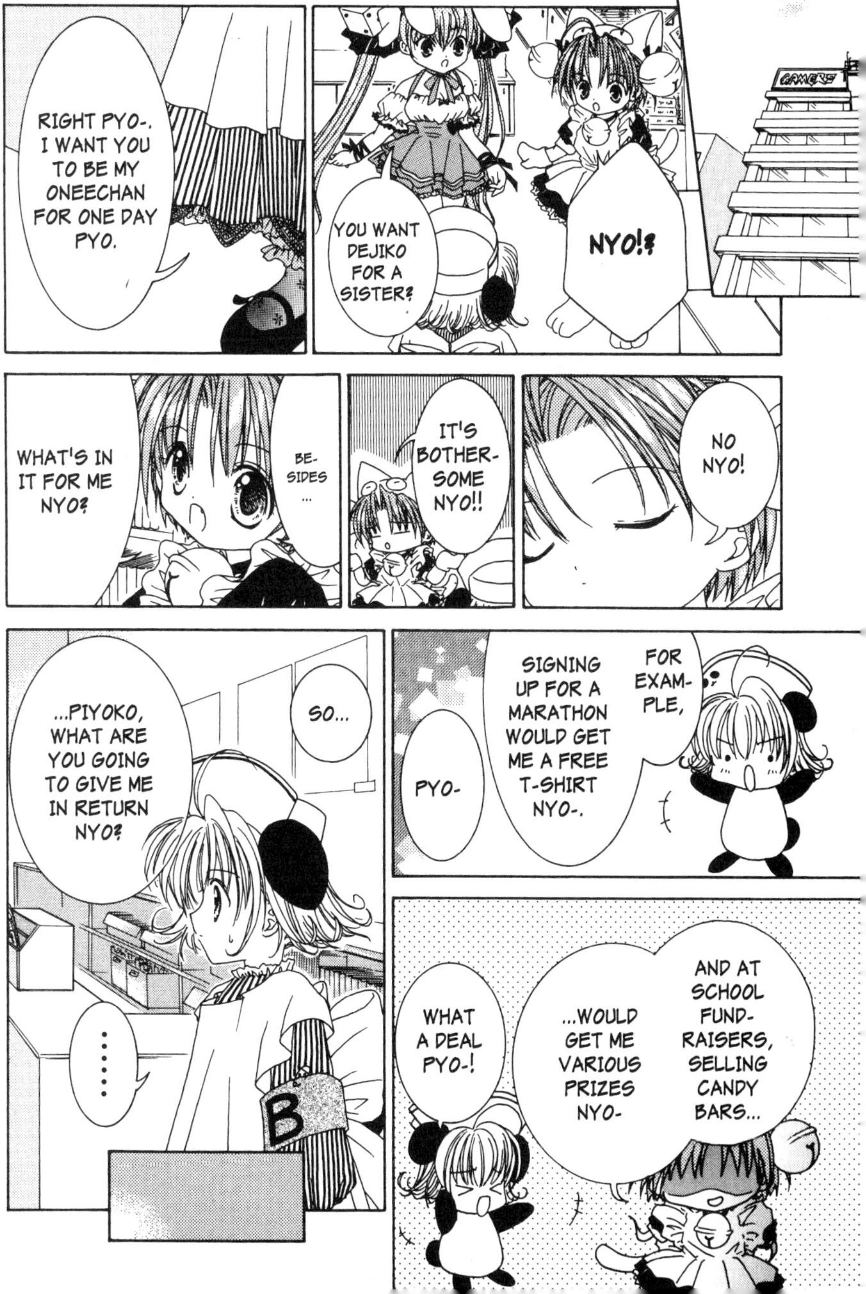
NYO!?
YOU WANT DEJIKO FOR A SISTER?
RIGHT PYO-. I WANT YOU TO BE MY ONEECHAN FOR ONE DAY PYO.
NO NYO!
IT'S BOTHER-SOME NYO!!
BE-SIDES ...
WHAT'S IN IT FOR ME NYO?
FOR EXAM-PLE,
SIGNING UP FOR A MARATHON WOULD GET ME A FREE T-SHIRT NYO-.
PYO-
AND AT SCHOOL FUND-RAISERS, SELLING CANDY BARS...
...WOULD GET ME VARIOUS PRIZES NYO-
WHAT A DEAL PYO-!
SO...
...PIYOKO, WHAT ARE YOU GOING TO GIVE ME IN RETURN NYO?
......

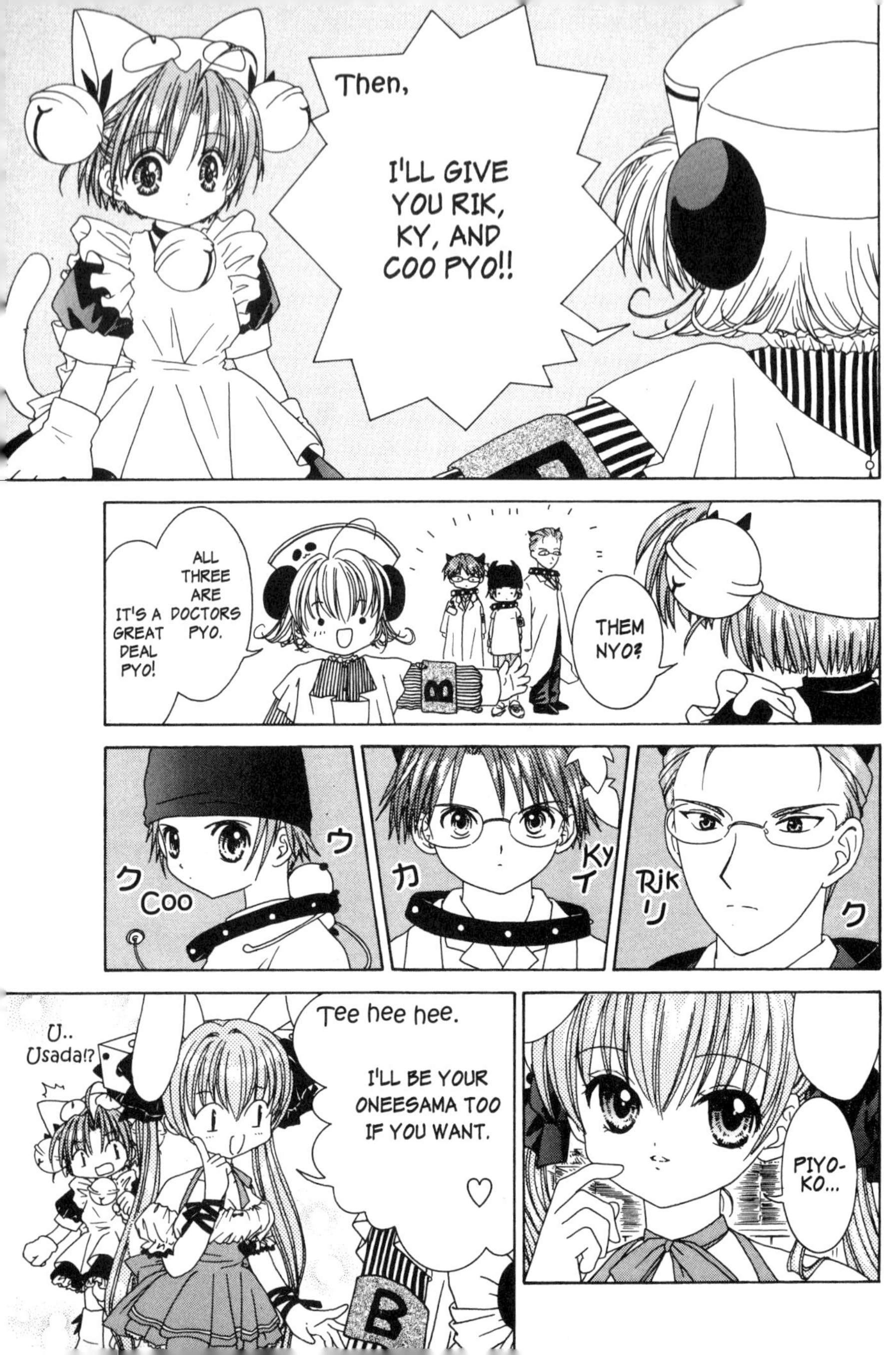
Then,
I'LL GIVE YOU RIK, KY, AND COO PYO!!
THEM NYO?
ALL THREE ARE DOCTORS PYO.
IT'S A GREAT DEAL PYO!
Rik
リク
Ky
カイ
Coo
クウ
PIYO-KO...
Tee hee hee.
I'LL BE YOUR ONEESAMA TOO IF YOU WANT. ♡
U.. Usada!?

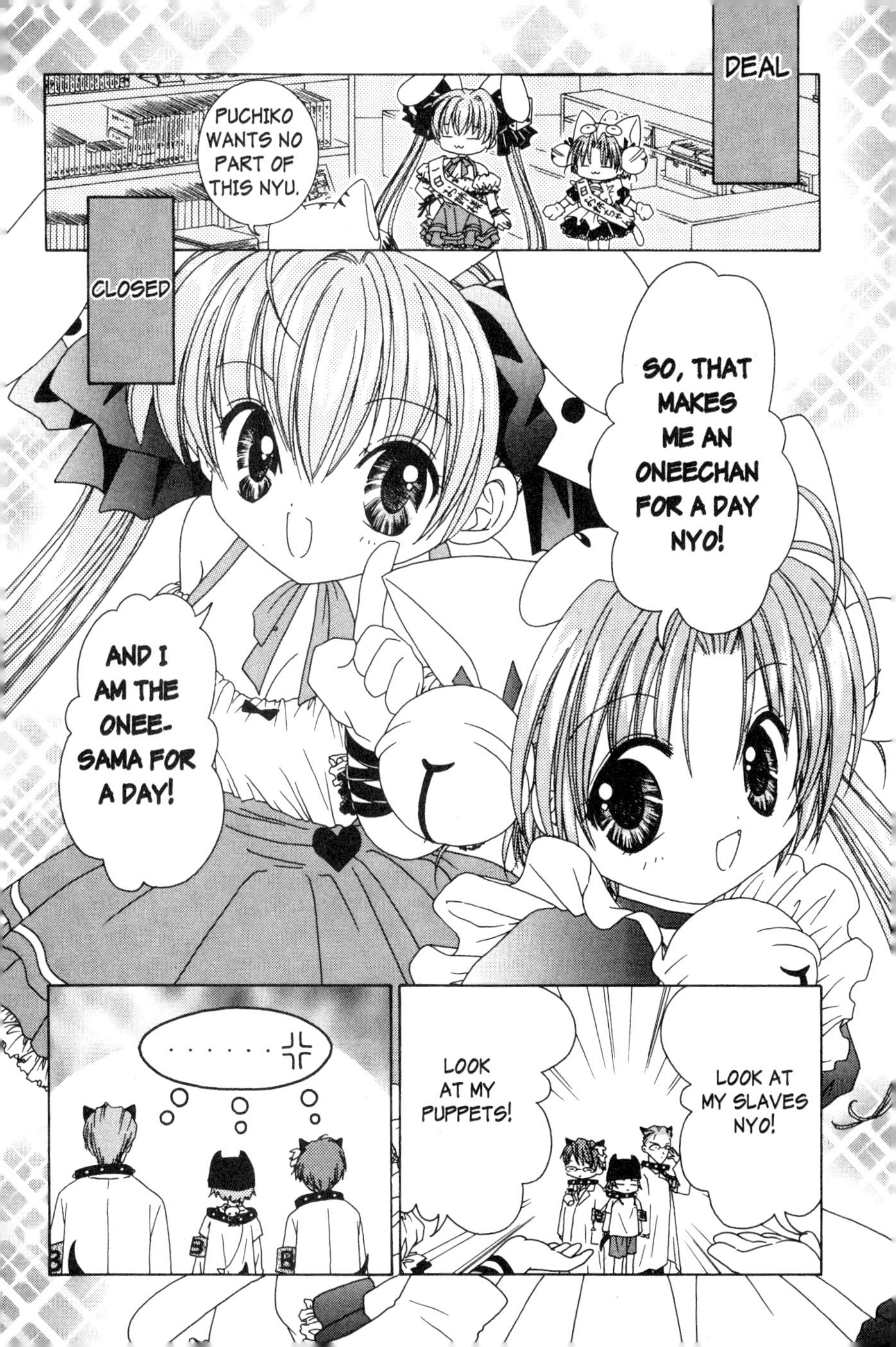
DEAL
PUCHIKO WANTS NO PART OF THIS NYU.
CLOSED
SO, THAT MAKES ME AN ONEECHAN FOR A DAY NYO!
AND I AM THE ONEE-SAMA FOR A DAY!
LOOK AT MY SLAVES NYO!
LOOK AT MY PUPPETS!
....

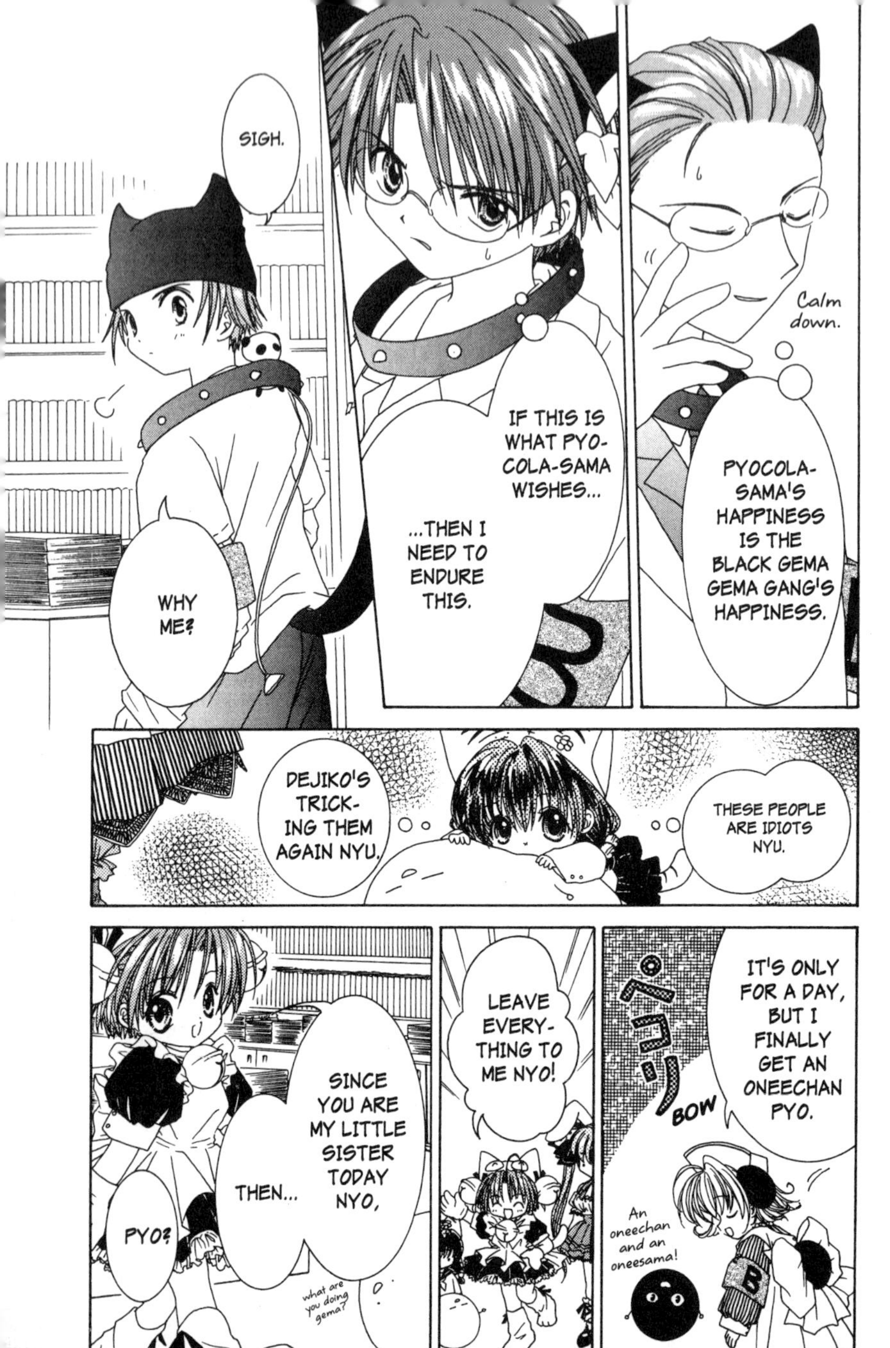
Calm down.
PYOCOLA-SAMA'S HAPPINESS IS THE BLACK GEMA GEMA GANG'S HAPPINESS.
IF THIS IS WHAT PYO-COLA-SAMA WISHES...
...THEN I NEED TO ENDURE THIS.
SIGH.
WHY ME?
THESE PEOPLE ARE IDIOTS NYU.
DEJIKO'S TRICK-ING THEM AGAIN NYU.
IT'S ONLY FOR A DAY, BUT I FINALLY GET AN ONEECHAN PYO.
BOW
An oneechan and an oneesama!
LEAVE EVERY-THING TO ME NYO!
SINCE YOU ARE MY LITTLE SISTER TODAY NYO,
THEN...
PYO?
what are you doing gema?

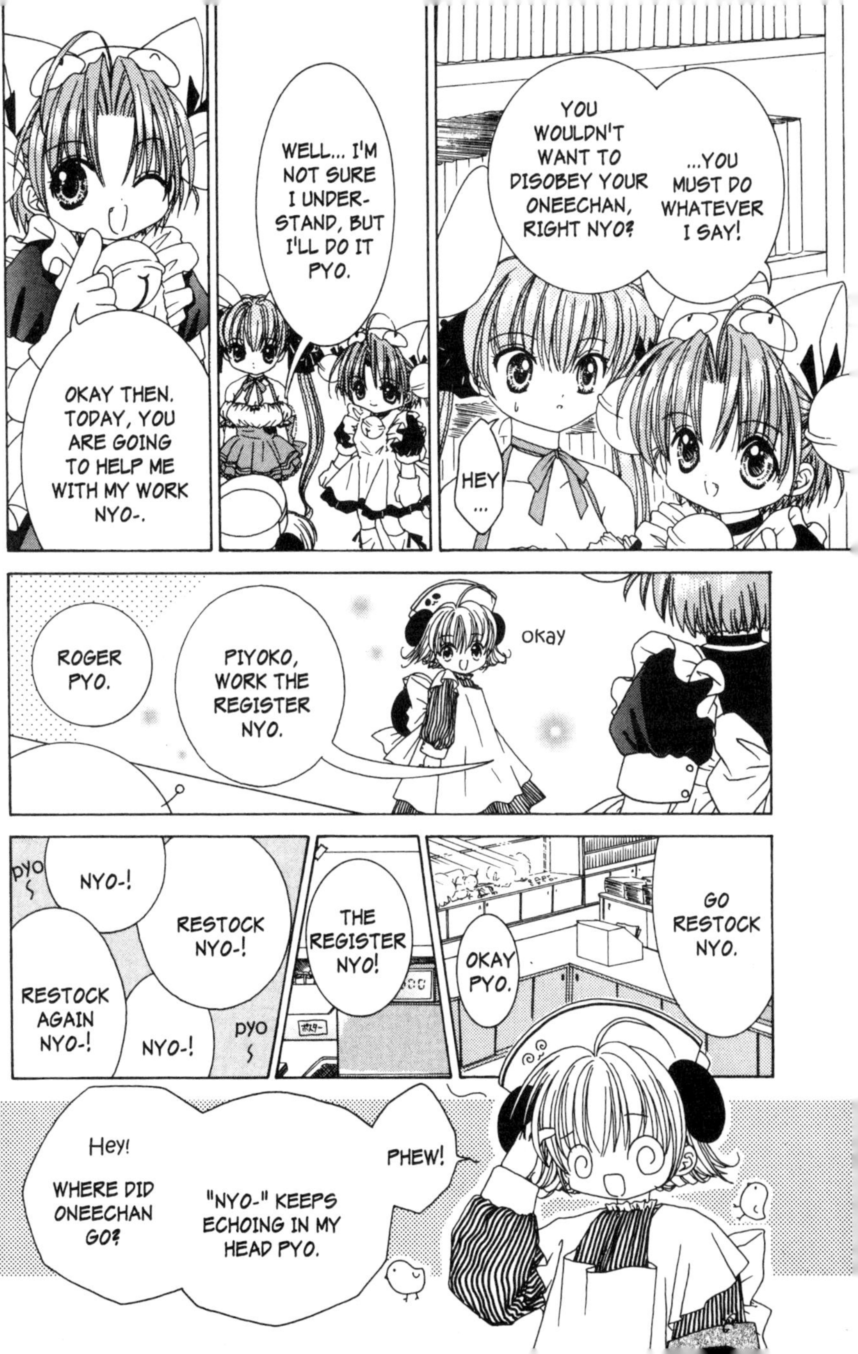
YOU WOULDN'T WANT TO DISOBEY YOUR ONEECHAN, RIGHT NYO?
...YOU MUST DO WHATEVER I SAY!
HEY ...
WELL... I'M NOT SURE I UNDER-STAND, BUT I'LL DO IT PYO.
OKAY THEN. TODAY, YOU ARE GOING TO HELP ME WITH MY WORK NYO-.
okay
PIYOKO, WORK THE REGISTER NYO.
ROGER PYO.
GO RESTOCK NYO.
OKAY PYO.
THE REGISTER NYO!
NYO-!
RESTOCK NYO-!
pyo
RESTOCK AGAIN NYO-!
NYO-!
pyo
PHEW!
"NYO-" KEEPS ECHOING IN MY HEAD PYO.
Hey!
WHERE DID ONEECHAN GO?

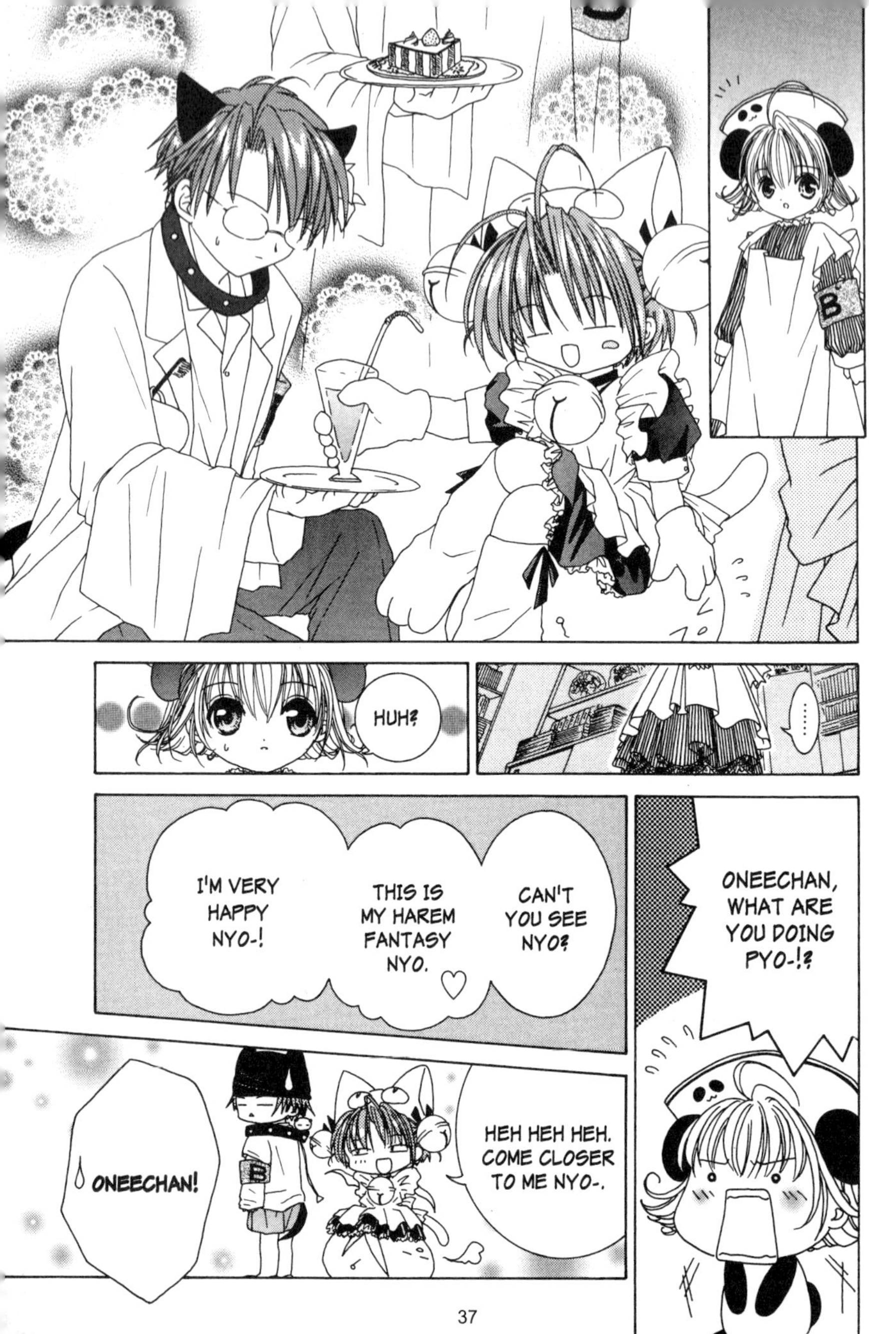
......
HUH?
ONEECHAN, WHAT ARE YOU DOING PYO-!?
CAN'T YOU SEE NYO?
THIS IS MY HAREM FANTASY NYO. ♡
I'M VERY HAPPY NYO-!
HEH HEH HEH. COME CLOSER TO ME NYO-.
ONEECHAN!

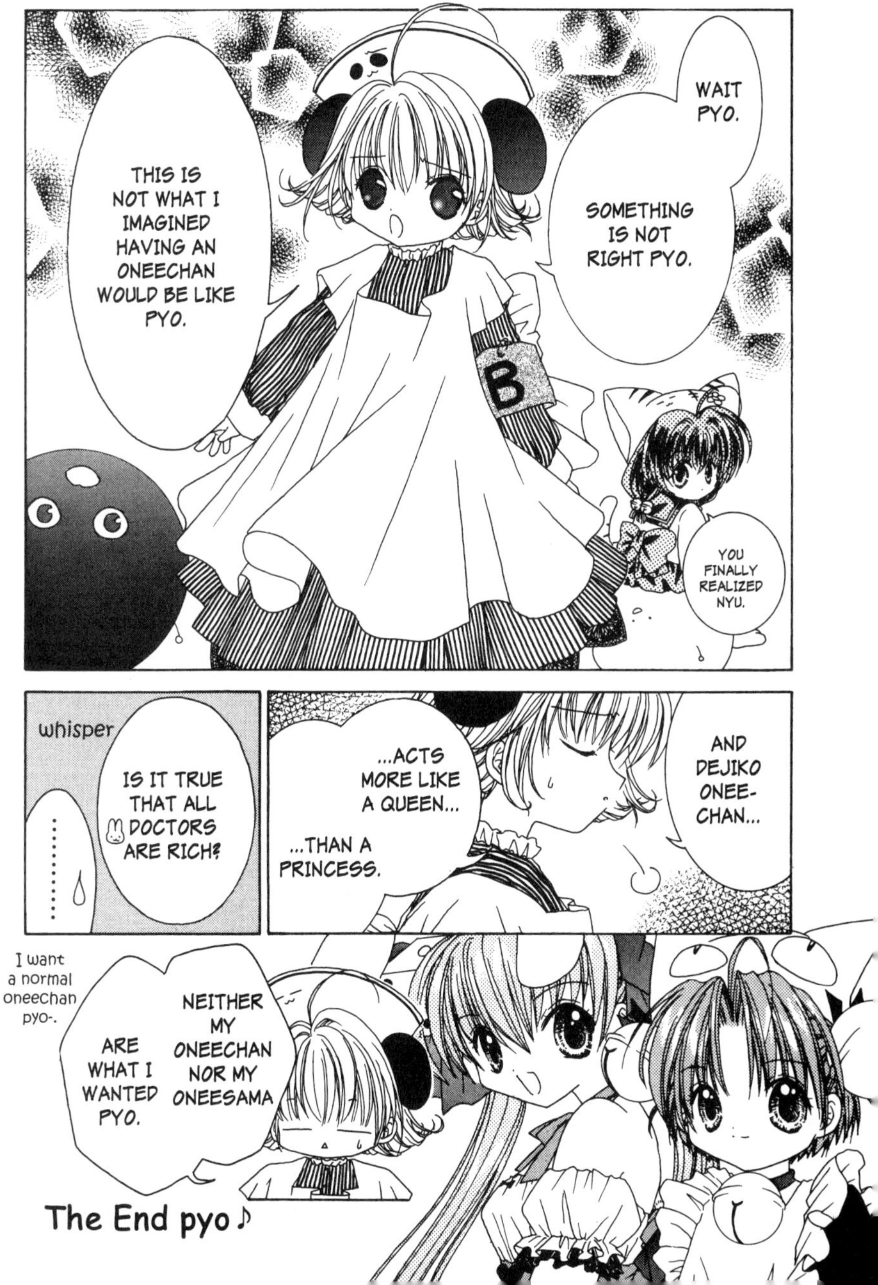
WAIT PYO.
SOMETHING IS NOT RIGHT PYO.
THIS IS NOT WHAT I IMAGINED HAVING AN ONEECHAN WOULD BE LIKE PYO.
YOU FINALLY REALIZED NYU.
AND DEJIKO ONEE-CHAN...
...ACTS MORE LIKE A QUEEN...
...THAN A PRINCESS.
whisper
IS IT TRUE THAT ALL DOCTORS ARE RICH?
......
NEITHER MY ONEECHAN NOR MY ONEESAMA
ARE WHAT I WANTED PYO.
I want a normal oneechan pyo-.
The End pyo♪

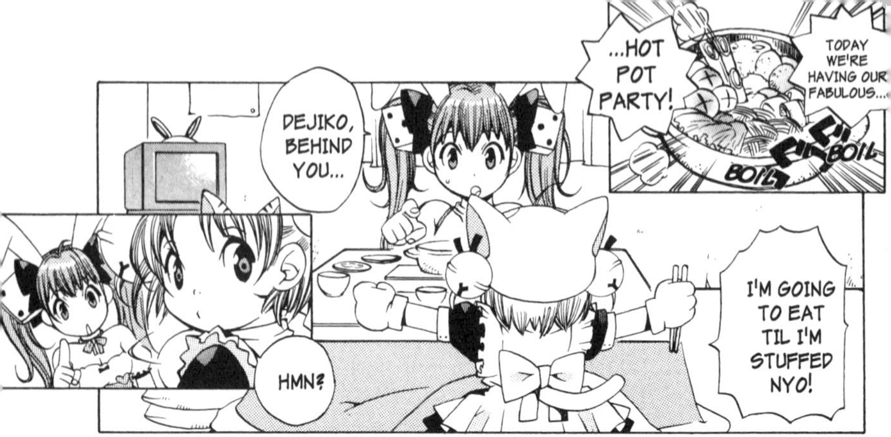
TODAY WE'RE HAVING OUR FABULOUS...
...HOT POT PARTY!
BOIL BOIL
I'M GOING TO EAT TIL I'M STUFFED NYO!
DEJIKO, BEHIND YOU...
HMN?

Piyoko Gets A Cavity

Towa Oozora

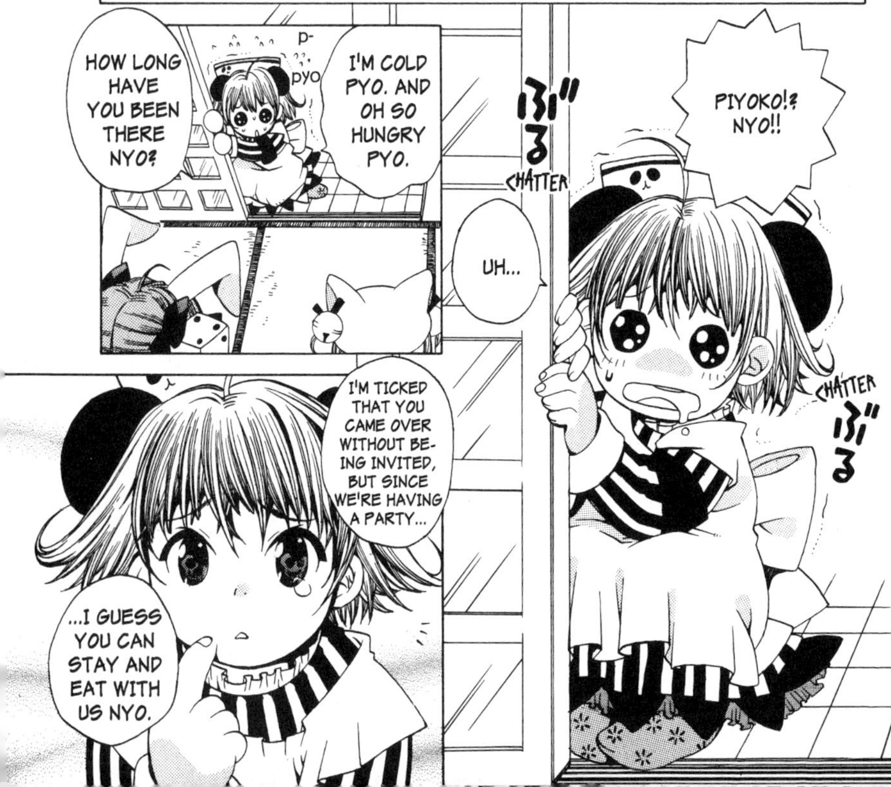
PIYOKO!? NYO!!
ぶる
CHATTER
ぶる
CHATTER
I'M COLD PYO. AND OH SO HUNGRY PYO.
p-pyo
HOW LONG HAVE YOU BEEN THERE NYO?
UH...
I'M TICKED THAT YOU CAME OVER WITHOUT BE-ING INVITED, BUT SINCE WE'RE HAVING A PARTY...
...I GUESS YOU CAN STAY AND EAT WITH US NYO.

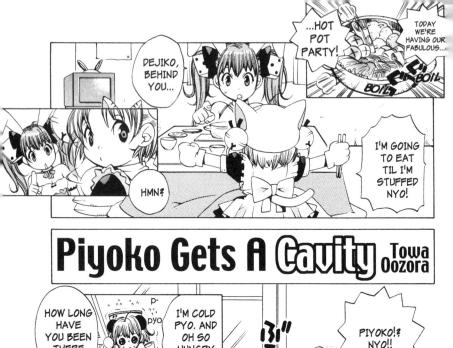

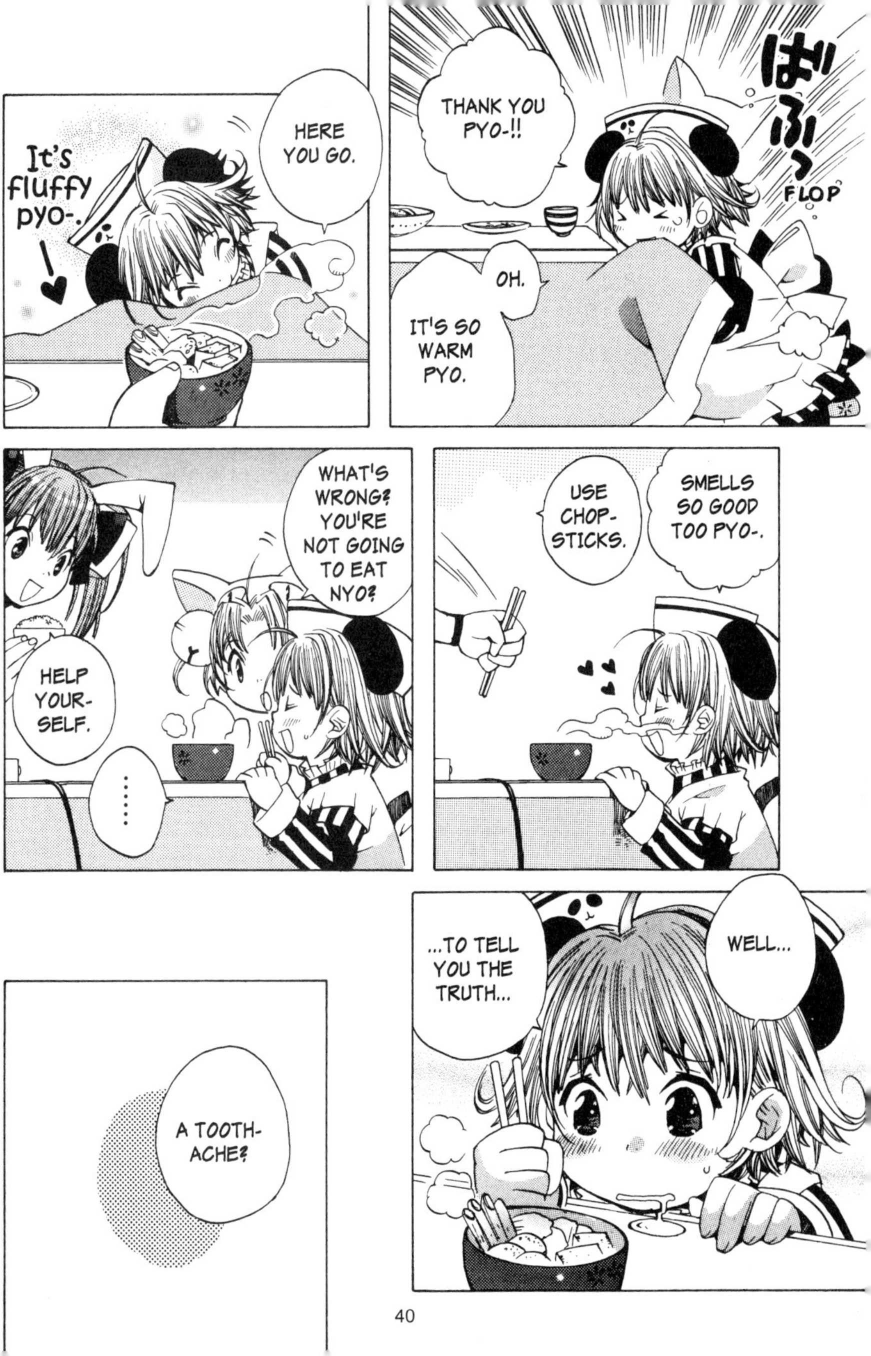
THANK YOU PYO-!!
ばふっ
FLOP
OH.
IT'S SO WARM PYO.
HERE YOU GO.
It's fluffy pyo-.
SMELLS SO GOOD TOO PYO-.
USE CHOP-STICKS.
WHAT'S WRONG? YOU'RE NOT GOING TO EAT NYO?
HELP YOUR-SELF.
......
WELL...
...TO TELL YOU THE TRUTH...
A TOOTH-ACHE?

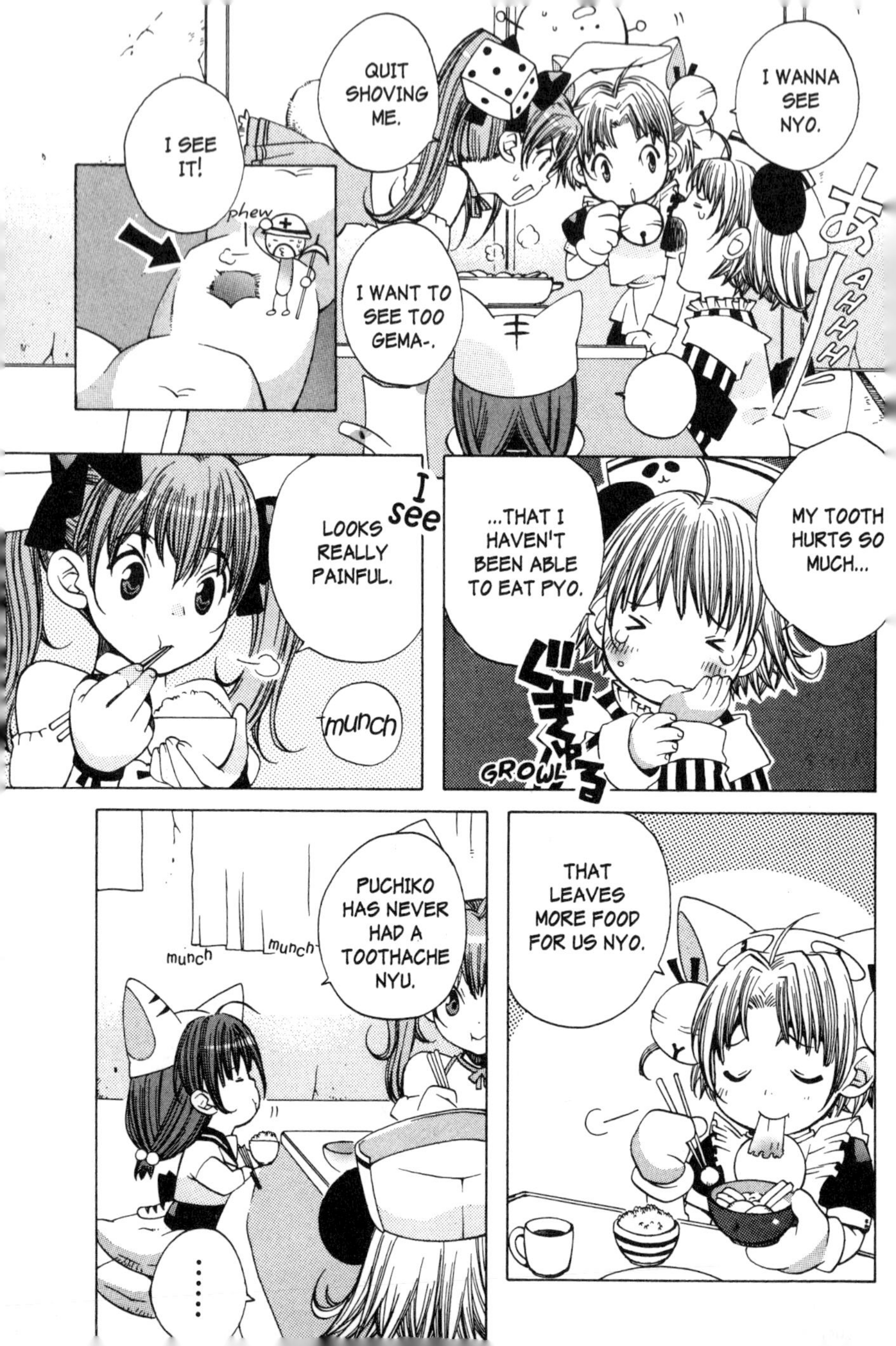

I WANNA SEE NYO.
あ AHHHH!
QUIT SHOVING ME.
I WANT TO SEE TOO GEMA-.
I SEE IT!
phew
MY TOOTH HURTS SO MUCH...
...THAT I HAVEN'T BEEN ABLE TO EAT PYO.
ぐぎゅる
GROWL
I see
LOOKS REALLY PAINFUL.
munch
THAT LEAVES MORE FOOD FOR US NYO.
PUCHIKO HAS NEVER HAD A TOOTHACHE NYU.
munch
munch
......

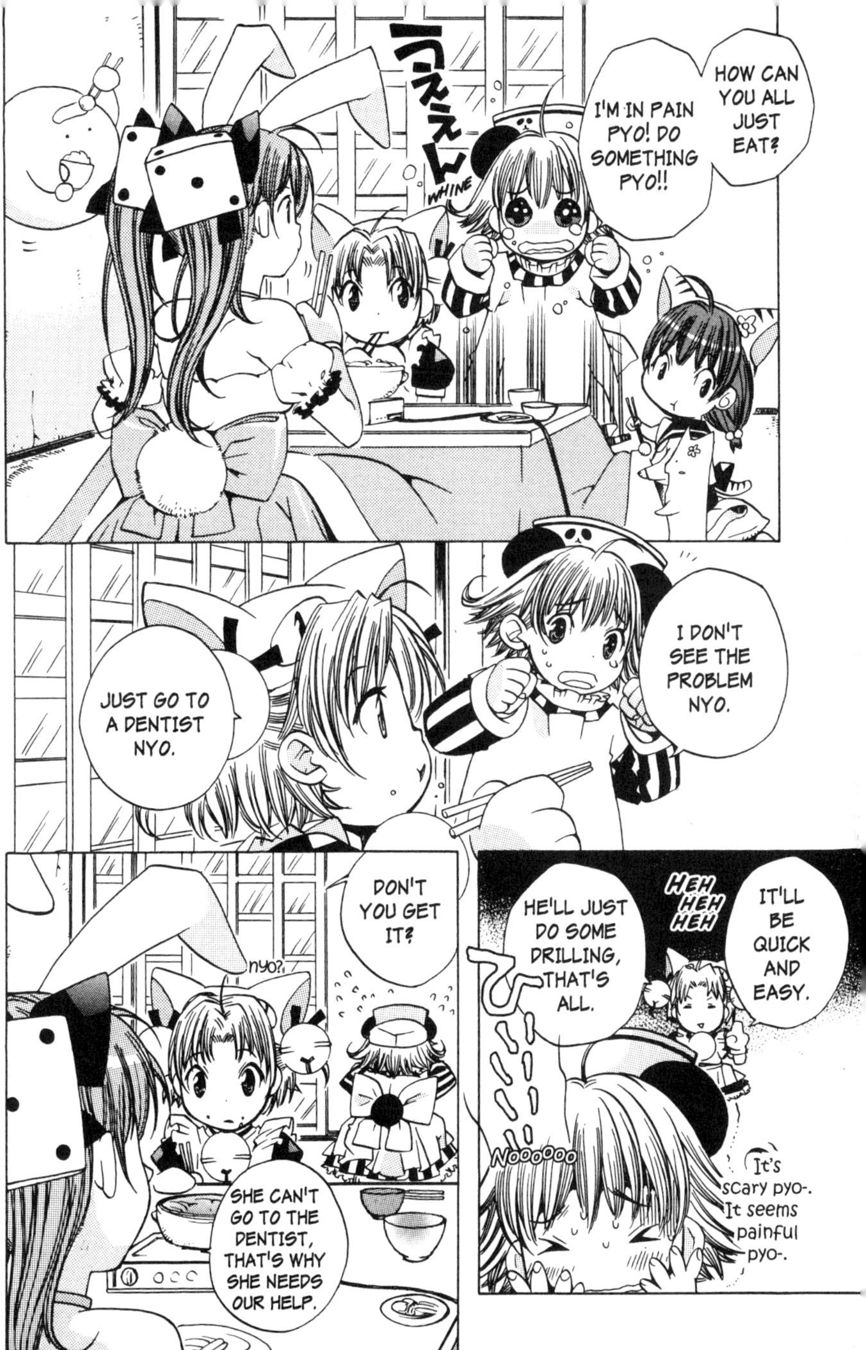
HOW CAN YOU ALL JUST EAT?
I'M IN PAIN PYO! DO SOMETHING PYO!!
うえぇん
WHINE
I DON'T SEE THE PROBLEM NYO.
JUST GO TO A DENTIST NYO.
IT'LL BE QUICK AND EASY.
HEH HEH HEH
HE'LL JUST DO SOME DRILLING, THAT'S ALL.
NOooooo
It's scary pyo-. It seems painful pyo-.
DON'T YOU GET IT?
nyo?
SHE CAN'T GO TO THE DENTIST, THAT'S WHY SHE NEEDS OUR HELP.

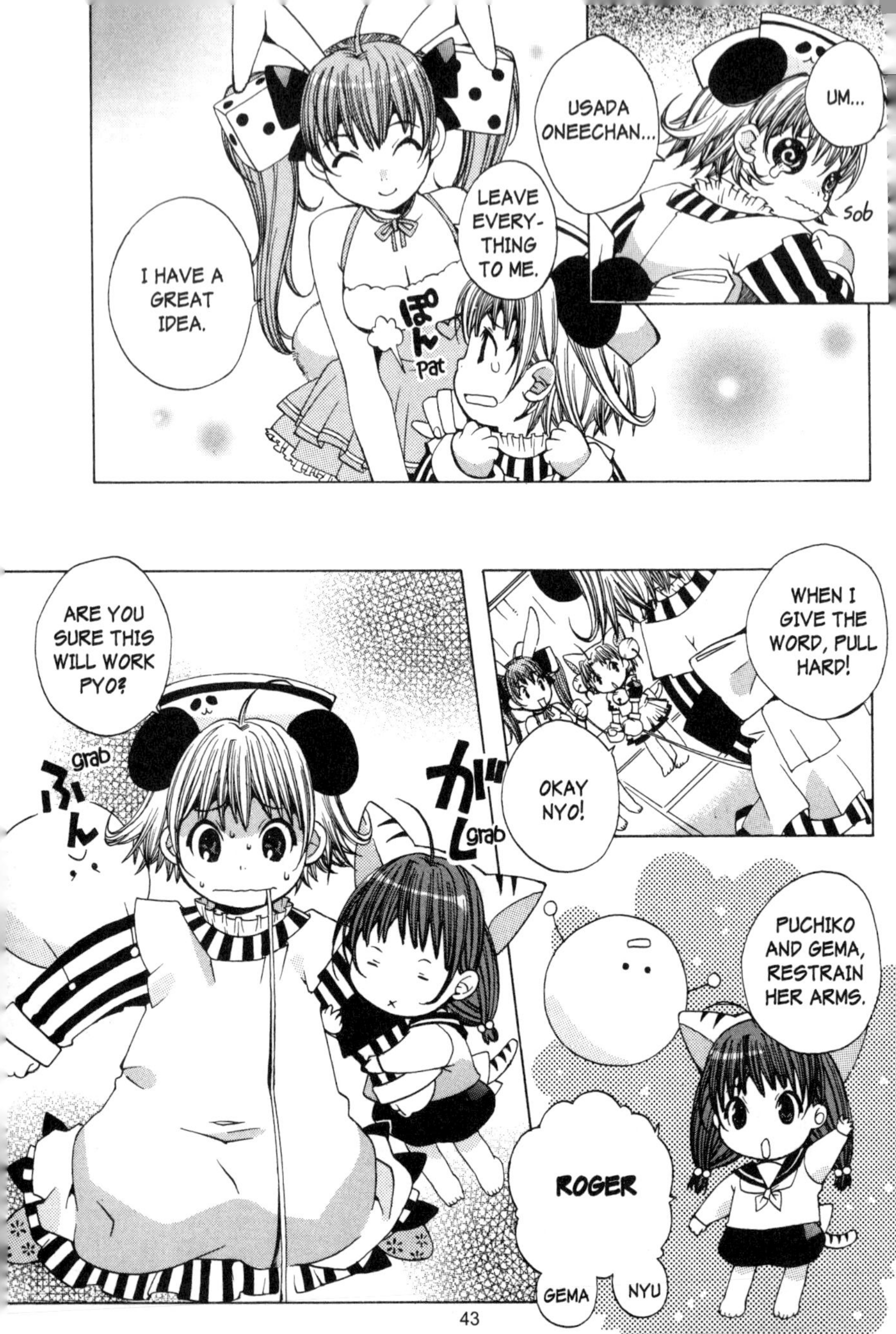
UM...
USADA ONEECHAN...
sob
LEAVE EVERY-THING TO ME.
ぽん pat
I HAVE A GREAT IDEA.
WHEN I GIVE THE WORD, PULL HARD!
OKAY NYO!
PUCHIKO AND GEMA, RESTRAIN HER ARMS.
ROGER
NYU
GEMA
ARE YOU SURE THIS WILL WORK PYO?
がし grab
ふん grab

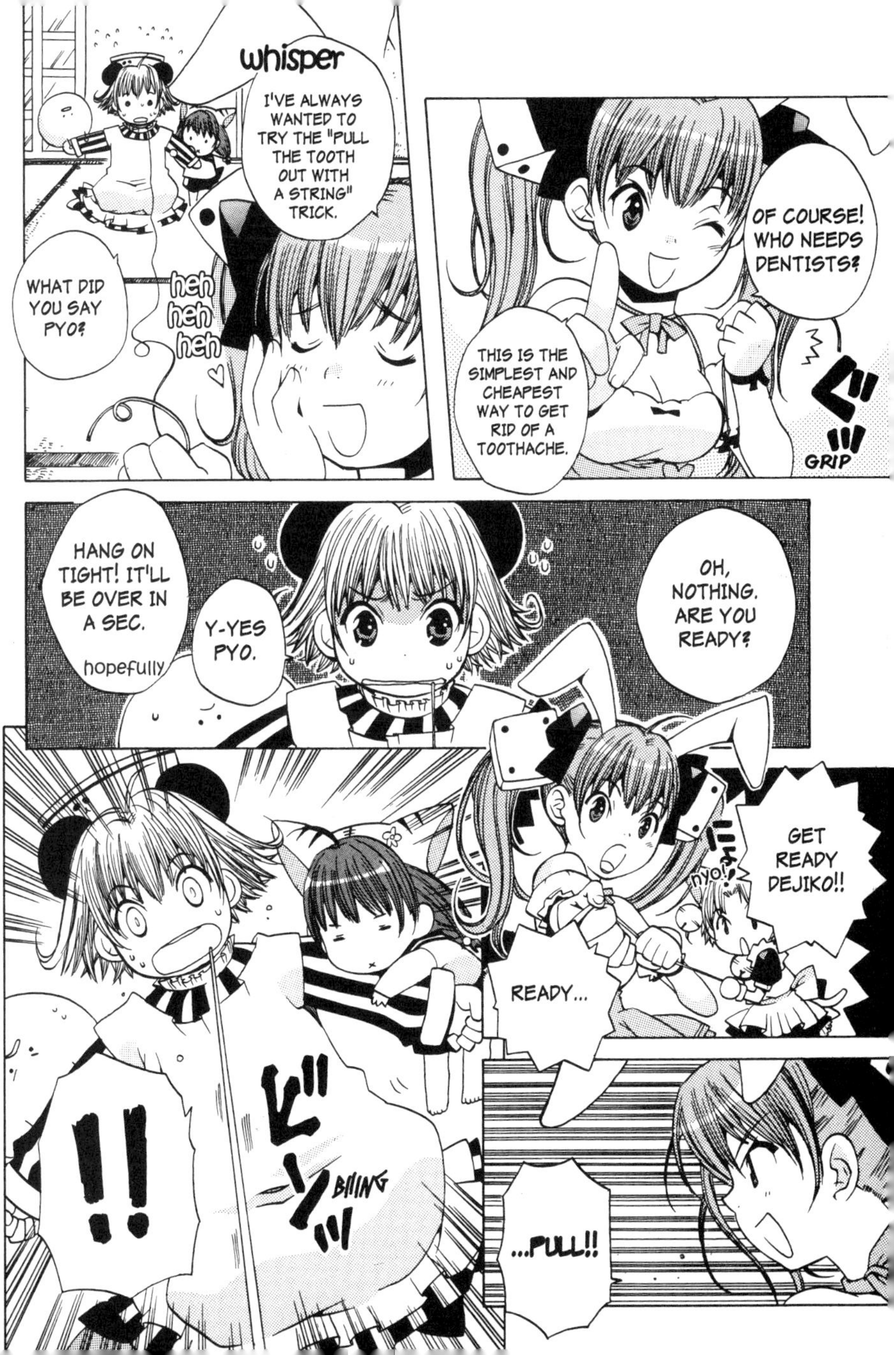
OF COURSE! WHO NEEDS DENTISTS?
THIS IS THE SIMPLEST AND CHEAPEST WAY TO GET RID OF A TOOTHACHE.
GRIP
whisper
I'VE ALWAYS WANTED TO TRY THE "PULL THE TOOTH OUT WITH A STRING" TRICK.
heh heh heh
WHAT DID YOU SAY PYO?
OH, NOTHING. ARE YOU READY?
Y-YES PYO.
HANG ON TIGHT! IT'LL BE OVER IN A SEC.
hopefully
GET READY DEJIKO!!
nyo!
READY...
...PULL!!
BIIING
!!

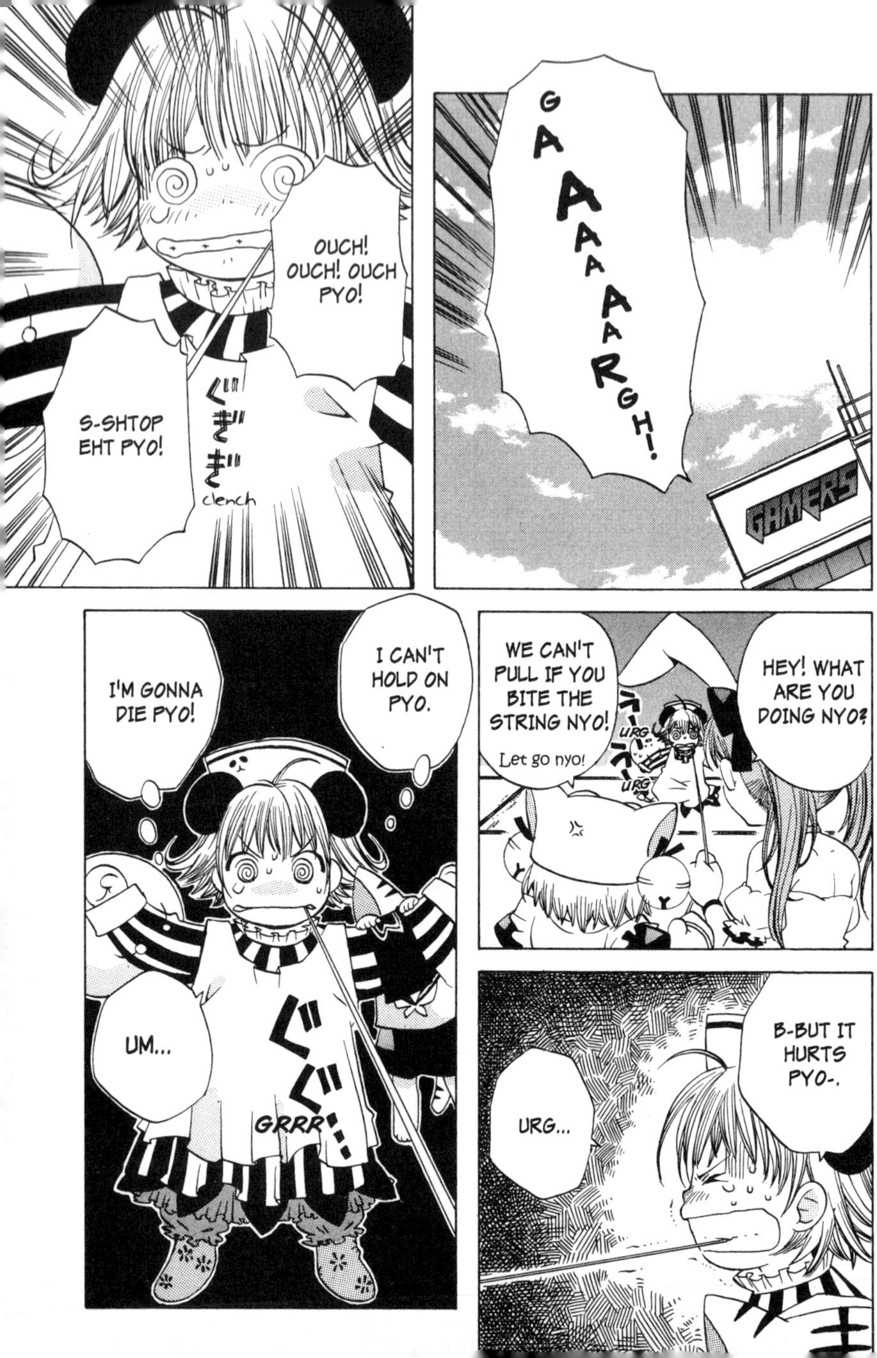
GAAAAAARGH!
GAMERS
OUCH! OUCH! OUCH PYO!
S-SHTOP EHT PYO!
ぐぎぎ
clench
HEY! WHAT ARE YOU DOING NYO?
WE CAN'T PULL IF YOU BITE THE STRING NYO!
Let go nyo!
URG
URG
B-BUT IT HURTS PYO-.
URG...
I CAN'T HOLD ON PYO.
I'M GONNA DIE PYO!
UM...
ぐぐぐ...
GRRR

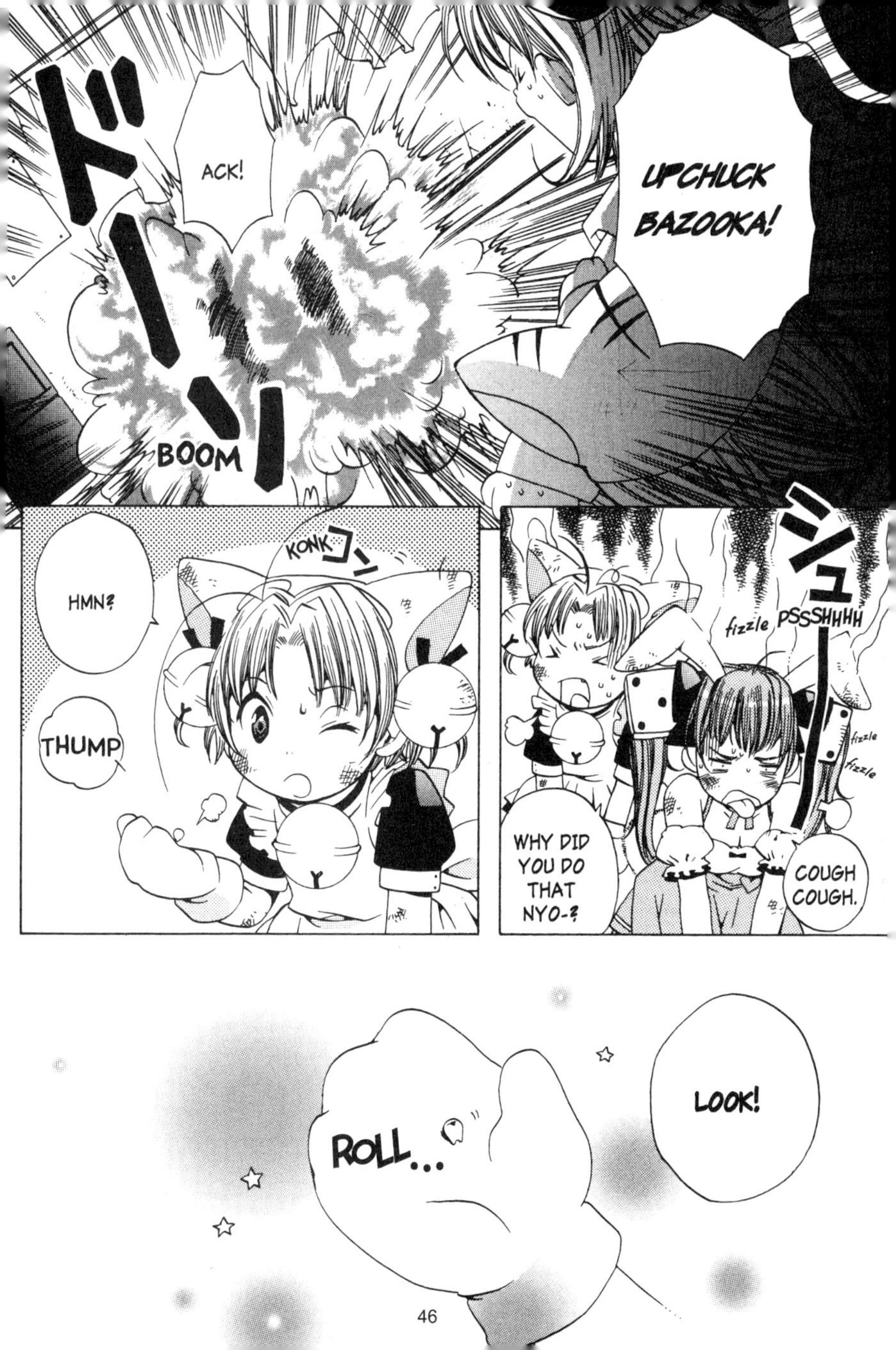
UPCHUCK BAZOOKA!
ACK!
BOOM
fizzle PSSSHHHH
fizzle
fizzle
COUGH COUGH.
WHY DID YOU DO THAT NYO-?
KONK
HMN?
THUMP
LOOK!
ROLL...

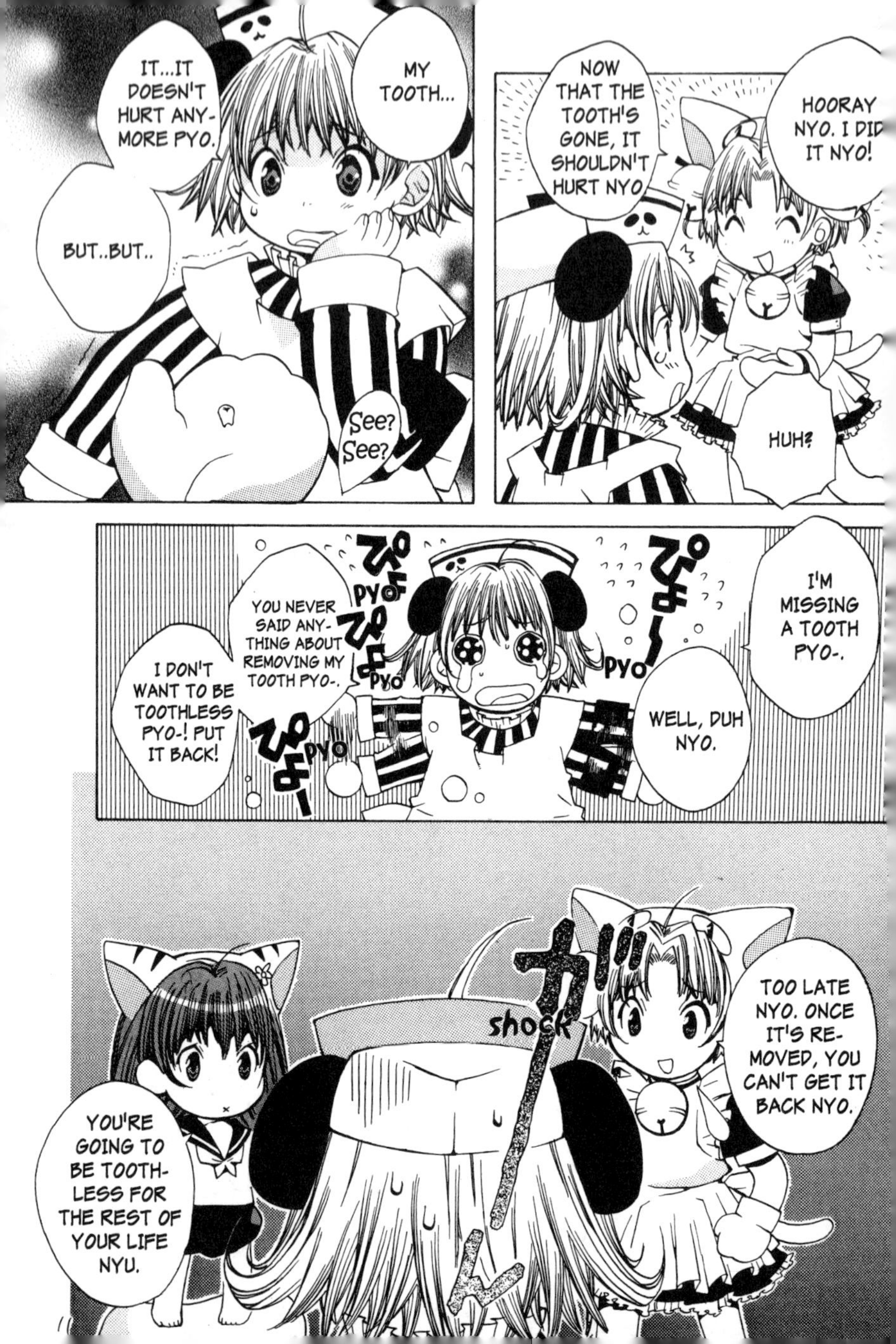

HOORAY NYO. I DID IT NYO!
NOW THAT THE TOOTH'S GONE, IT SHOULDN'T HURT NYO.
HUH?
MY TOOTH...
IT...IT DOESN'T HURT ANY-MORE PYO.
BUT..BUT..
See? See?
I'M MISSING A TOOTH PYO-.
WELL, DUH NYO.
PYO
PYO
YOU NEVER SAID ANY-THING ABOUT REMOVING MY TOOTH PYO-.
PYO
I DON'T WANT TO BE TOOTHLESS PYO-! PUT IT BACK!
PYO
shock
TOO LATE NYO. ONCE IT'S RE-MOVED, YOU CAN'T GET IT BACK NYO.
YOU'RE GOING TO BE TOOTH-LESS FOR THE REST OF YOUR LIFE NYU.

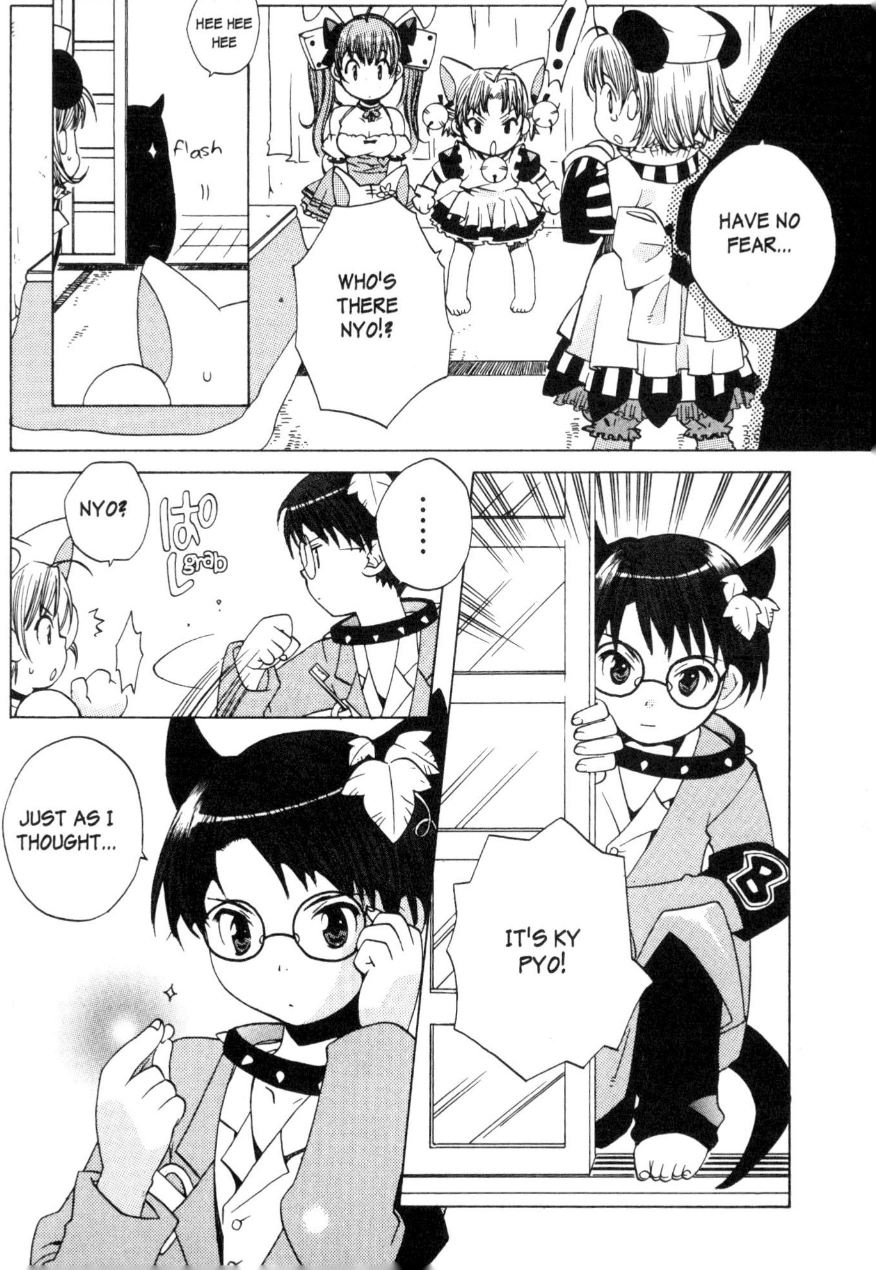
HAVE NO FEAR...
WHO'S THERE NYO!?
HEE HEE HEE
flash
IT'S KY PYO!
......
NYO?
grab
JUST AS I THOUGHT...

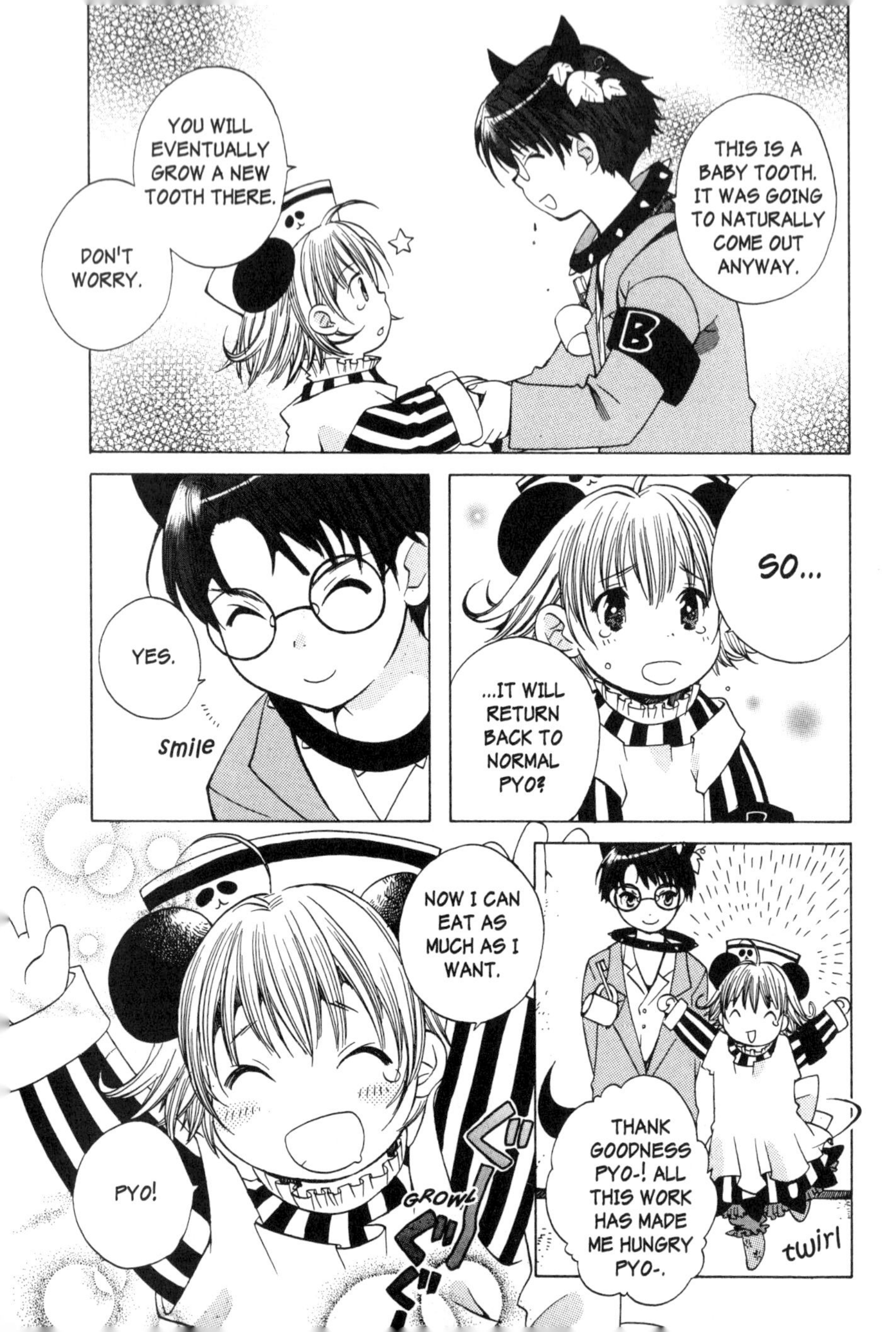
THIS IS A BABY TOOTH. IT WAS GOING TO NATURALLY COME OUT ANYWAY.
YOU WILL EVENTUALLY GROW A NEW TOOTH THERE.
DON'T WORRY.
SO...
...IT WILL RETURN BACK TO NORMAL PYO?
YES.
smile
THANK GOODNESS PYO-! ALL THIS WORK HAS MADE ME HUNGRY PYO-.
twirl
NOW I CAN EAT AS MUCH AS I WANT.
PYO!
GROWL

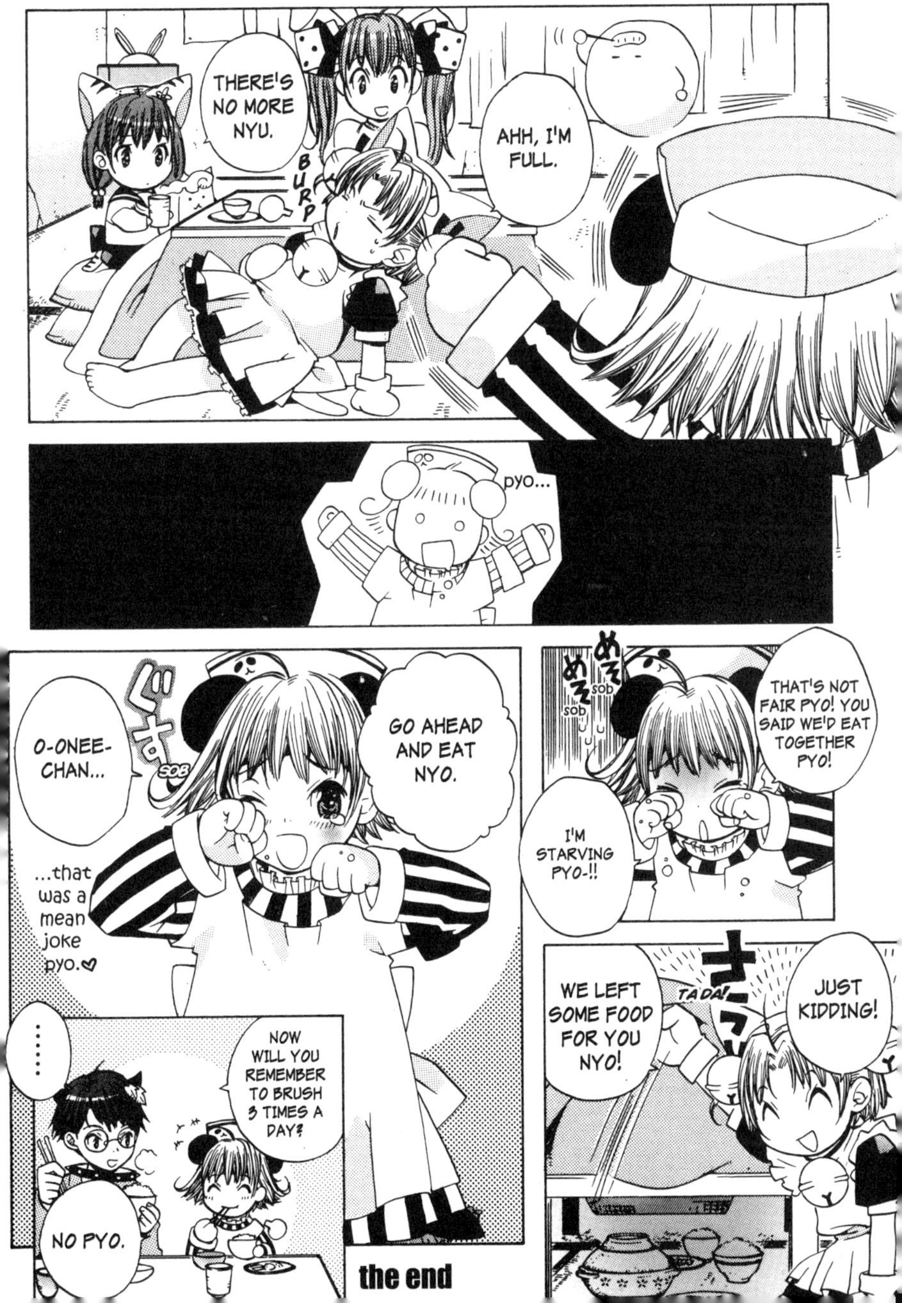
AHH, I'M FULL.
THERE'S NO MORE NYU.
BURP
pyo...
めそ めそ
sob sob
THAT'S NOT FAIR PYO! YOU SAID WE'D EAT TOGETHER PYO!
I'M STARVING PYO-!!
JUST KIDDING!
TA DA!
WE LEFT SOME FOOD FOR YOU NYO!
GO AHEAD AND EAT NYO.
ぐす
SOB
O-ONEE-CHAN...
...that was a mean joke pyo.♡
NOW WILL YOU REMEMBER TO BRUSH 3 TIMES A DAY?
......
NO PYO.
the end

A Message to Piyoko-sama!

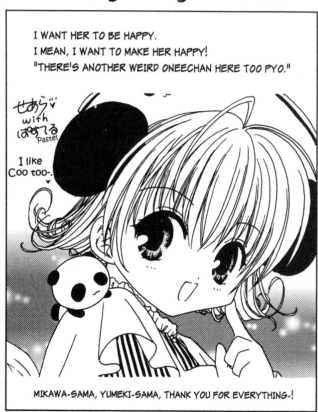

I WANT HER TO BE HAPPY.
I MEAN, I WANT TO MAKE HER HAPPY!
"THERE'S ANOTHER WEIRD ONEECHAN HERE TOO PYO."

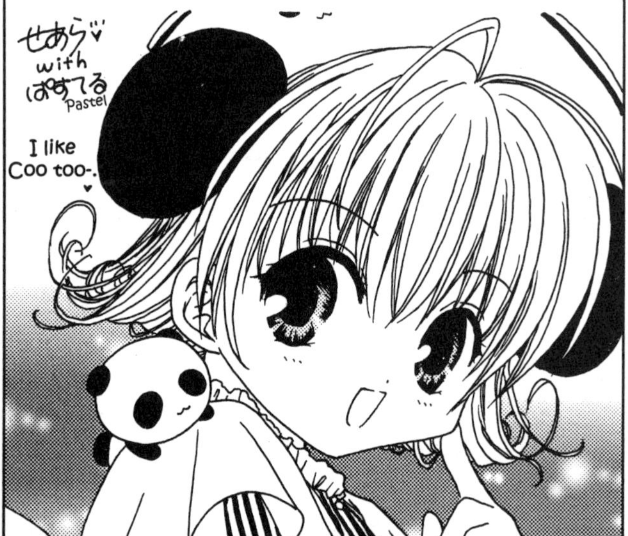
せあら♥
with
ぱすてる
Pastel
I like
Coo too-.

MIKAWA-SAMA, YUMEKI-SAMA, THANK YOU FOR EVERYTHING-!

B

Seara

A Message to Piyoko-sama!

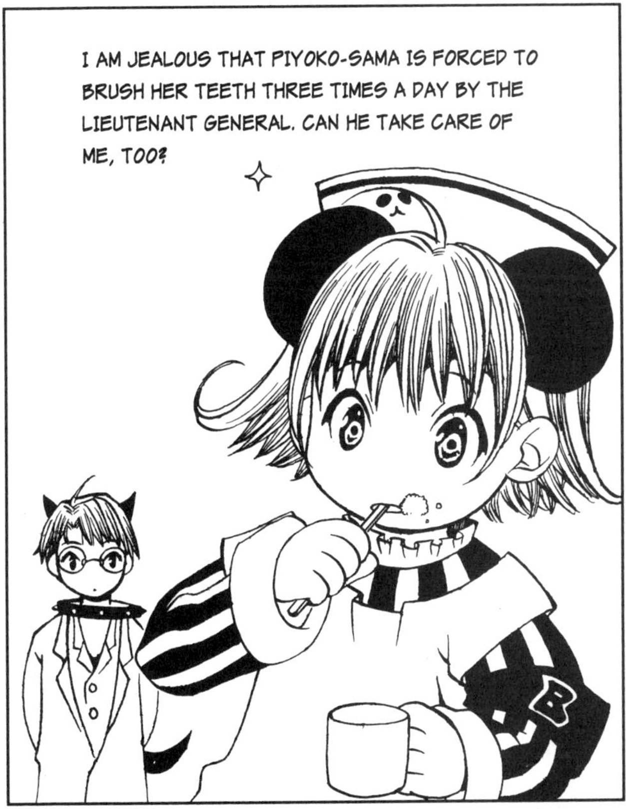
I AM JEALOUS THAT PIYOKO-SAMA IS FORCED TO BRUSH HER TEETH THREE TIMES A DAY BY THE LIEUTENANT GENERAL. CAN HE TAKE CARE OF ME, TOO?
B

Towa Oozora

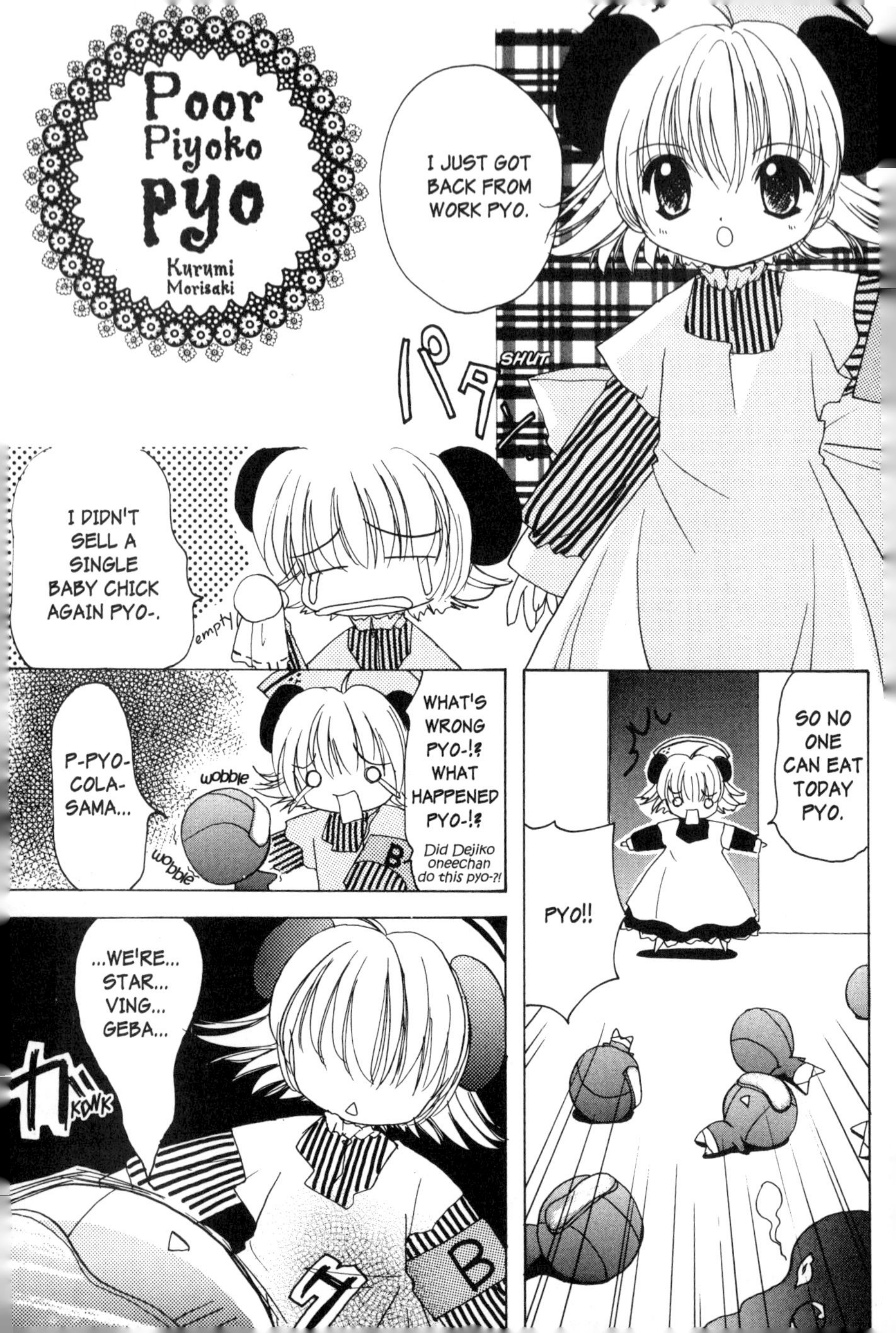
Poor Piyoko Pyo
Kurumi Morisaki
I JUST GOT BACK FROM WORK PYO.
SHUT
I DIDN'T SELL A SINGLE BABY CHICK AGAIN PYO-.
empty
SO NO ONE CAN EAT TODAY PYO.
PYO!!
WHAT'S WRONG PYO-!? WHAT HAPPENED PYO-!?
Did Dejiko oneechan do this pyo-?!
P-PYO-COLA-SAMA...
wobble
wobble
...WE'RE... STAR... VING... GEBA...
KONK

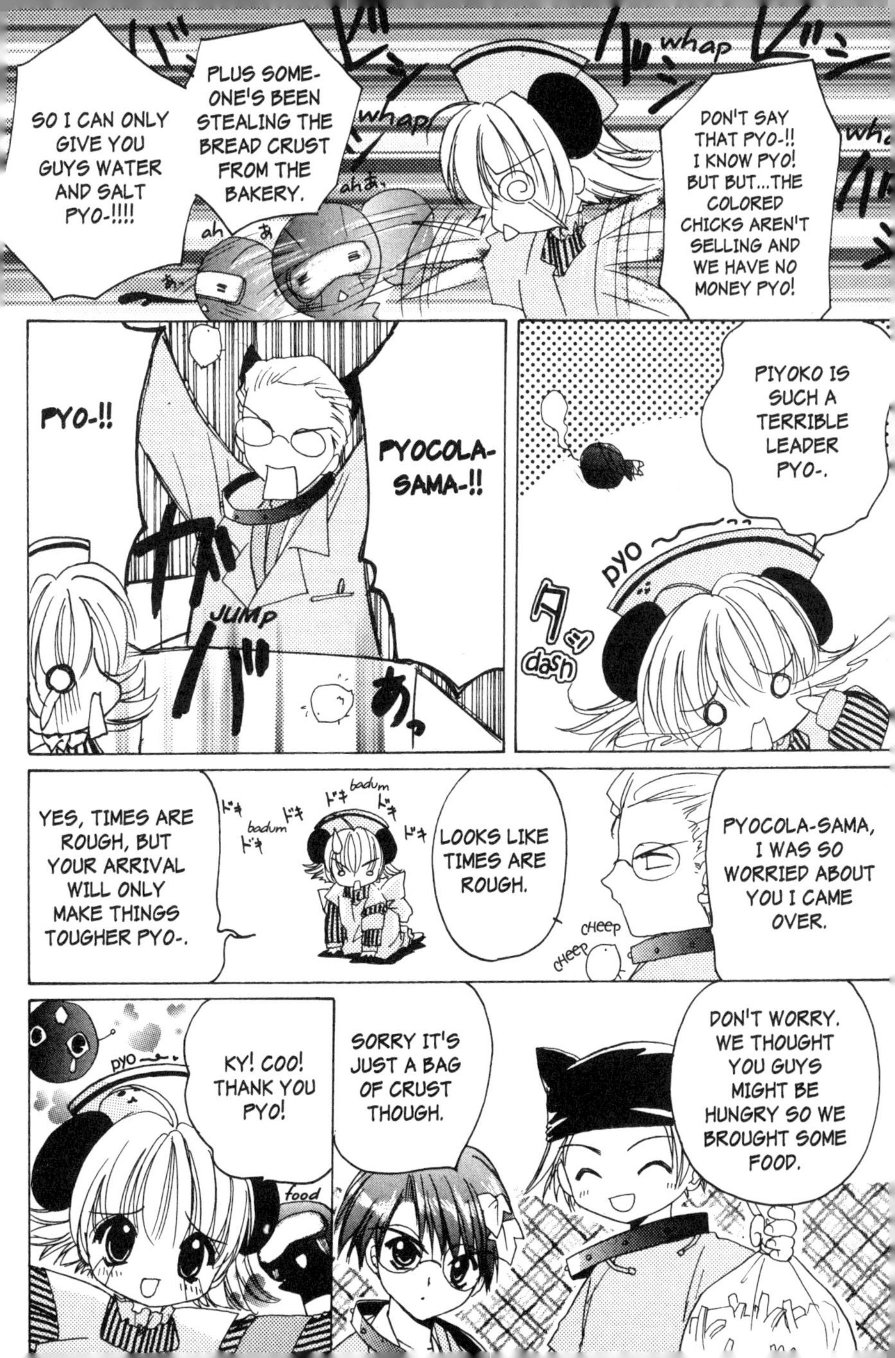

whap
DON'T SAY THAT PYO-!! I KNOW PYO! BUT BUT...THE COLORED CHICKS AREN'T SELLING AND WE HAVE NO MONEY PYO!
whap
PLUS SOME-ONE'S BEEN STEALING THE BREAD CRUST FROM THE BAKERY.
ah
ah
SO I CAN ONLY GIVE YOU GUYS WATER AND SALT PYO-!!!!
PIYOKO IS SUCH A TERRIBLE LEADER PYO-.
PYO
dash
PYOCOLA-SAMA-!!
PYO-!!
JUMP
PYOCOLA-SAMA, I WAS SO WORRIED ABOUT YOU I CAME OVER.
CHEEP
CHEEP
LOOKS LIKE TIMES ARE ROUGH.
badum
badum
YES, TIMES ARE ROUGH, BUT YOUR ARRIVAL WILL ONLY MAKE THINGS TOUGHER PYO-.
DON'T WORRY. WE THOUGHT YOU GUYS MIGHT BE HUNGRY SO WE BROUGHT SOME FOOD.
SORRY IT'S JUST A BAG OF CRUST THOUGH.
KY! COO! THANK YOU PYO!
pyo
food

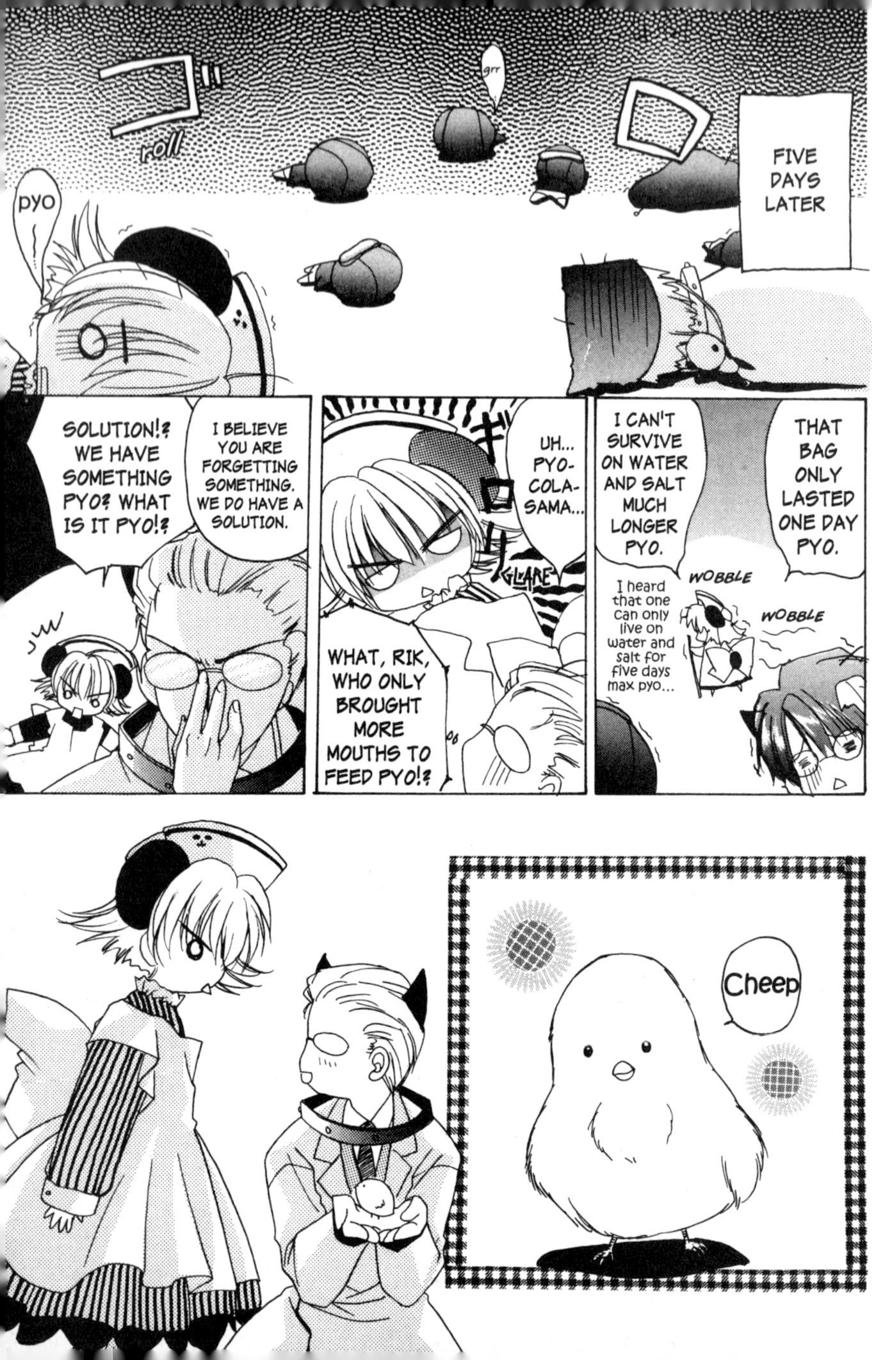
FIVE DAYS LATER
grr
roll
pyo
THAT BAG ONLY LASTED ONE DAY PYO.
I CAN'T SURVIVE ON WATER AND SALT MUCH LONGER PYO.
WOBBLE
WOBBLE
I heard that one can only live on water and salt for five days max pyo...
UH... PYO-COLA-SAMA...
GLARE
WHAT, RIK, WHO ONLY BROUGHT MORE MOUTHS TO FEED PYO!?
I BELIEVE YOU ARE FORGETTING SOMETHING. WE DO HAVE A SOLUTION.
SOLUTION!? WE HAVE SOMETHING PYO? WHAT IS IT PYO!?
Cheep

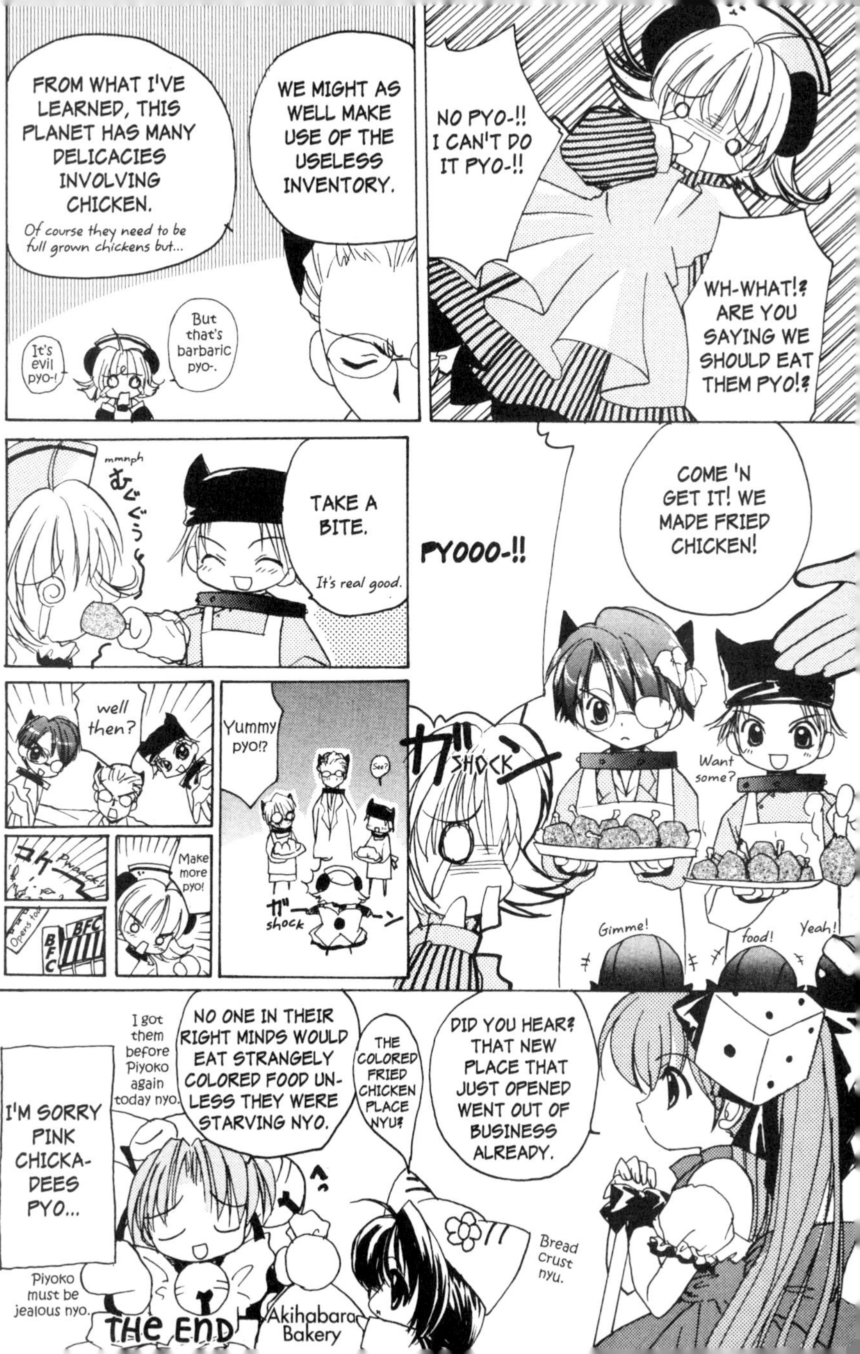
WH-WHAT!? ARE YOU SAYING WE SHOULD EAT THEM PYO!?
NO PYO-!! I CAN'T DO IT PYO-!!
WE MIGHT AS WELL MAKE USE OF THE USELESS INVENTORY.
FROM WHAT I'VE LEARNED, THIS PLANET HAS MANY DELICACIES INVOLVING CHICKEN.
Of course they need to be full grown chickens but...
But that's barbaric pyo-.
It's evil pyo-!
COME 'N GET IT! WE MADE FRIED CHICKEN!
PYOOO-!!
SHOCK
Want some?
Yeah!
food!
Gimme!
TAKE A BITE.
It's real good.
mmnph
むぐぐう
Yummy pyo!?
See?
shock
well then?
Make more pyo!
Pwaack!
BFC
DID YOU HEAR? THAT NEW PLACE THAT JUST OPENED WENT OUT OF BUSINESS ALREADY.
THE COLORED FRIED CHICKEN PLACE NYU?
Bread crust nyu.
NO ONE IN THEIR RIGHT MINDS WOULD EAT STRANGELY COLORED FOOD UNLESS THEY WERE STARVING NYO.
I got them before Piyoko again today nyo.
I'M SORRY PINK CHICKA-DEES PYO...
Piyoko must be jealous nyo.
THE END
Akihabara Bakery

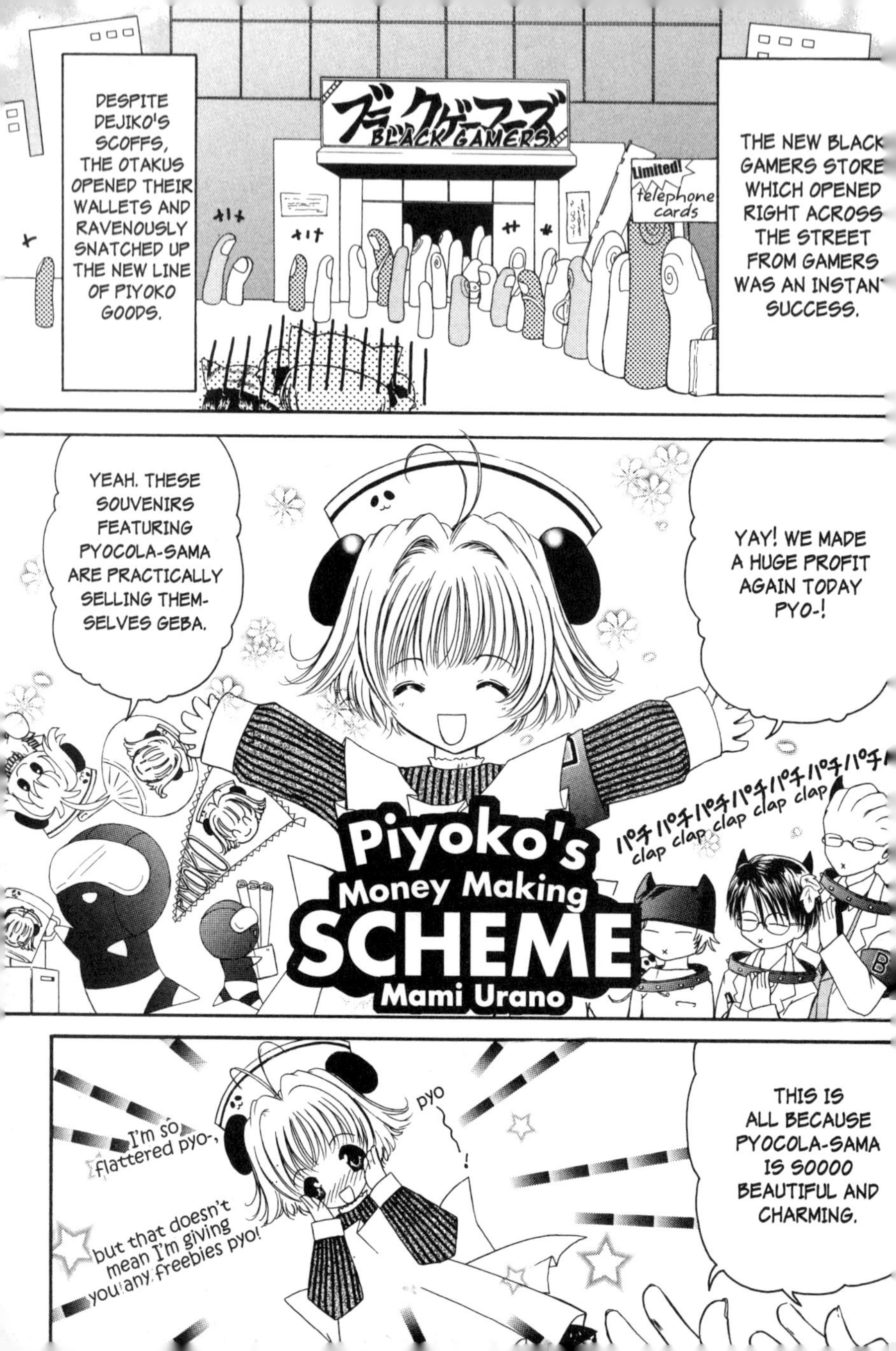
THE NEW BLACK GAMERS STORE WHICH OPENED RIGHT ACROSS THE STREET FROM GAMERS WAS AN INSTANT SUCCESS.
ブラックゲーマーズ
BLACK GAMERS
Limited!
telephone cards
DESPITE DEJIKO'S SCOFFS, THE OTAKUS OPENED THEIR WALLETS AND RAVENOUSLY SNATCHED UP THE NEW LINE OF PIYOKO GOODS.
YAY! WE MADE A HUGE PROFIT AGAIN TODAY PYO-!
YEAH. THESE SOUVENIRS FEATURING PYOCOLA-SAMA ARE PRACTICALLY SELLING THEM-SELVES GEBA.
パチパチパチパチパチパチパチパチ
clap clap clap clap clap
Piyoko's Money Making SCHEME
Mami Urano
THIS IS ALL BECAUSE PYOCOLA-SAMA IS SOOOO BEAUTIFUL AND CHARMING.
pyo
!
I'm so flattered pyo-,
but that doesn't mean I'm giving you any freebies pyo!

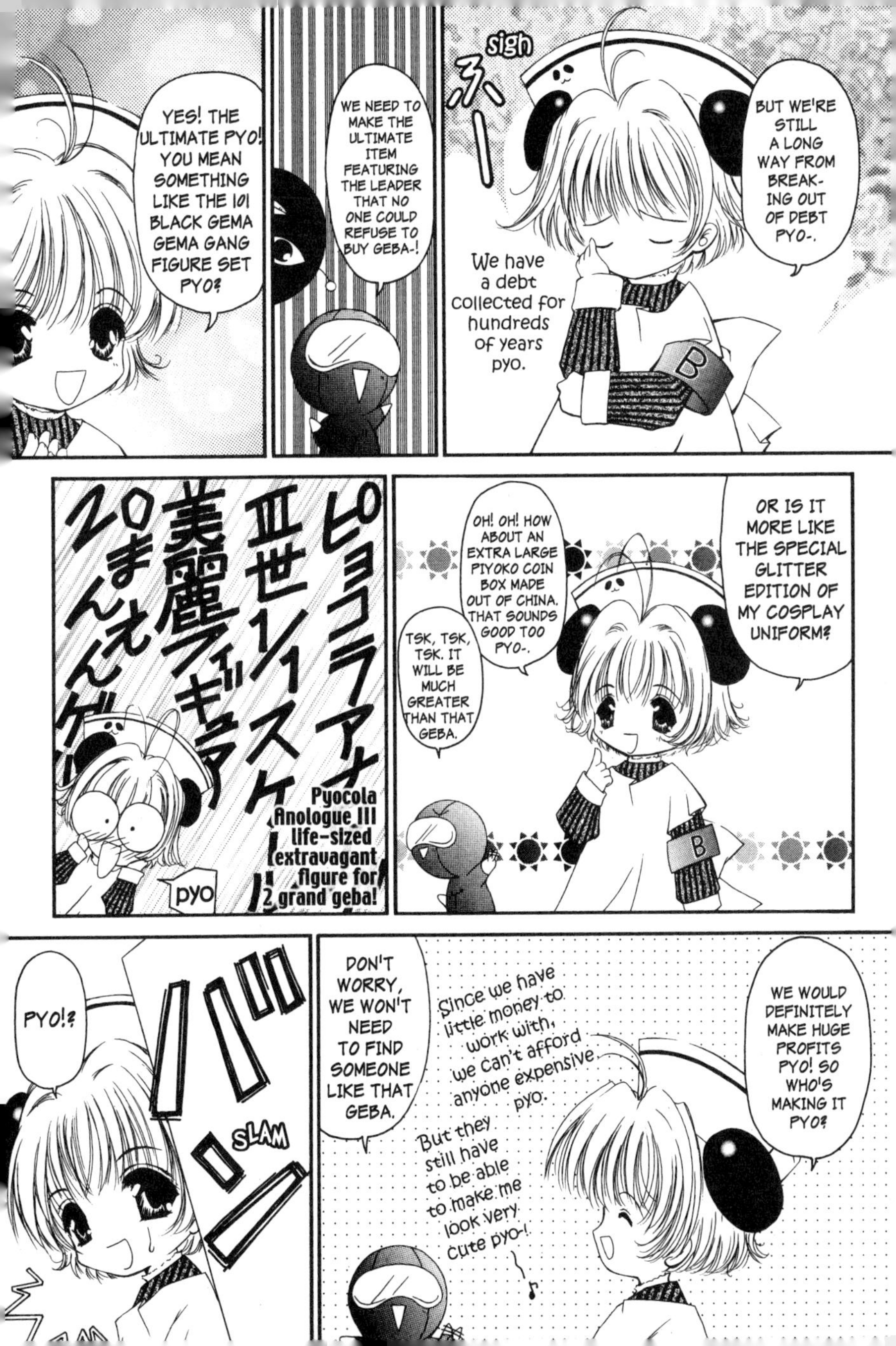
sigh
ふー
BUT WE'RE STILL A LONG WAY FROM BREAK-ING OUT OF DEBT PYO-.
We have a debt collected for hundreds of years pyo.
WE NEED TO MAKE THE ULTIMATE ITEM FEATURING THE LEADER THAT NO ONE COULD REFUSE TO BUY GEBA-!
YES! THE ULTIMATE PYO! YOU MEAN SOMETHING LIKE THE 101 BLACK GEMA GEMA GANG FIGURE SET PYO?
OR IS IT MORE LIKE THE SPECIAL GLITTER EDITION OF MY COSPLAY UNIFORM?
OH! OH! HOW ABOUT AN EXTRA LARGE PIYOKO COIN BOX MADE OUT OF CHINA. THAT SOUNDS GOOD TOO PYO-.
TSK, TSK, TSK. IT WILL BE MUCH GREATER THAN THAT GEBA.
ピョコラアナIII世1/1スケ美麗フィギュア20まんえんゲバ!
Pyocola Anologue III life-sized extravagant figure for 2 grand geba!
pyo
WE WOULD DEFINITELY MAKE HUGE PROFITS PYO! SO WHO'S MAKING IT PYO?
DON'T WORRY, WE WON'T NEED TO FIND SOMEONE LIKE THAT GEBA.
Since we have little money to work with, we can't afford anyone expensive pyo.
But they still have to be able to make me look very cute pyo-!
PYO!?
バン
SLAM

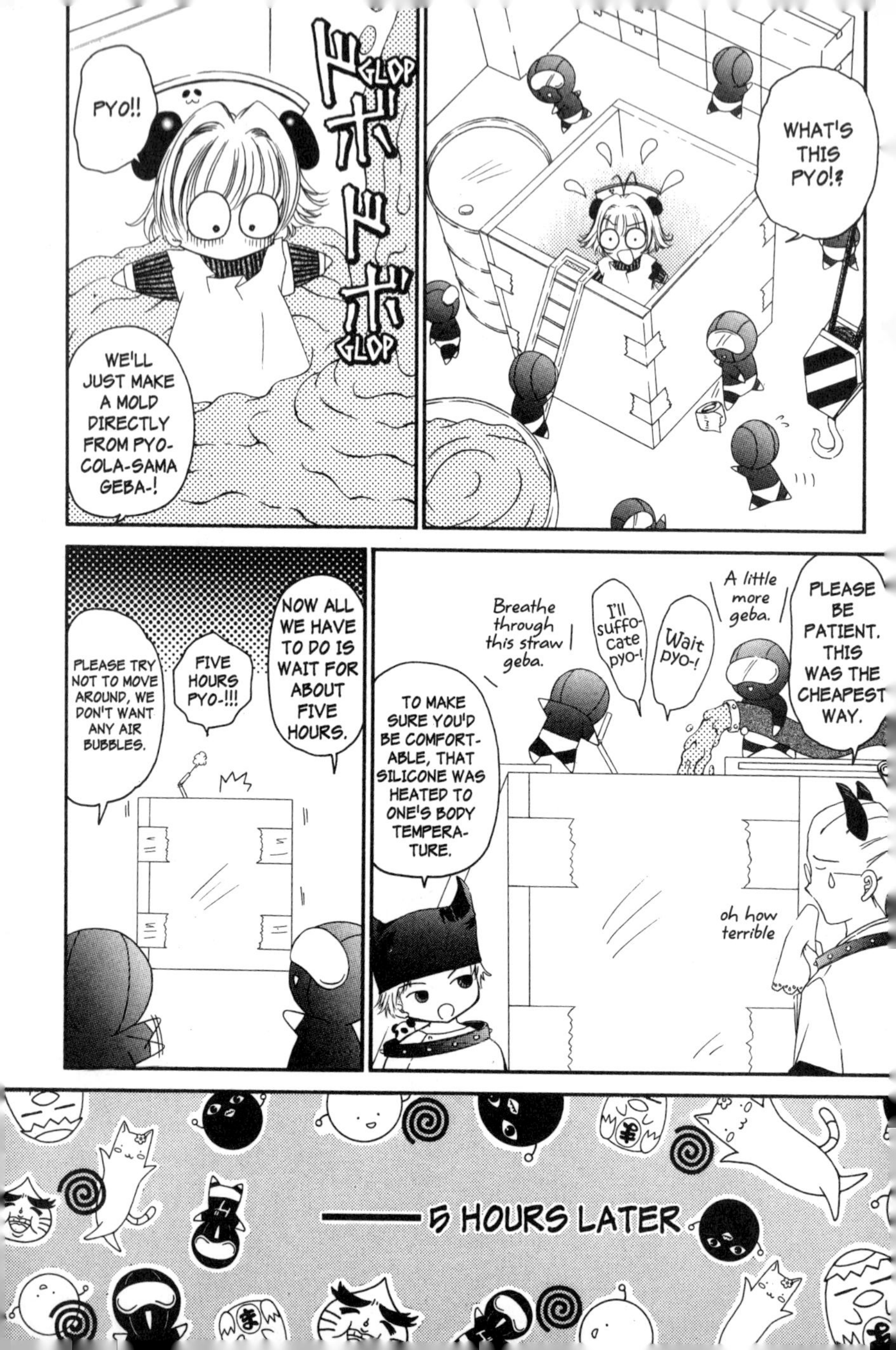
WHAT'S THIS PYO!?
PYO!!
GLOP GLOP
WE'LL JUST MAKE A MOLD DIRECTLY FROM PYO-COLA-SAMA GEBA-!
PLEASE BE PATIENT. THIS WAS THE CHEAPEST WAY.
A little more geba.
Wait pyo-!
I'll suffocate pyo-!
Breathe through this straw geba.
TO MAKE SURE YOU'D BE COMFORTABLE, THAT SILICONE WAS HEATED TO ONE'S BODY TEMPERATURE.
oh how terrible
NOW ALL WE HAVE TO DO IS WAIT FOR ABOUT FIVE HOURS.
FIVE HOURS PYO-!!!
PLEASE TRY NOT TO MOVE AROUND, WE DON'T WANT ANY AIR BUBBLES.
—5 HOURS LATER

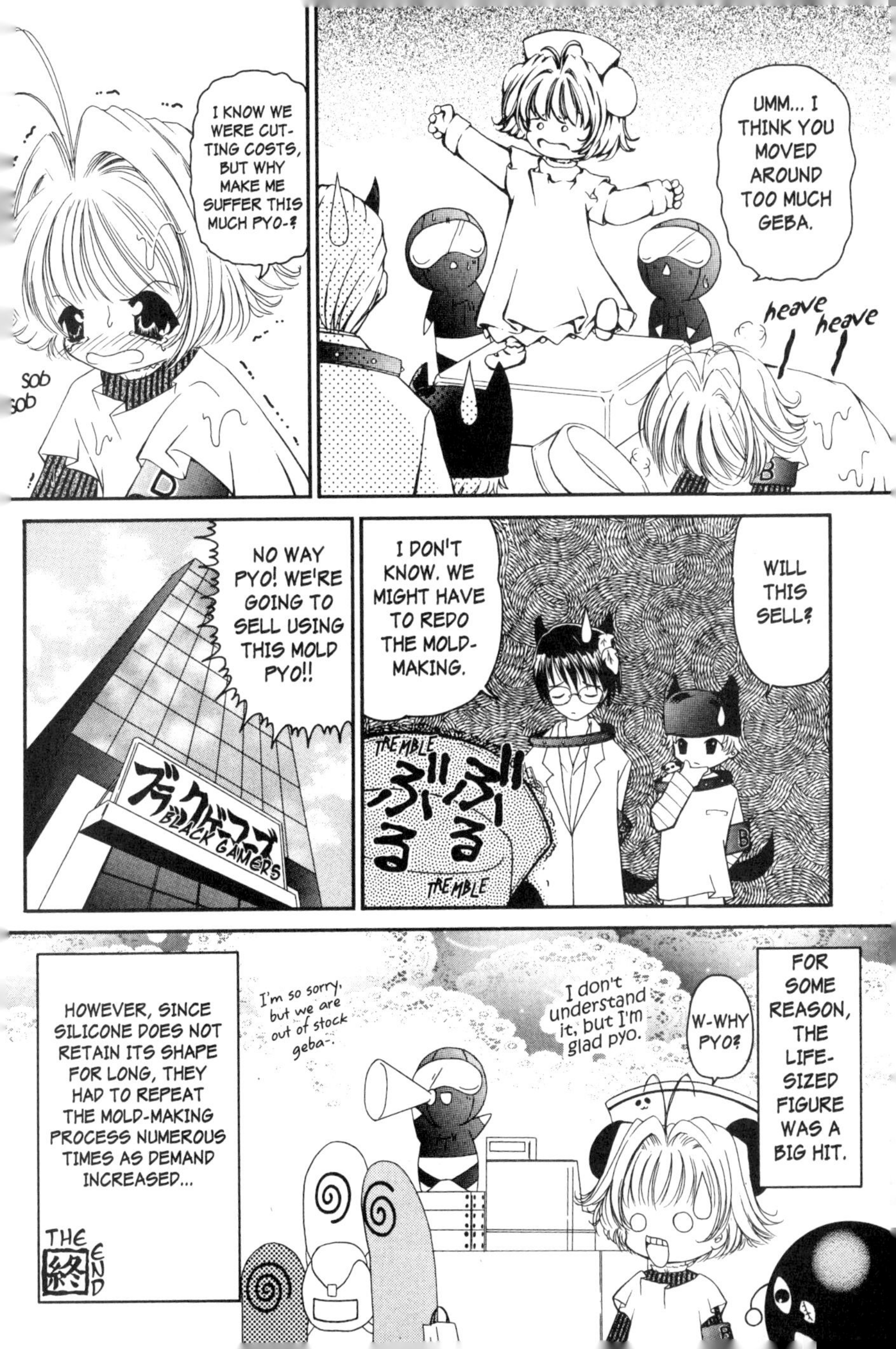
UMM... I THINK YOU MOVED AROUND TOO MUCH GEBA.
heave heave
I KNOW WE WERE CUT-TING COSTS, BUT WHY MAKE ME SUFFER THIS MUCH PYO-?
sob sob
WILL THIS SELL?
I DON'T KNOW. WE MIGHT HAVE TO REDO THE MOLD-MAKING.
TREMBLE
ぶるぶる
TREMBLE
NO WAY PYO! WE'RE GOING TO SELL USING THIS MOLD PYO!!
ブラックゲーマーズ
BLACK GAMERS
FOR SOME REASON, THE LIFE-SIZED FIGURE WAS A BIG HIT.
W-WHY PYO?
I don't understand it, but I'm glad pyo.
I'm so sorry, but we are out of stock geba-.
HOWEVER, SINCE SILICONE DOES NOT RETAIN ITS SHAPE FOR LONG, THEY HAD TO REPEAT THE MOLD-MAKING PROCESS NUMEROUS TIMES AS DEMAND INCREASED...
THE 終 END

A Message to Piyoko-sama!

PLEASE FORGIVE ME FOR MAKING HER LOOK LIKE THIS 80 PERCENT OF THE TIME. I'M SSSOORRRY!

sorry!
by 森崎

HOW SAD PYO-!!

Kurumi Morisaki

A Message to Piyoko-sama!

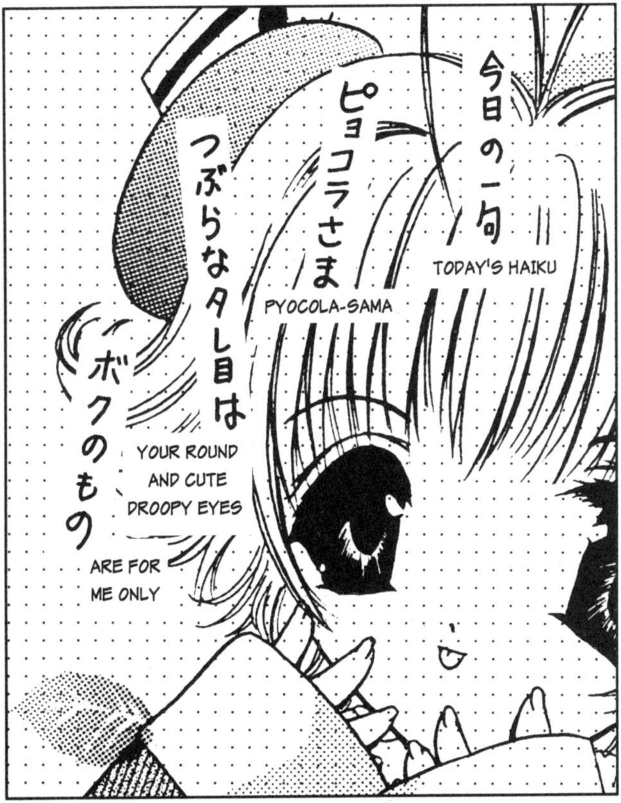
今日の一句
TODAY'S HAIKU
ピョコラさま
PYOCOLA-SAMA
つぶらなタレ目は
YOUR ROUND AND CUTE DROOPY EYES
ボクのもの
ARE FOR ME ONLY

Mami Urano

Piyoko's Gold Rush

Yuzuru Asahina

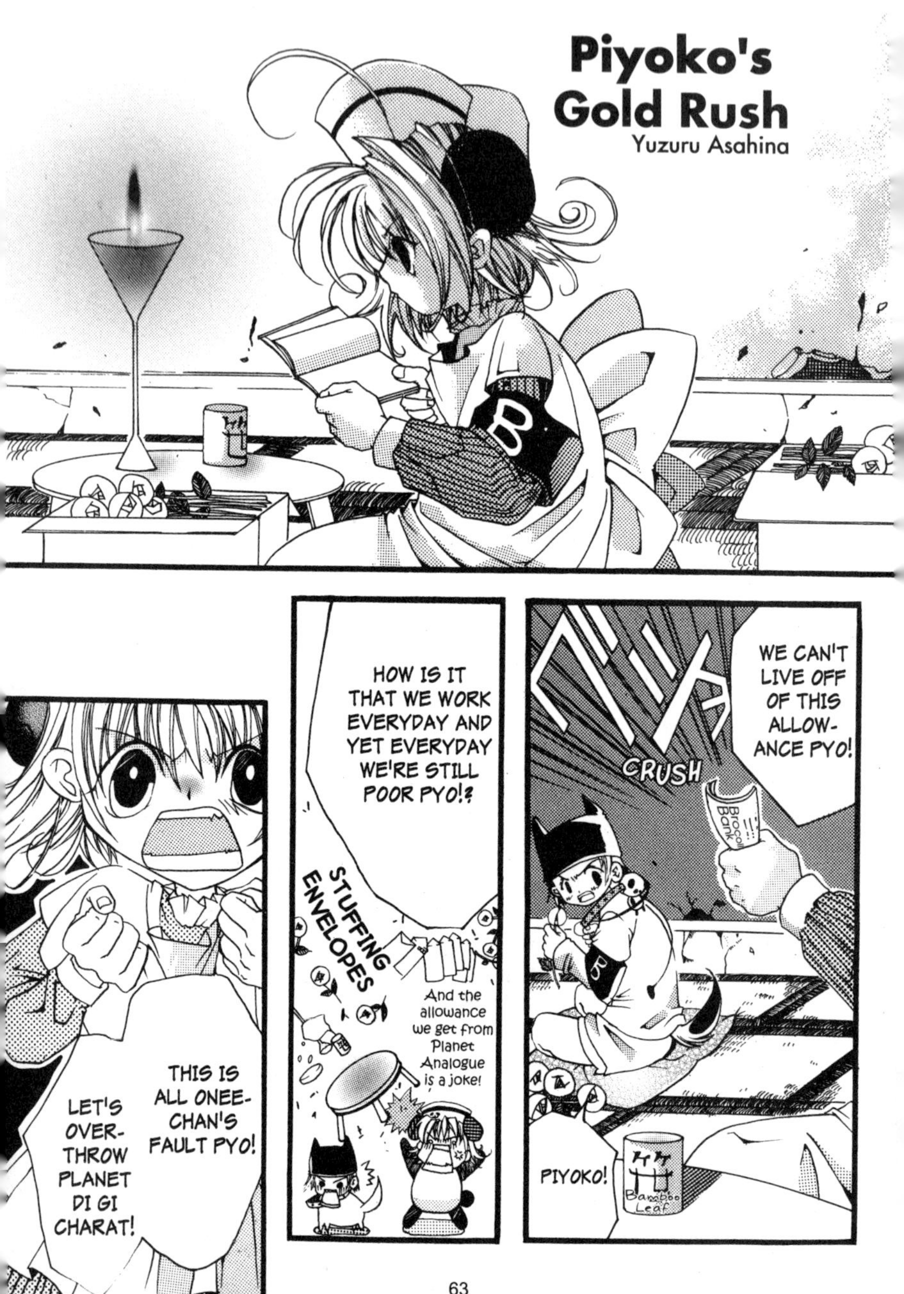

WE CAN'T LIVE OFF OF THIS ALLOW-ANCE PYO!
CRUSH
Broccoli Bank
PIYOKO!
Bamboo Leaf
HOW IS IT THAT WE WORK EVERYDAY AND YET EVERYDAY WE'RE STILL POOR PYO!?
STUFFING ENVELOPES
And the allowance we get from Planet Analogue is a joke!
THIS IS ALL ONEE-CHAN'S FAULT PYO!
LET'S OVER-THROW PLANET DI GI CHARAT!

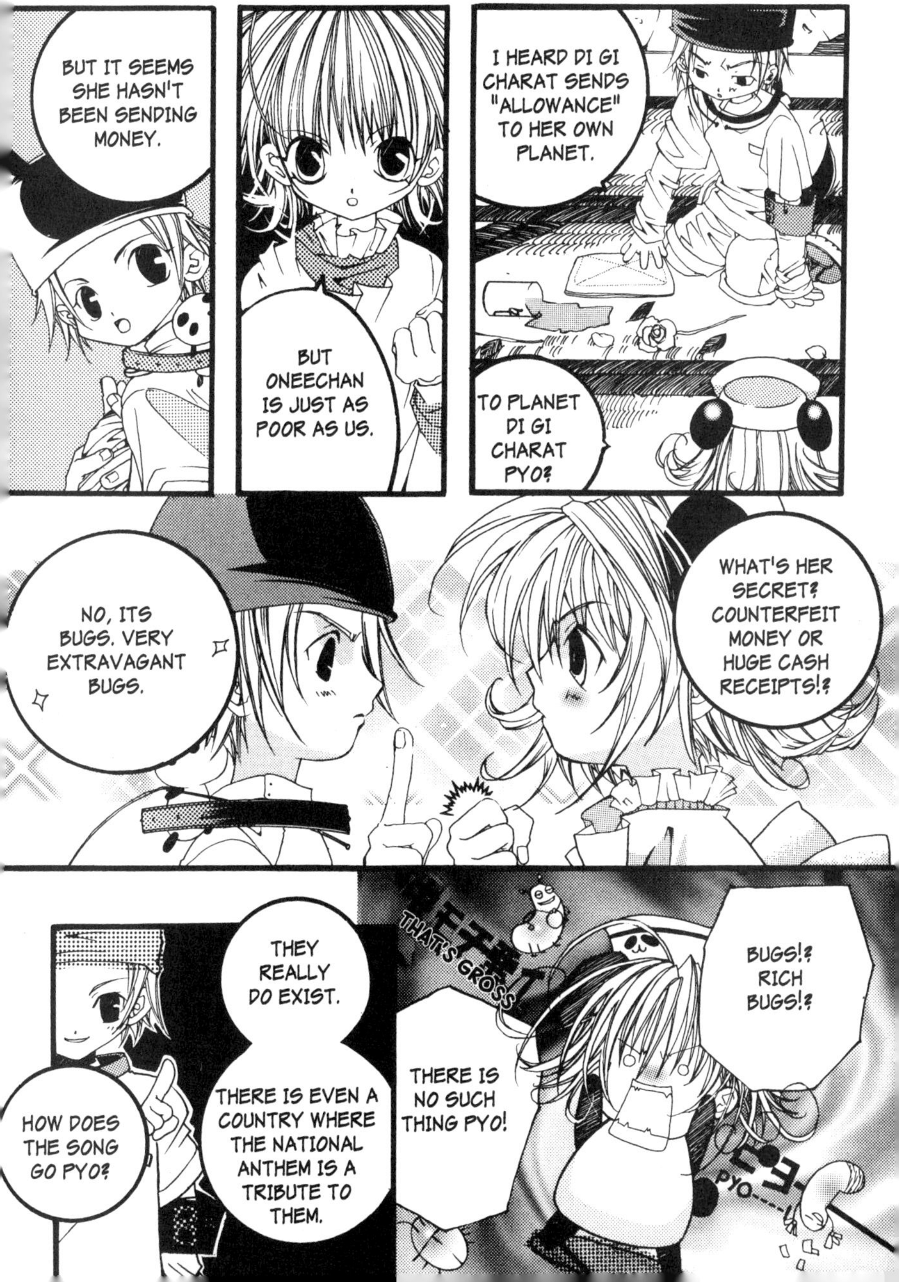
I HEARD DI GI CHARAT SENDS "ALLOWANCE" TO HER OWN PLANET.
TO PLANET DI GI CHARAT PYO?
BUT ONEECHAN IS JUST AS POOR AS US.
BUT IT SEEMS SHE HASN'T BEEN SENDING MONEY.
WHAT'S HER SECRET? COUNTERFEIT MONEY OR HUGE CASH RECEIPTS!?
NO, ITS BUGS. VERY EXTRAVAGANT BUGS.
BUGS!? RICH BUGS!?
THAT'S GROSS
THERE IS NO SUCH THING PYO!
PYO---!
THEY REALLY DO EXIST.
THERE IS EVEN A COUNTRY WHERE THE NATIONAL ANTHEM IS A TRIBUTE TO THEM.
HOW DOES THE SONG GO PYO?

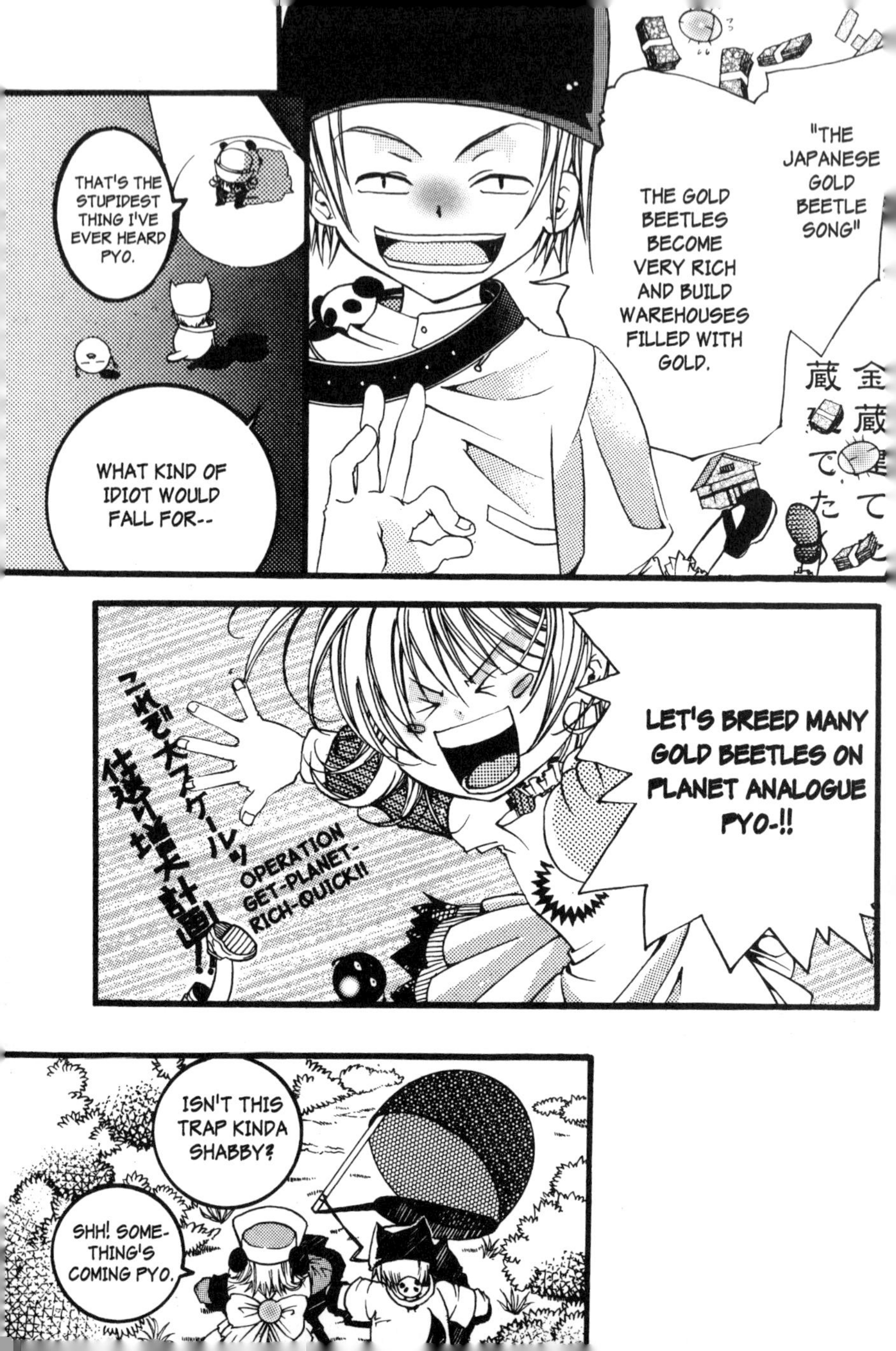
"THE JAPANESE GOLD BEETLE SONG"
THE GOLD BEETLES BECOME VERY RICH AND BUILD WAREHOUSES FILLED WITH GOLD.
THAT'S THE STUPIDEST THING I'VE EVER HEARD PYO.
WHAT KIND OF IDIOT WOULD FALL FOR--
LET'S BREED MANY GOLD BEETLES ON PLANET ANALOGUE PYO-!!
OPERATION GET-PLANET-RICH-QUICK!!
ISN'T THIS TRAP KINDA SHABBY?
SHH! SOMETHING'S COMING PYO.

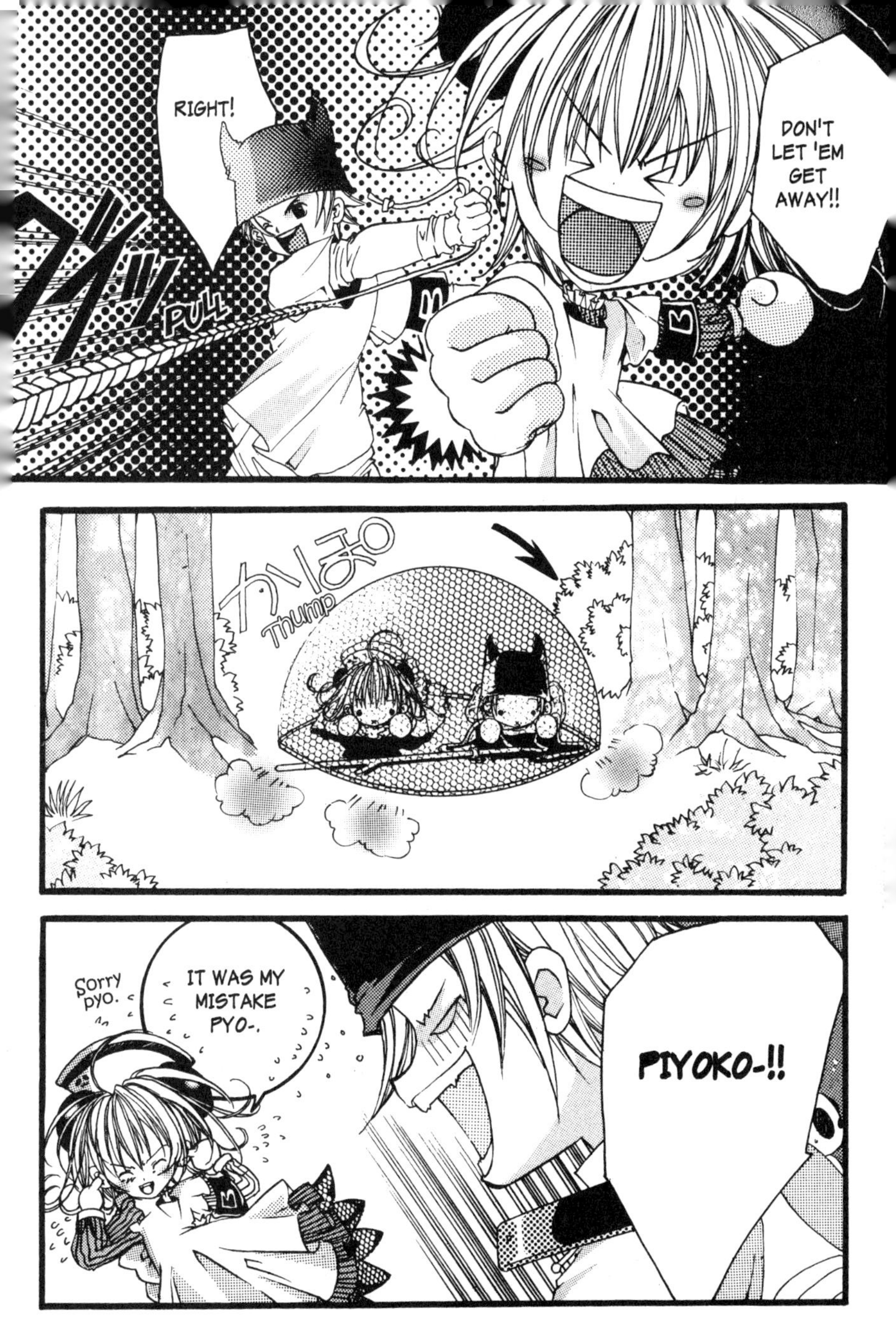
DON'T LET 'EM GET AWAY!!
RIGHT!
PULL
THUMP
PIYOKO-!!
IT WAS MY MISTAKE PYO-.
Sorry pyo.

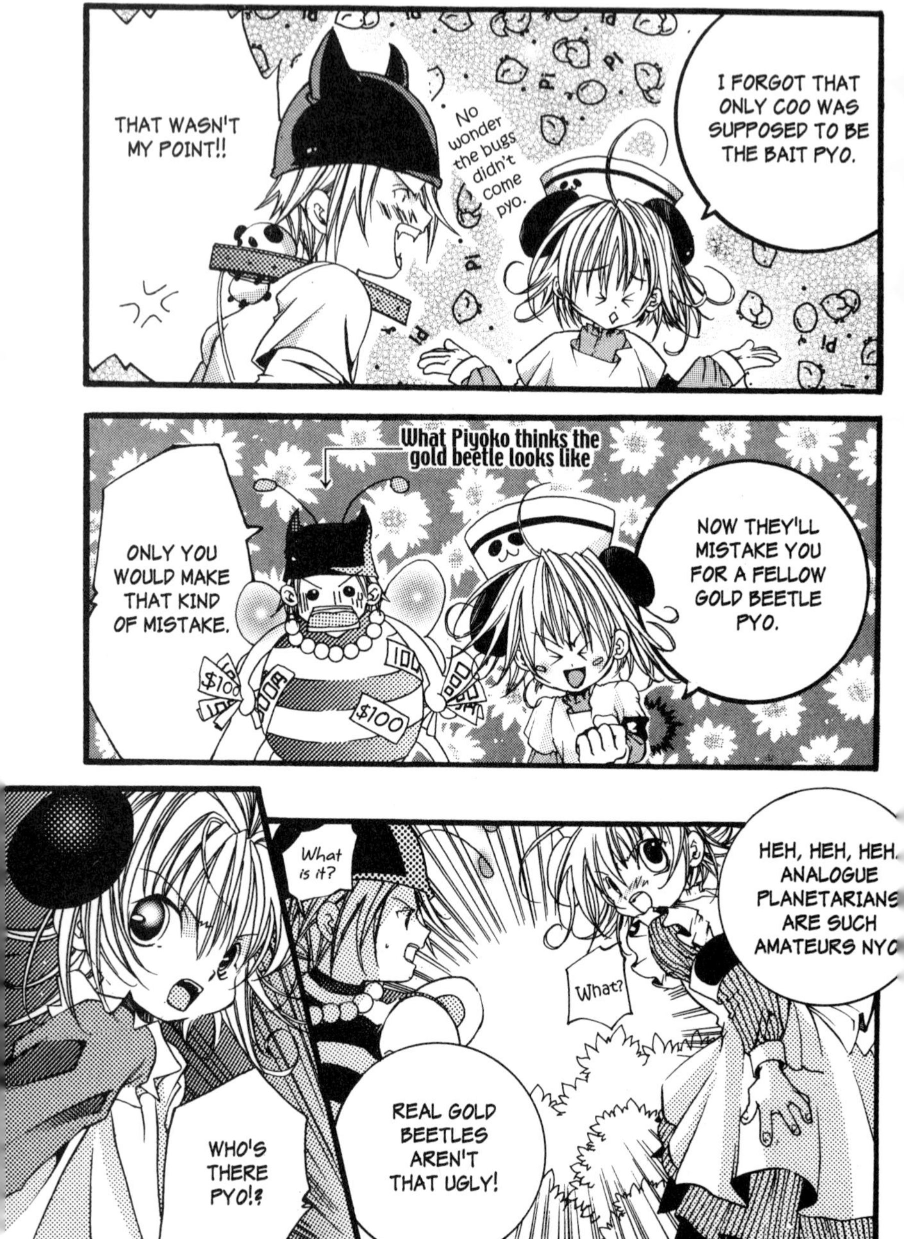
I FORGOT THAT ONLY COO WAS SUPPOSED TO BE THE BAIT PYO.
No wonder the bugs didn't come pyo.
THAT WASN'T MY POINT!!
NOW THEY'LL MISTAKE YOU FOR A FELLOW GOLD BEETLE PYO.
What Piyoko thinks the gold beetle looks like
ONLY YOU WOULD MAKE THAT KIND OF MISTAKE.
HEH, HEH, HEH. ANALOGUE PLANETARIANS ARE SUCH AMATEURS NYO
REAL GOLD BEETLES AREN'T THAT UGLY!
What?
What is it?
WHO'S THERE PYO!?

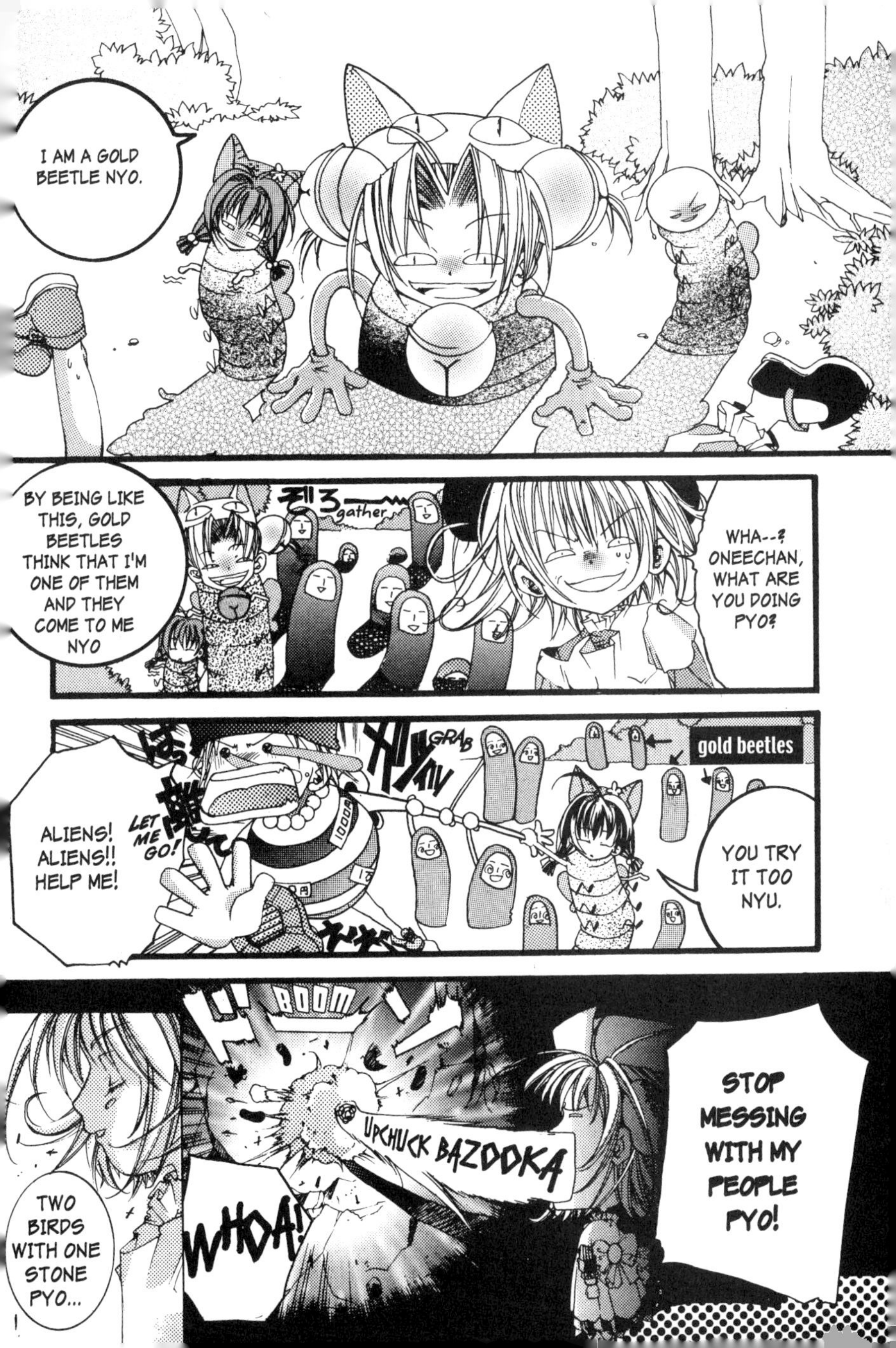
I AM A GOLD BEETLE NYO.
WHA--? ONEECHAN, WHAT ARE YOU DOING PYO?
gather
BY BEING LIKE THIS, GOLD BEETLES THINK THAT I'M ONE OF THEM AND THEY COME TO ME NYO
gold beetles
YOU TRY IT TOO NYU.
GRAB
LET ME GO!
ALIENS! ALIENS!! HELP ME!
STOP MESSING WITH MY PEOPLE PYO!
BOOM
UPCHUCK BAZOOKA
WHOA!
TWO BIRDS WITH ONE STONE PYO...

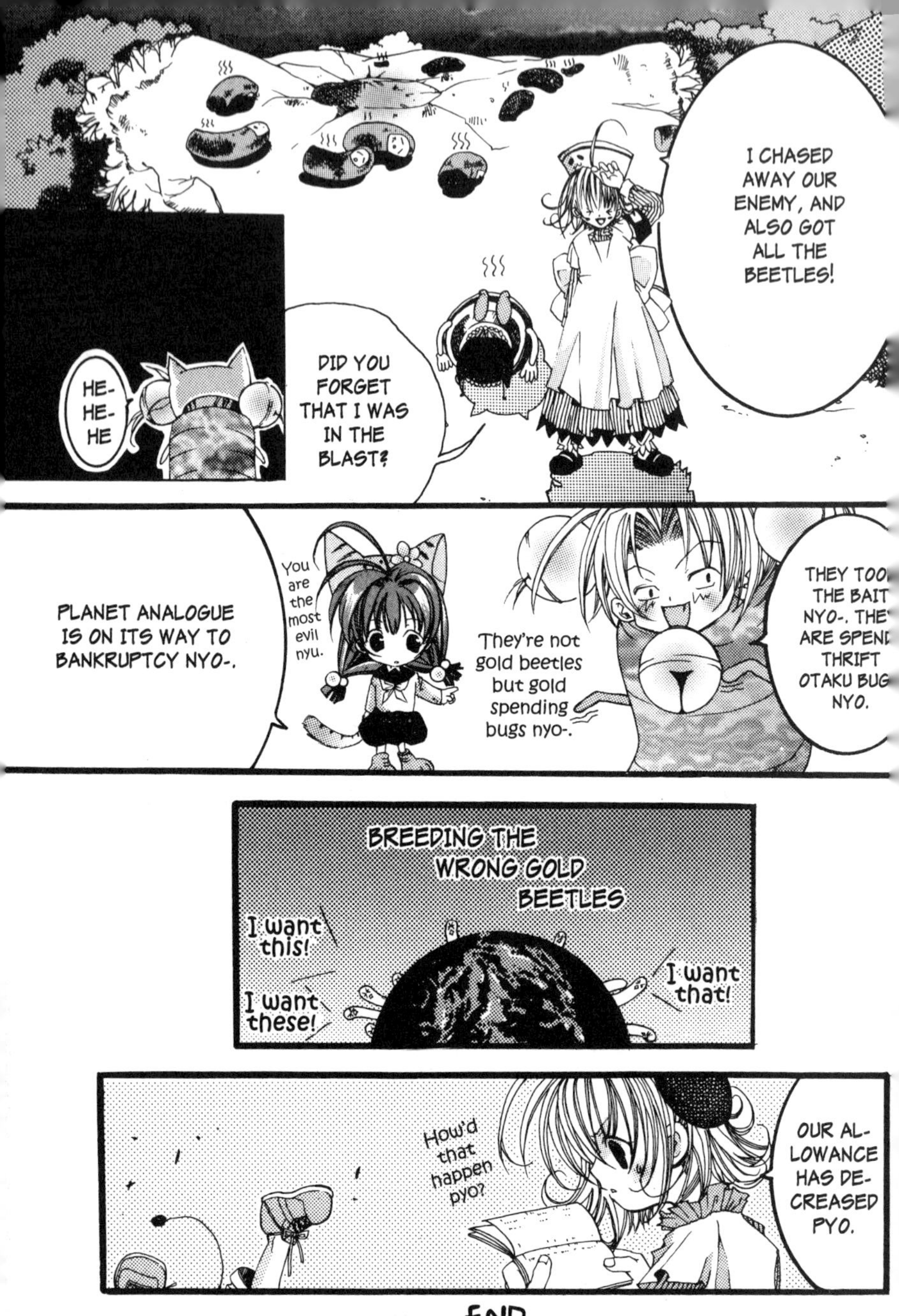
I CHASED AWAY OUR ENEMY, AND ALSO GOT ALL THE BEETLES!
DID YOU FORGET THAT I WAS IN THE BLAST?
HE-HE-HE
THEY TOO THE BAIT NYO-. THE ARE SPEND THRIFT OTAKU BUG NYO.
They're not gold beetles but gold spending bugs nyo-.
You are the most evil nyu.
PLANET ANALOGUE IS ON ITS WAY TO BANKRUPTCY NYO-.
BREEDING THE WRONG GOLD BEETLES
I want that!
I want this!
I want these!
OUR AL-LOWANCE HAS DE-CREASED PYO.
How'd that happen pyo?

END

Pyocola-sama and Me

Yuzuru Asahina

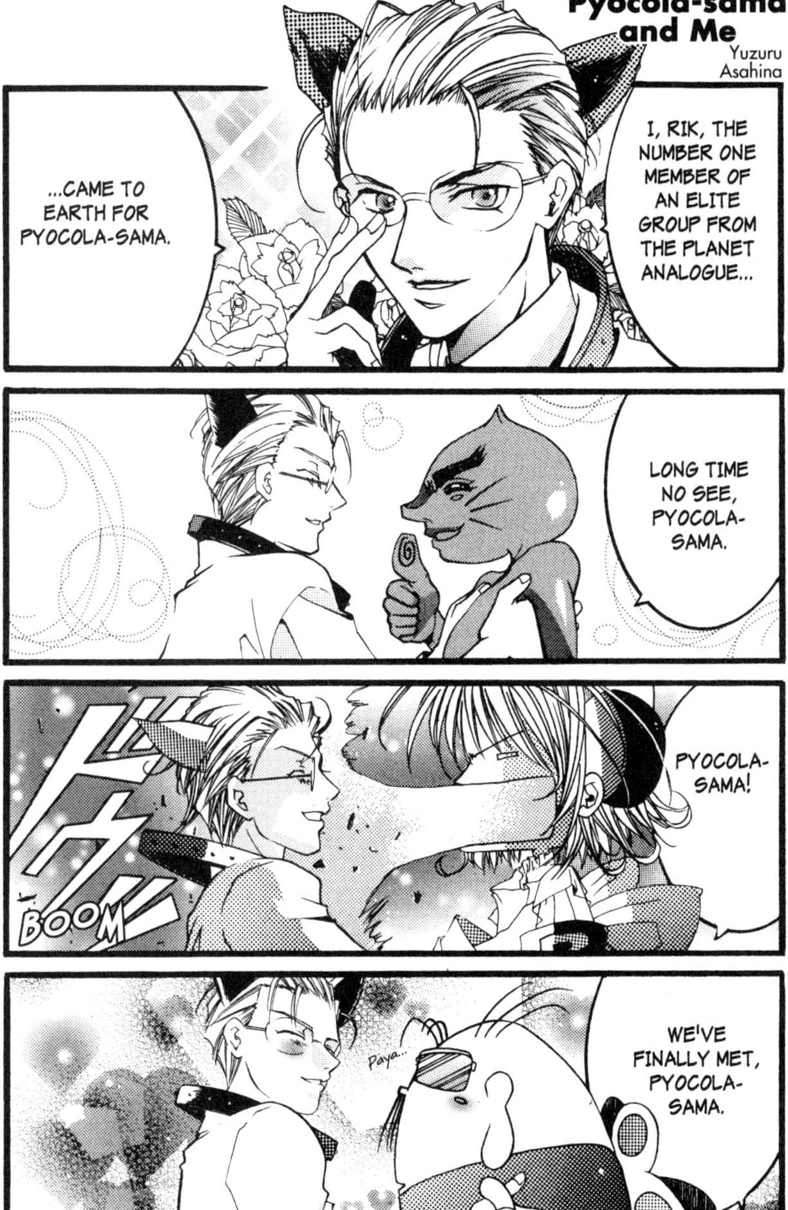
I, RIK, THE NUMBER ONE MEMBER OF AN ELITE GROUP FROM THE PLANET ANALOGUE...
...CAME TO EARTH FOR PYOCOLA-SAMA.
LONG TIME NO SEE, PYOCOLA-SAMA.
PYOCOLA-SAMA!
BOOM
WE'VE FINALLY MET, PYOCOLA-SAMA.
Paya...

END

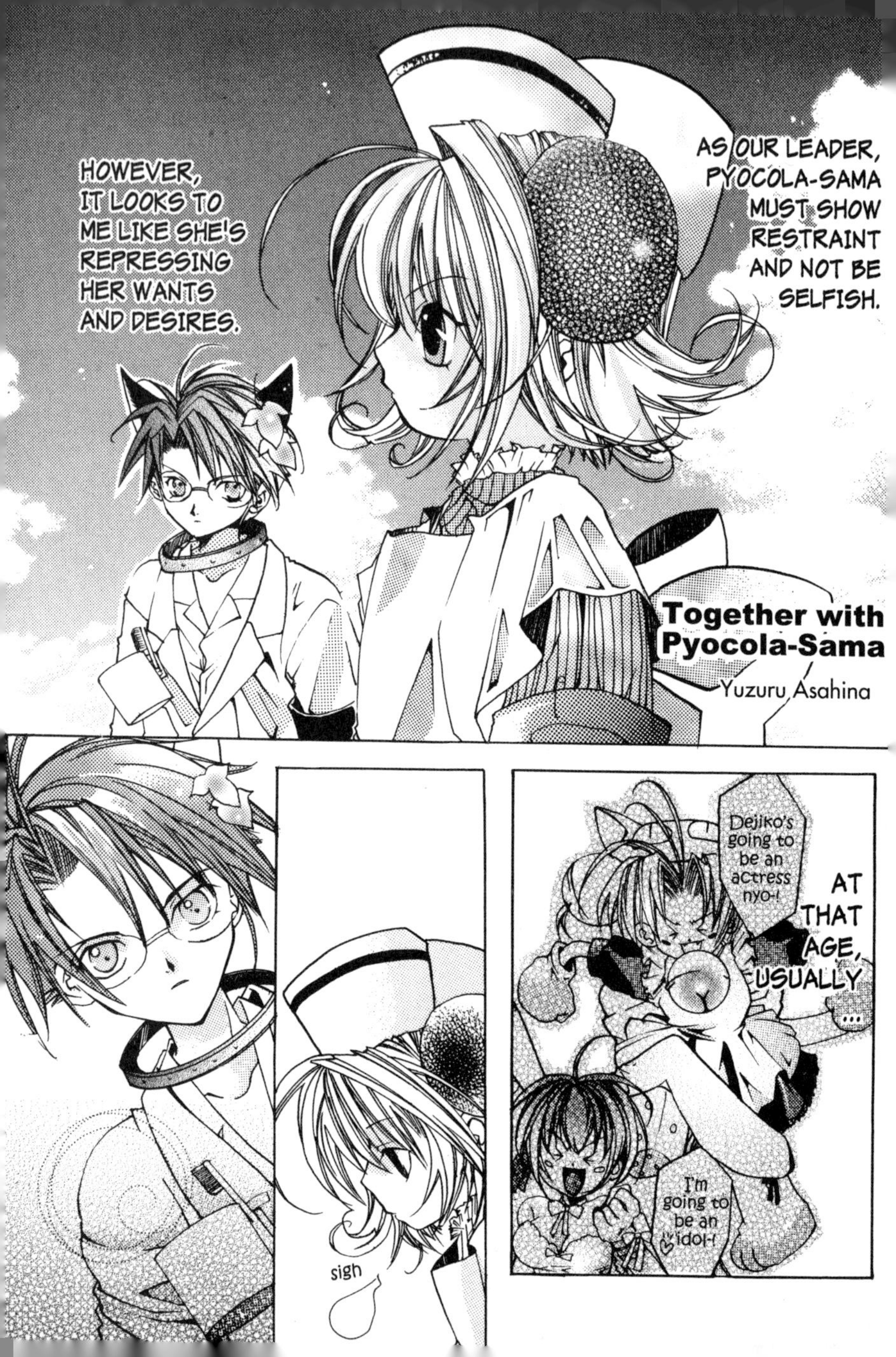
AS OUR LEADER, PYOCOLA-SAMA MUST SHOW RESTRAINT AND NOT BE SELFISH.
HOWEVER, IT LOOKS TO ME LIKE SHE'S REPRESSING HER WANTS AND DESIRES.
Together with Pyocola-Sama
Yuzuru Asahina
AT THAT AGE, USUALLY...
Dejiko's going to be an actress nyo-!
I'm going to be an idol-!
sigh

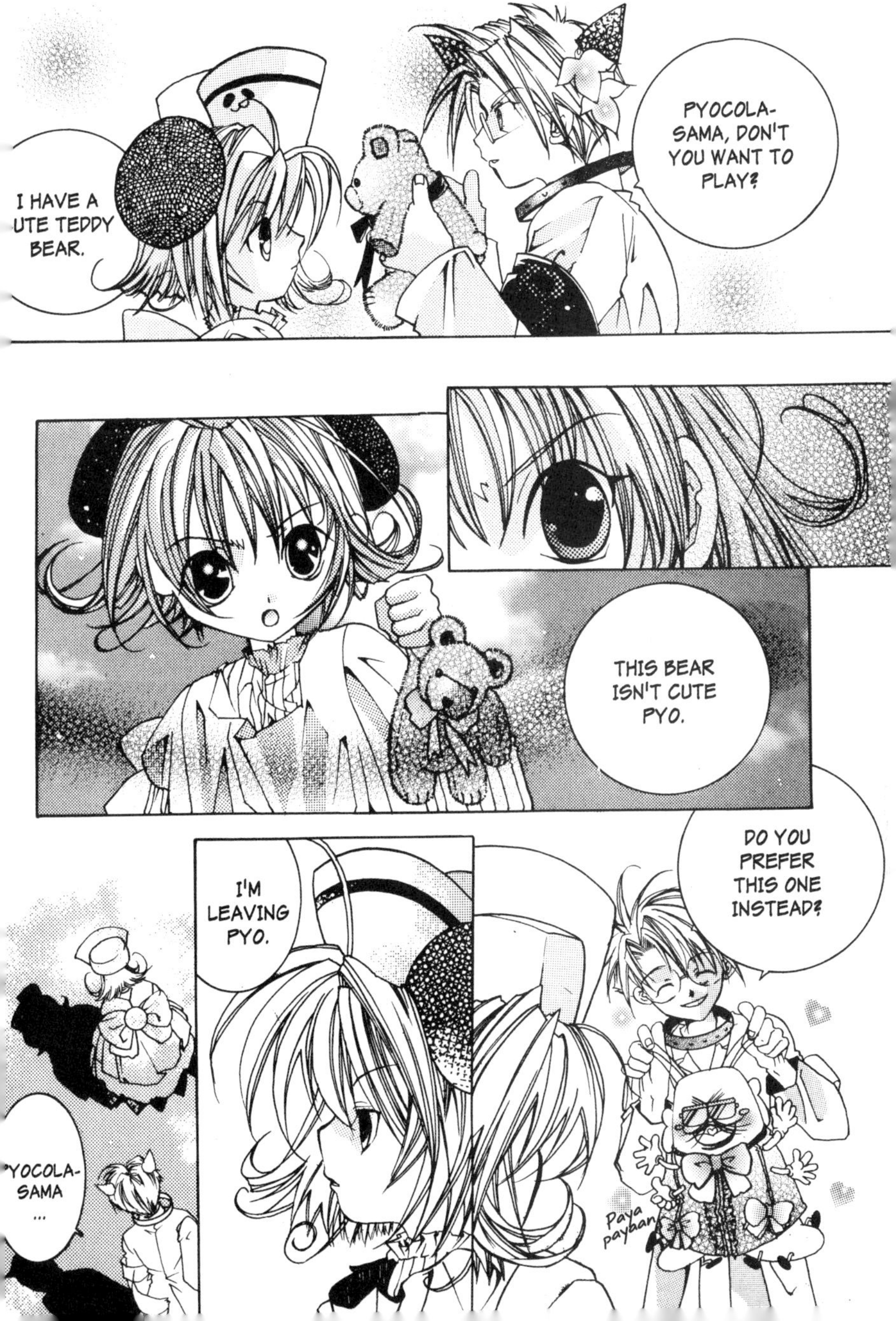
PYOCOLA-SAMA, DON'T YOU WANT TO PLAY?
I HAVE A UTE TEDDY BEAR.
THIS BEAR ISN'T CUTE PYO.
DO YOU PREFER THIS ONE INSTEAD?
Paya payban
I'M LEAVING PYO.
YOCOLA-SAMA ...

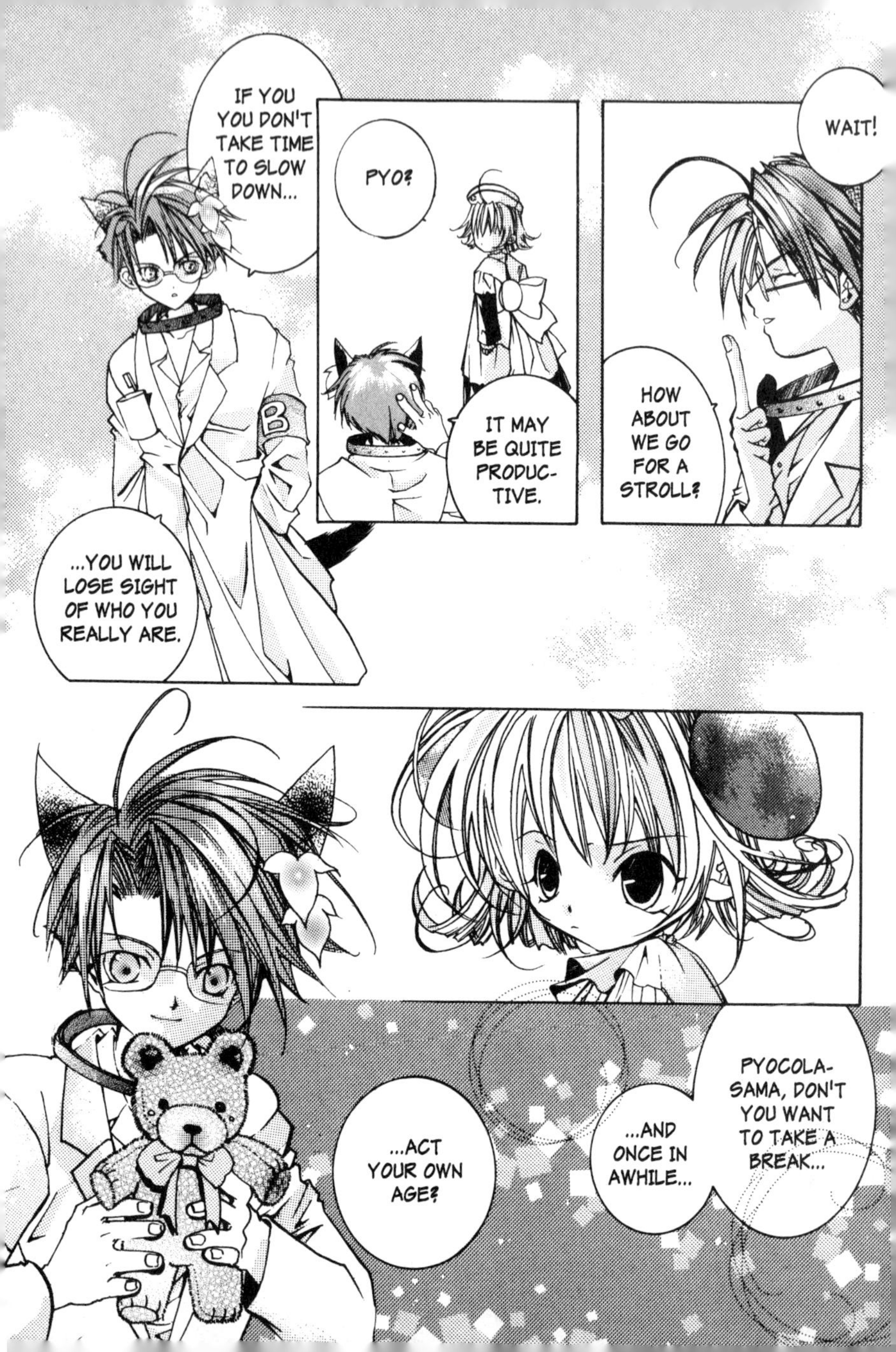
WAIT!
HOW ABOUT WE GO FOR A STROLL?
PYO?
IT MAY BE QUITE PRODUC-TIVE.
IF YOU YOU DON'T TAKE TIME TO SLOW DOWN...
...YOU WILL LOSE SIGHT OF WHO YOU REALLY ARE.
PYOCOLA-SAMA, DON'T YOU WANT TO TAKE A BREAK...
...AND ONCE IN AWHILE...
...ACT YOUR OWN AGE?

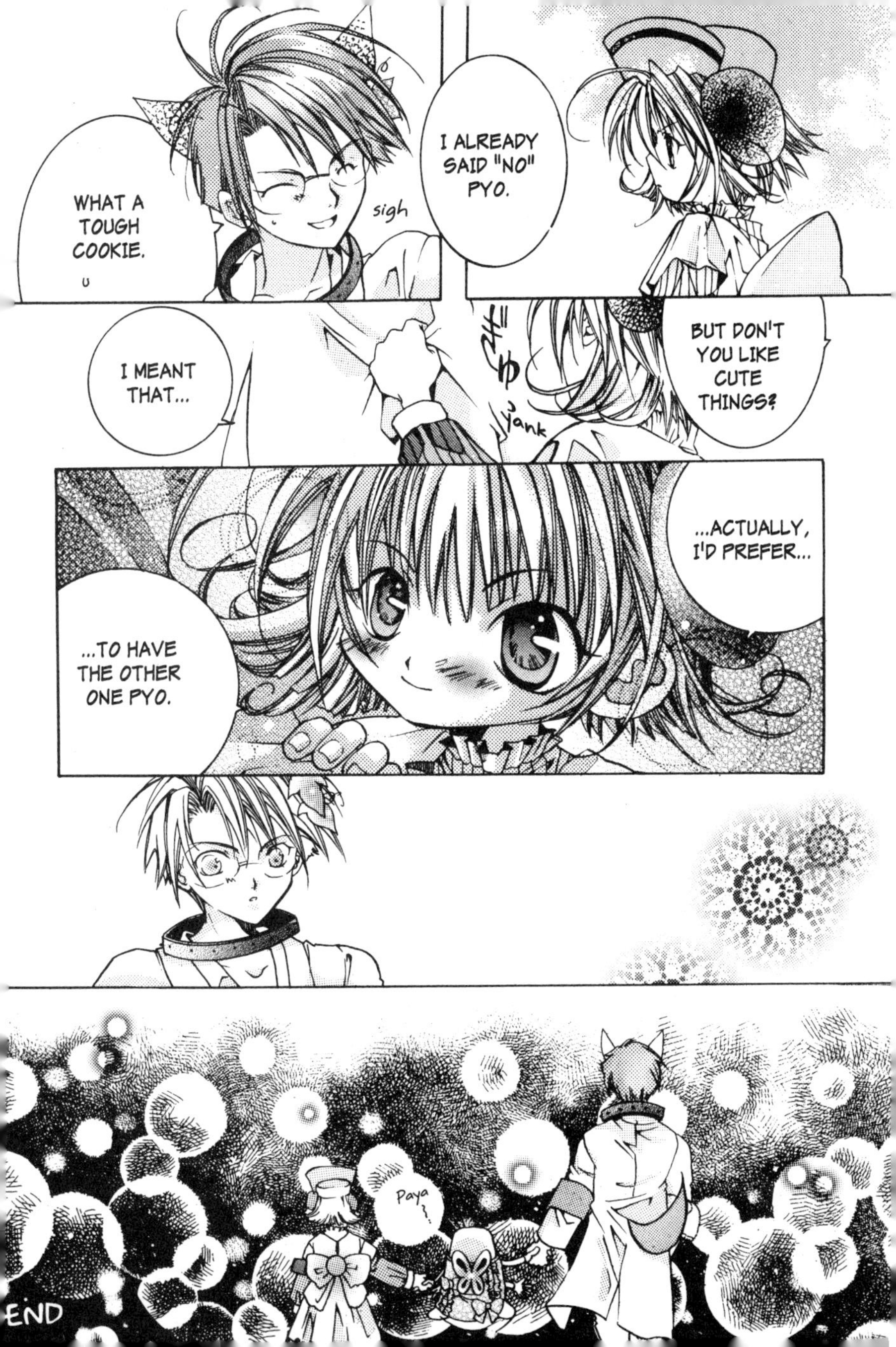
I ALREADY SAID "NO" PYO.
WHAT A TOUGH COOKIE.
sigh
BUT DON'T YOU LIKE CUTE THINGS?
yank
I MEANT THAT...
...ACTUALLY, I'D PREFER...
...TO HAVE THE OTHER ONE PYO.
Paya
END

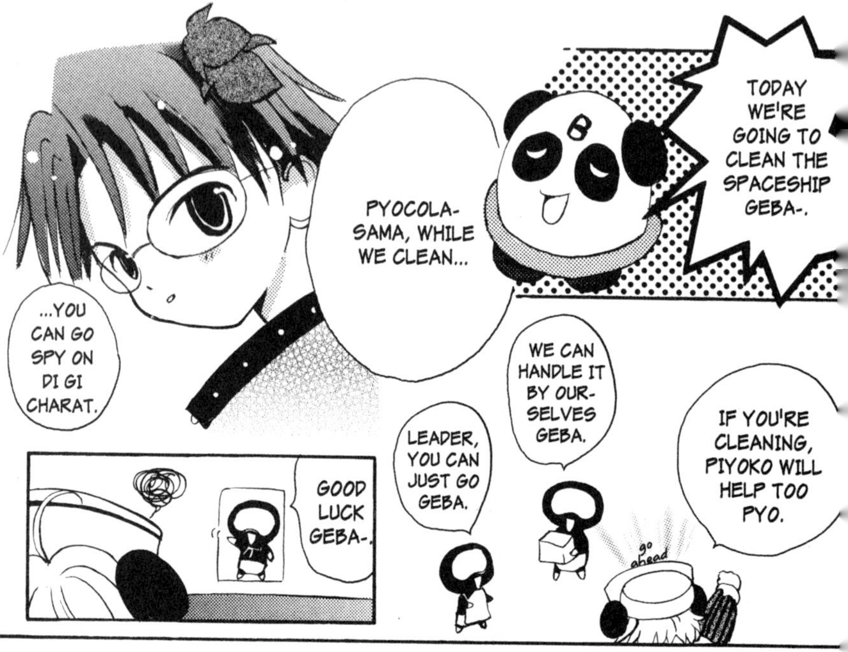
TODAY WE'RE GOING TO CLEAN THE SPACESHIP GEBA-.
PYOCOLA-SAMA, WHILE WE CLEAN...
...YOU CAN GO SPY ON DI GI CHARAT.
IF YOU'RE CLEANING, PIYOKO WILL HELP TOO PYO.
WE CAN HANDLE IT BY OUR-SELVES GEBA.
LEADER, YOU CAN JUST GO GEBA.
go ahead
GOOD LUCK GEBA-.

Lonely Day

Tsukiko

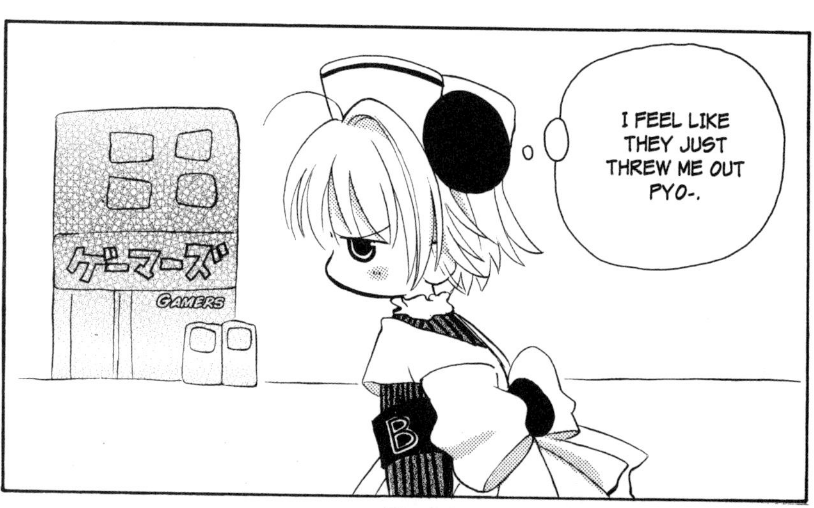
I FEEL LIKE THEY JUST THREW ME OUT PYO-.
ゲーマーズ
GAMERS

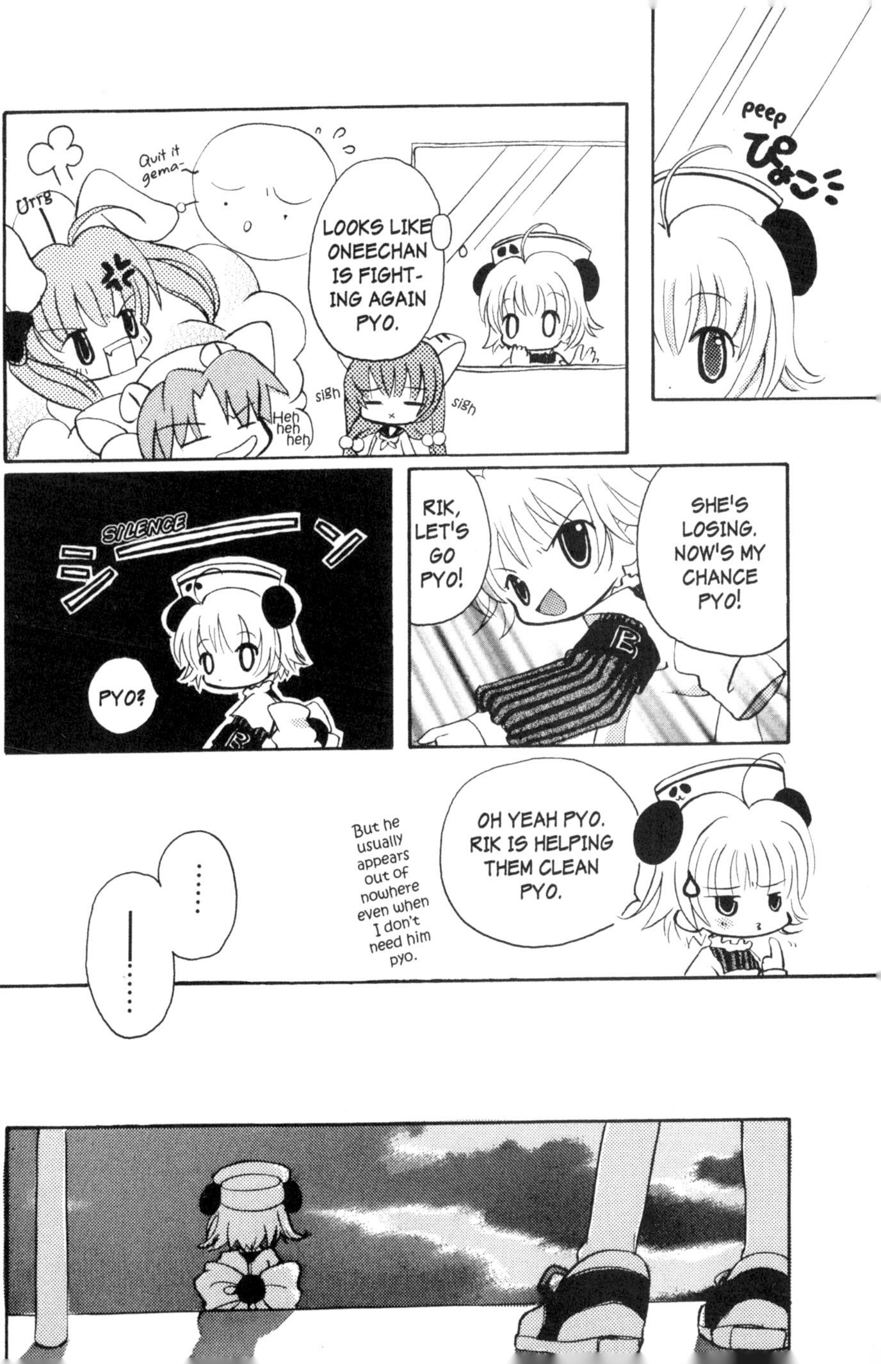
peep
ぴょこ
LOOKS LIKE ONEECHAN IS FIGHTING AGAIN PYO.
Quit it gema~
Urrg
sigh
sigh
Heh heh heh
SHE'S LOSING. NOW'S MY CHANCE PYO!
RIK, LET'S GO PYO!
SILENCE
ジーーーッ
PYO?
OH YEAH PYO. RIK IS HELPING THEM CLEAN PYO.
But he usually appears out of nowhere even when I don't need him pyo.
......
—......

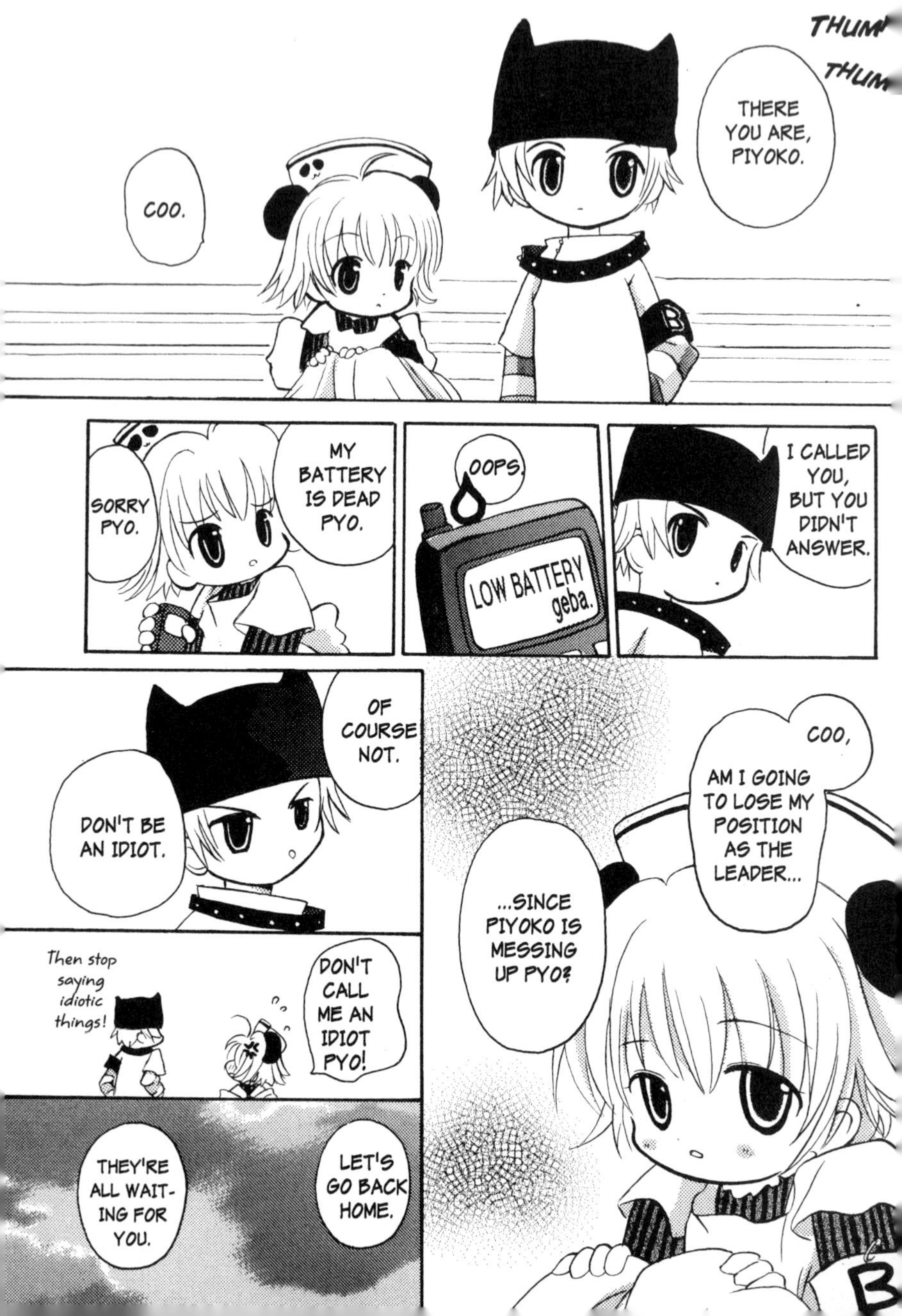
THUM
THUM
THERE YOU ARE, PIYOKO.
COO.
I CALLED YOU, BUT YOU DIDN'T ANSWER.
OOPS.
LOW BATTERY geba.
MY BATTERY IS DEAD PYO.
SORRY PYO.
COO, AM I GOING TO LOSE MY POSITION AS THE LEADER...
...SINCE PIYOKO IS MESSING UP PYO?
OF COURSE NOT.
DON'T BE AN IDIOT.
DON'T CALL ME AN IDIOT PYO!
Then stop saying idiotic things!
LET'S GO BACK HOME.
THEY'RE ALL WAITING FOR YOU.

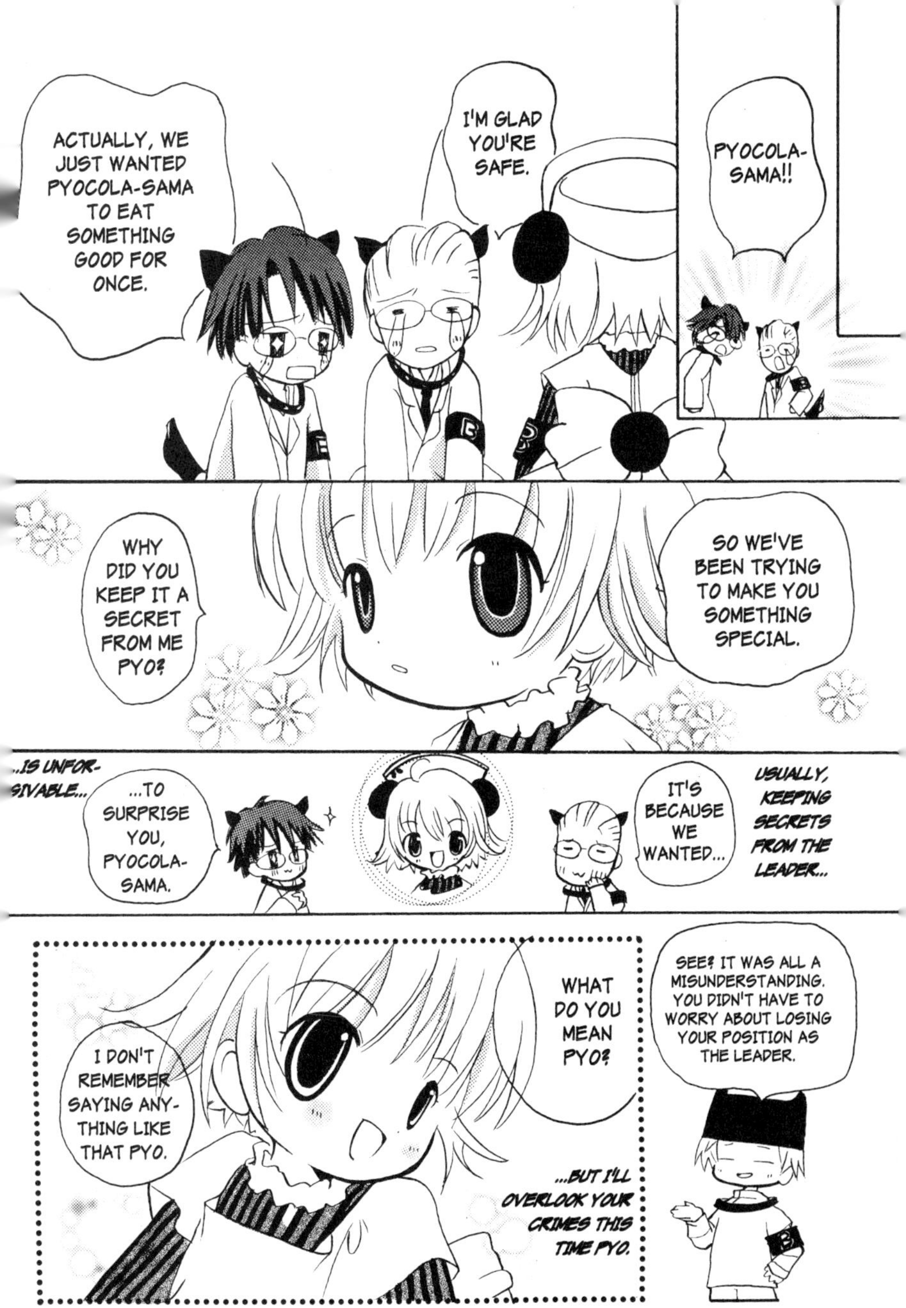
PYOCOLA-SAMA!!
I'M GLAD YOU'RE SAFE.
ACTUALLY, WE JUST WANTED PYOCOLA-SAMA TO EAT SOMETHING GOOD FOR ONCE.
SO WE'VE BEEN TRYING TO MAKE YOU SOMETHING SPECIAL.
WHY DID YOU KEEP IT A SECRET FROM ME PYO?
USUALLY, KEEPING SECRETS FROM THE LEADER...
IT'S BECAUSE WE WANTED...
...TO SURPRISE YOU, PYOCOLA-SAMA.
...IS UNFORGIVABLE...
SEE? IT WAS ALL A MISUNDERSTANDING. YOU DIDN'T HAVE TO WORRY ABOUT LOSING YOUR POSITION AS THE LEADER.
WHAT DO YOU MEAN PYO?
I DON'T REMEMBER SAYING ANYTHING LIKE THAT PYO.
...BUT I'LL OVERLOOK YOUR CRIMES THIS TIME PYO.

THE END

A Message to Piyoko-sama!

PIYOKO-SAMA
   I AM HONORED TO MEET YOU FOR THE FIRST TIME. I HEARD THAT PIYOKO-SAMA LIKES THE CREME-FILLED COOKIES THAT THE LIEUTENANT GENERAL MAKES FOR HER. DOES THAT MEAN THAT IF THOSE COOKIES GIVE YOU A TOOTHACHE, THE LIEUTENANT GENERAL MUST FIX IT?

Congratulations on opening Black Gamers!

I am also intrigued by the history between Piyoko-sama and Abare-sama. The Abare-Taiko drums...

 Yuzuru Asahina

A Message to Piyoko-sama!

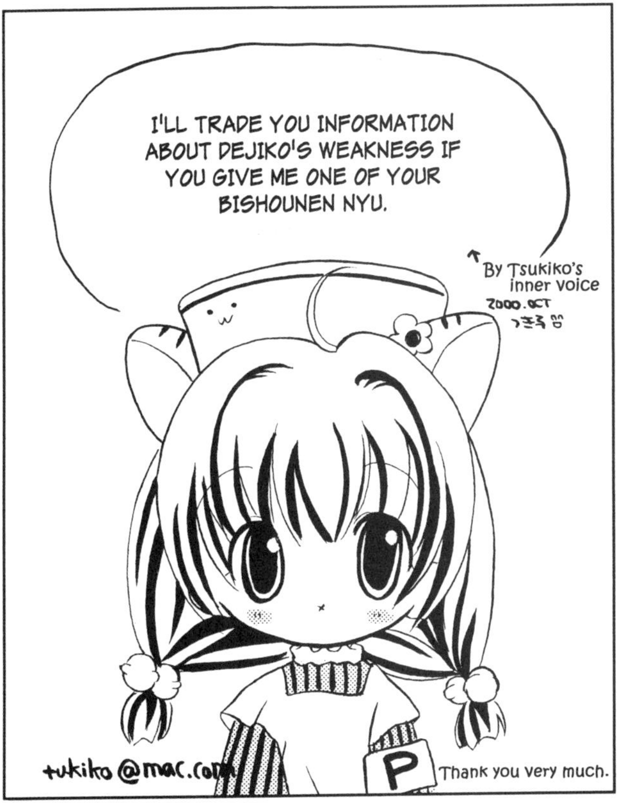
I'LL TRADE YOU INFORMATION ABOUT DEJIKO'S WEAKNESS IF YOU GIVE ME ONE OF YOUR BISHOUNEN NYU.
By Tsukiko's inner voice
2000.OCT
tukiko @mac.co
P
Thank you very much.

B

Tsukiko

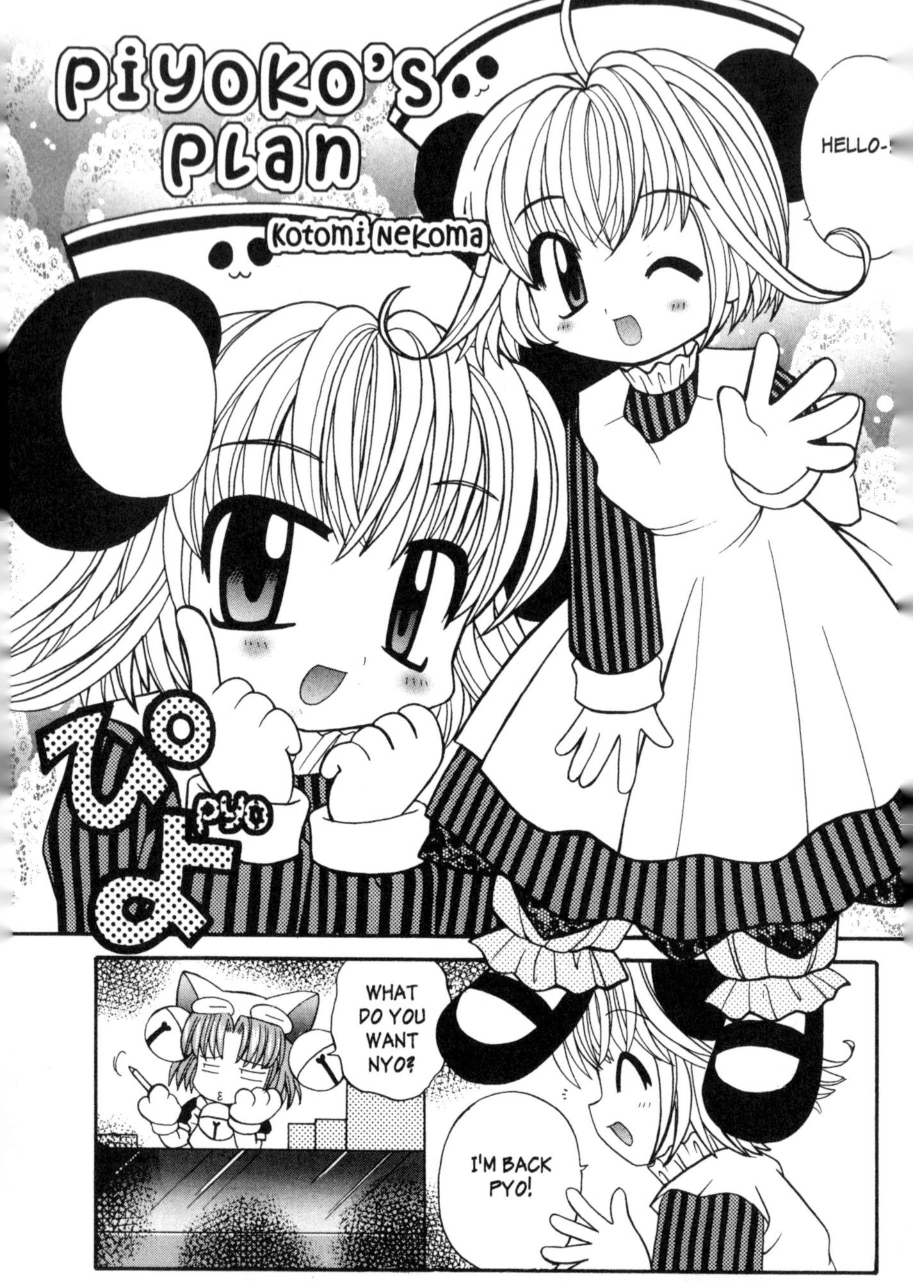
Piyoko's Plan
Kotomi Nekoma
HELLO-
ぴょ
PYO
I'M BACK PYO!
WHAT DO YOU WANT NYO?

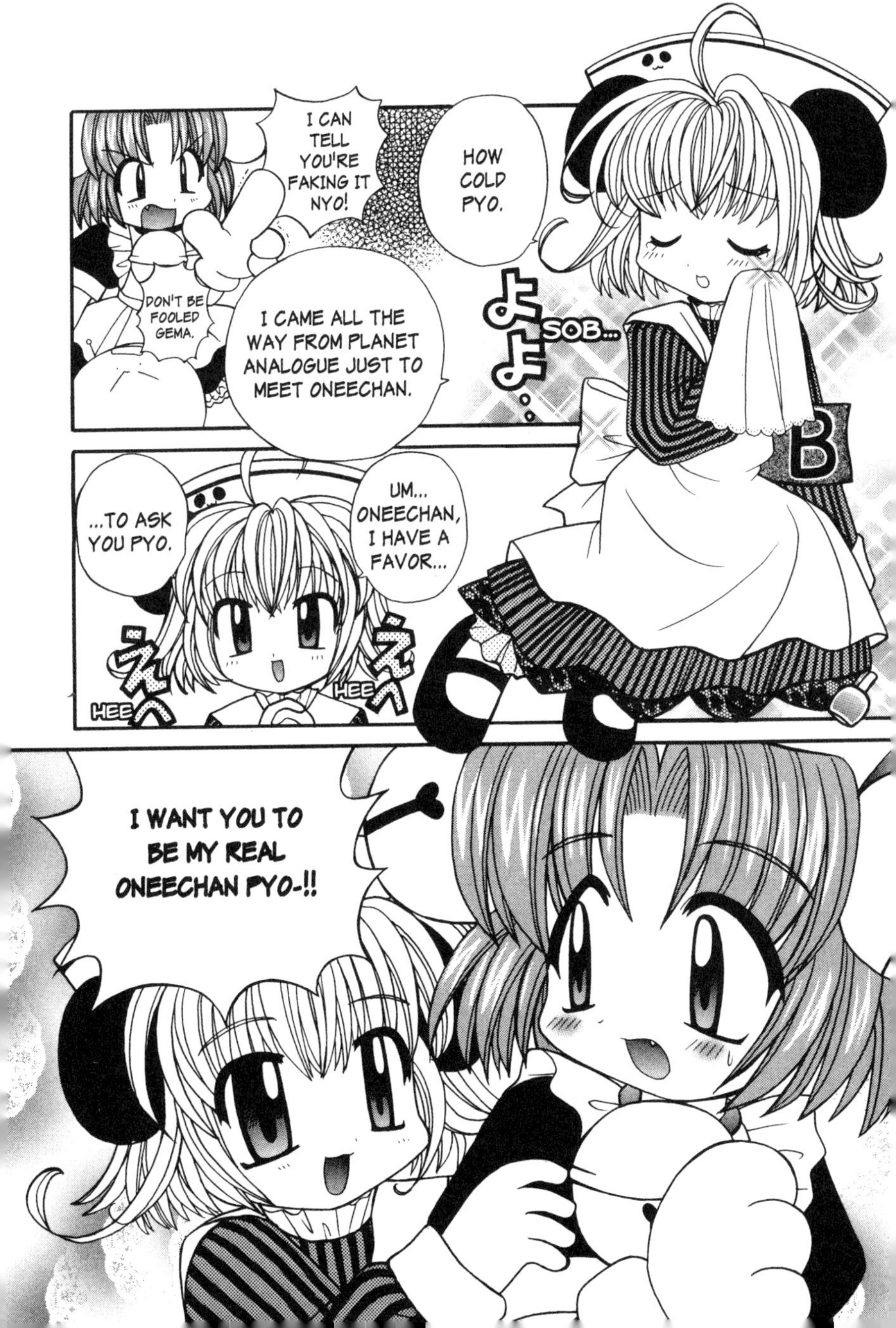
HOW COLD PYO.
よよ SOB...
I CAME ALL THE WAY FROM PLANET ANALOGUE JUST TO MEET ONEECHAN.
I CAN TELL YOU'RE FAKING IT NYO!
DON'T BE FOOLED GEMA.
B
UM... ONEECHAN, I HAVE A FAVOR...
...TO ASK YOU PYO.
えへ HEE
えへ HEE
I WANT YOU TO BE MY REAL ONEECHAN PYO-!!

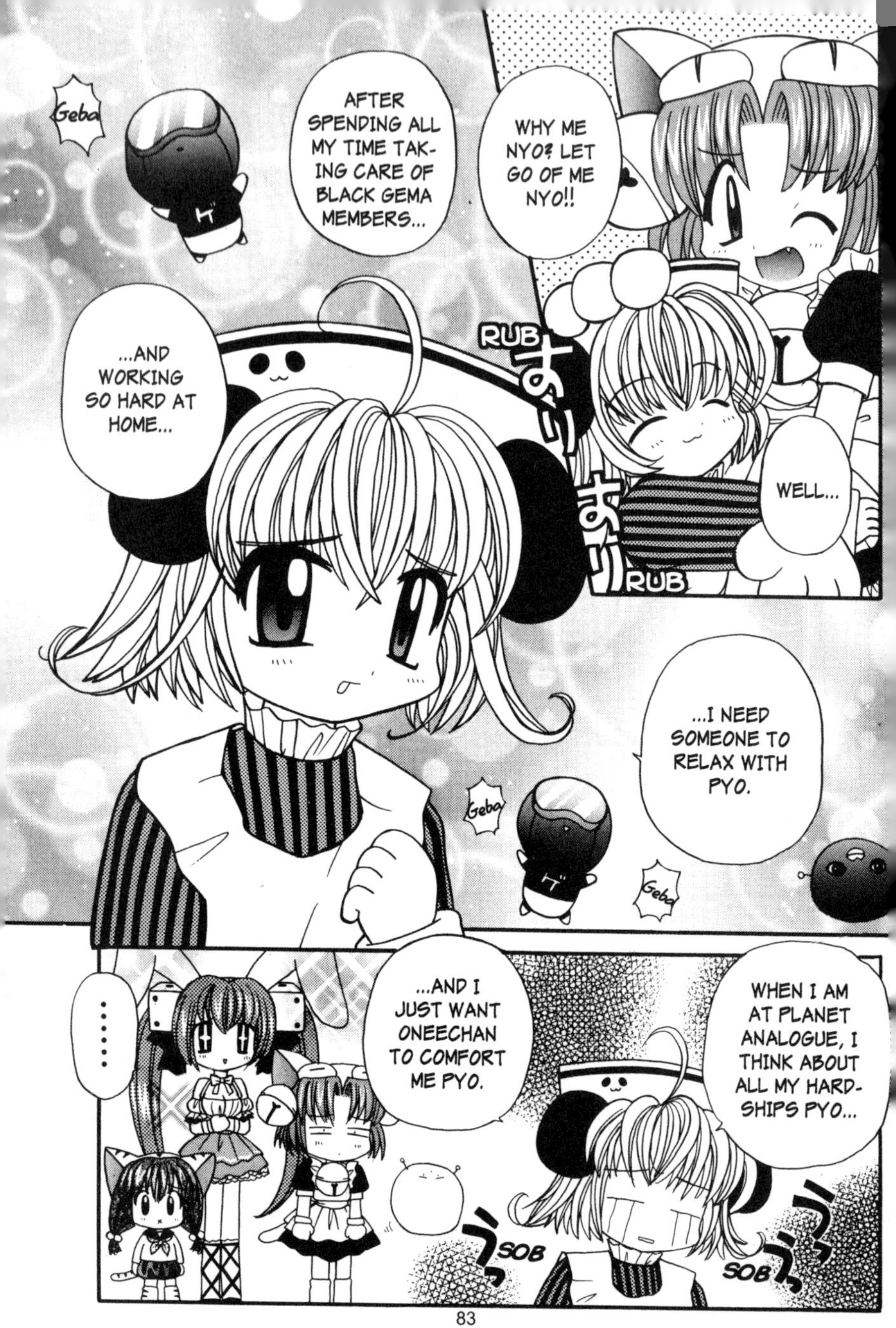
WHY ME NYO? LET GO OF ME NYO!!
RUB すり
すり RUB
WELL...
Geba
AFTER SPENDING ALL MY TIME TAKING CARE OF BLACK GEMA MEMBERS...
...AND WORKING SO HARD AT HOME...
...I NEED SOMEONE TO RELAX WITH PYO.
Geba
Geba
WHEN I AM AT PLANET ANALOGUE, I THINK ABOUT ALL MY HARDSHIPS PYO...
...AND I JUST WANT ONEECHAN TO COMFORT ME PYO.
......
SOB
SOB

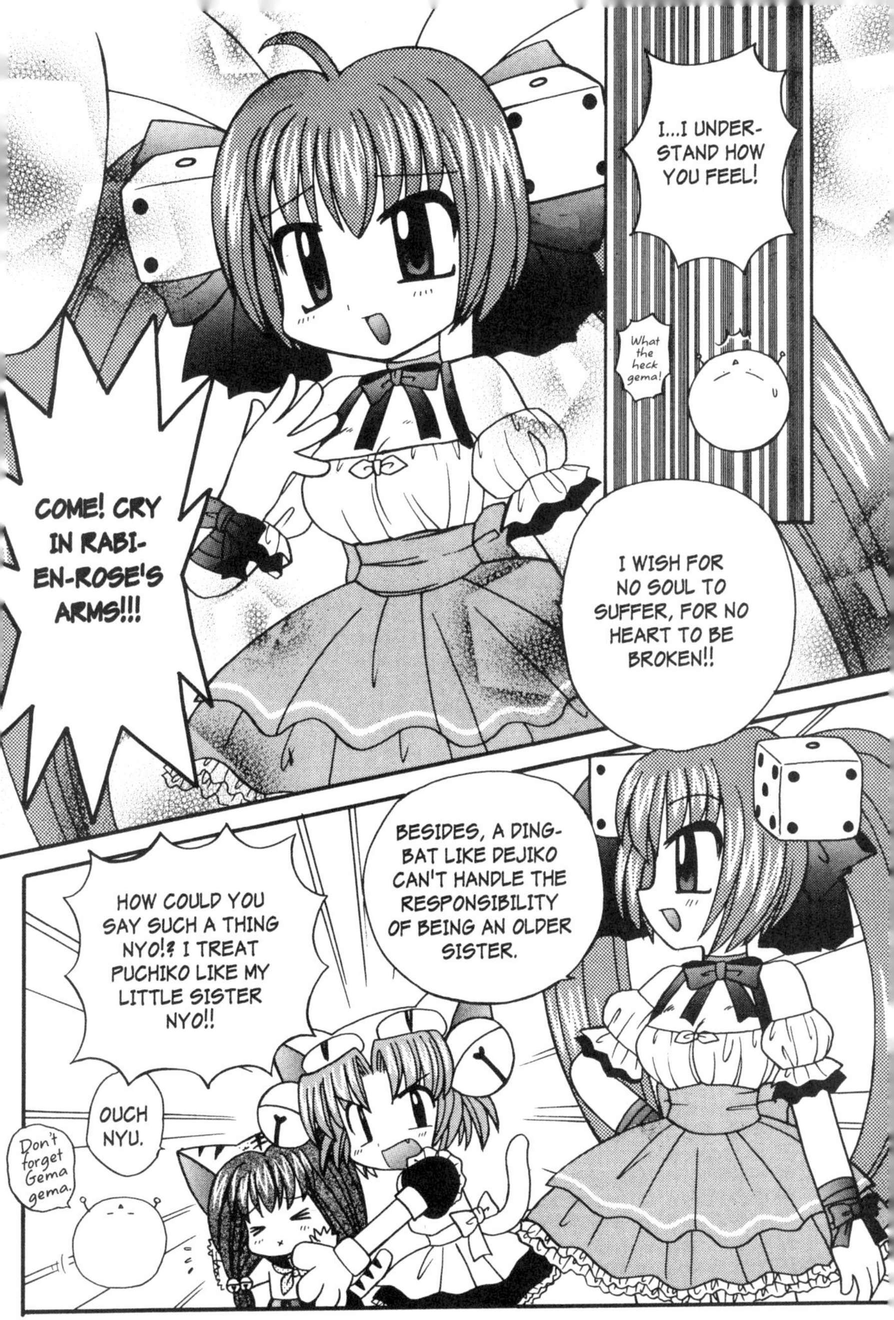
I...I UNDER-
STAND HOW
YOU FEEL!
What the heck gema!
I WISH FOR NO SOUL TO SUFFER, FOR NO HEART TO BE BROKEN!!
COME! CRY IN RABI-EN-ROSE'S ARMS!!!
BESIDES, A DING-BAT LIKE DEJIKO CAN'T HANDLE THE RESPONSIBILITY OF BEING AN OLDER SISTER.
HOW COULD YOU SAY SUCH A THING NYO!? I TREAT PUCHIKO LIKE MY LITTLE SISTER NYO!!
OUCH NYU.
Don't forget Gema gema.

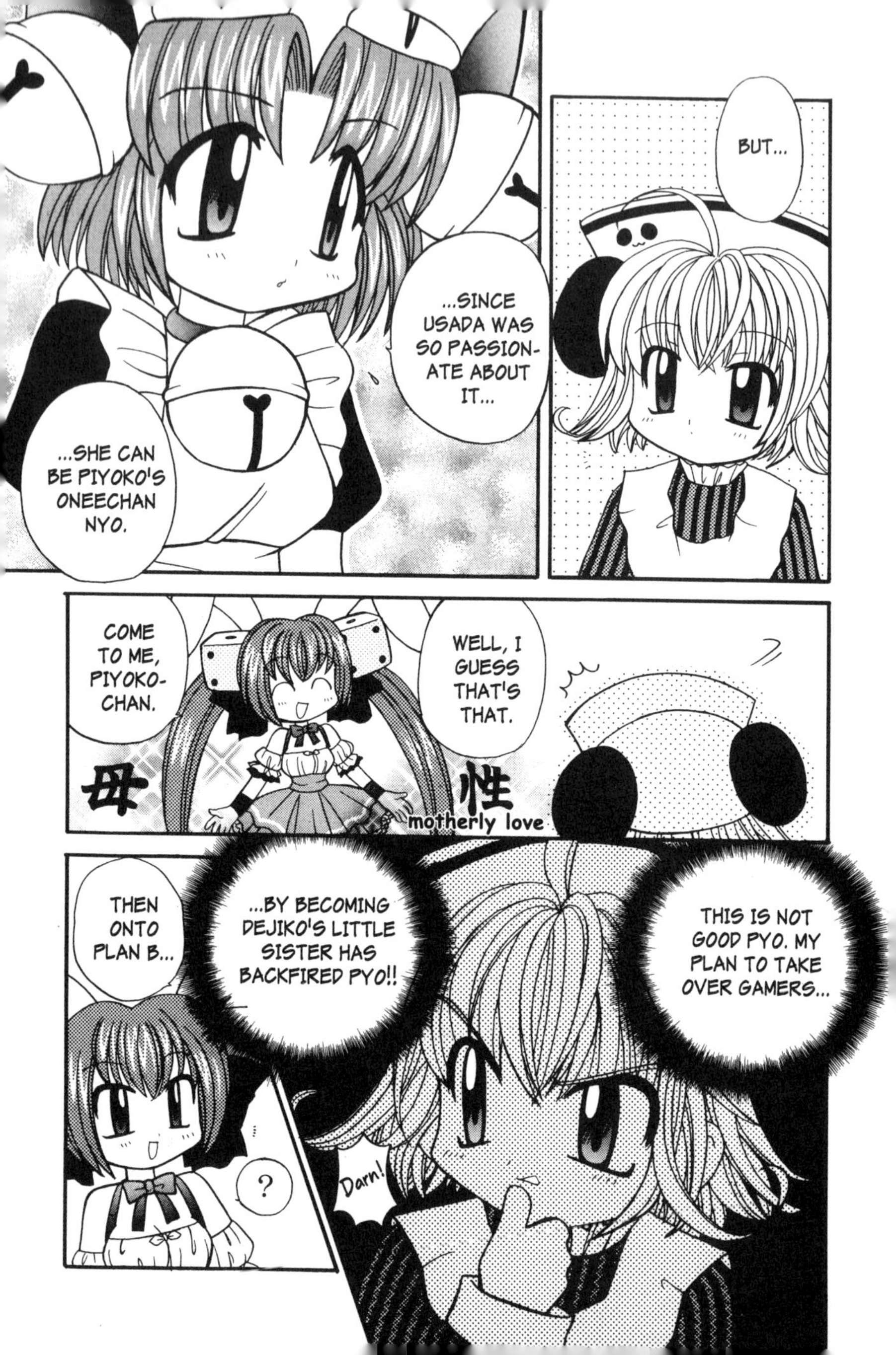
BUT...
...SINCE USADA WAS SO PASSION-ATE ABOUT IT...
...SHE CAN BE PIYOKO'S ONEECHAN NYO.
WELL, I GUESS THAT'S THAT.
COME TO ME, PIYOKO-CHAN.
母 性
motherly love
THIS IS NOT GOOD PYO. MY PLAN TO TAKE OVER GAMERS...
...BY BECOMING DEJIKO'S LITTLE SISTER HAS BACKFIRED PYO!!
Darn!
THEN ONTO PLAN B...
?

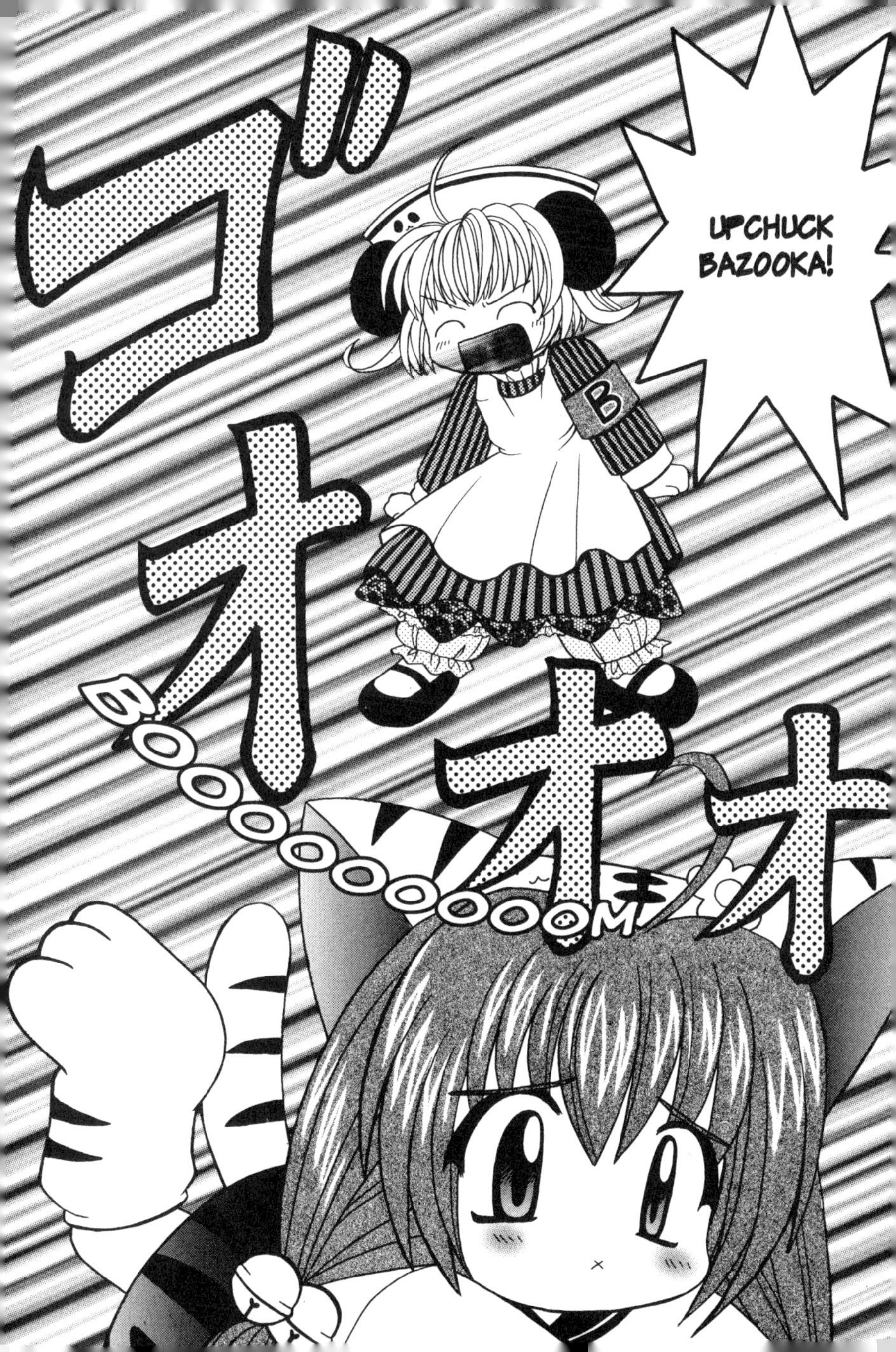
ゴオオオ
UPCHUCK BAZOOKA!
BOOOOOOOOOOM

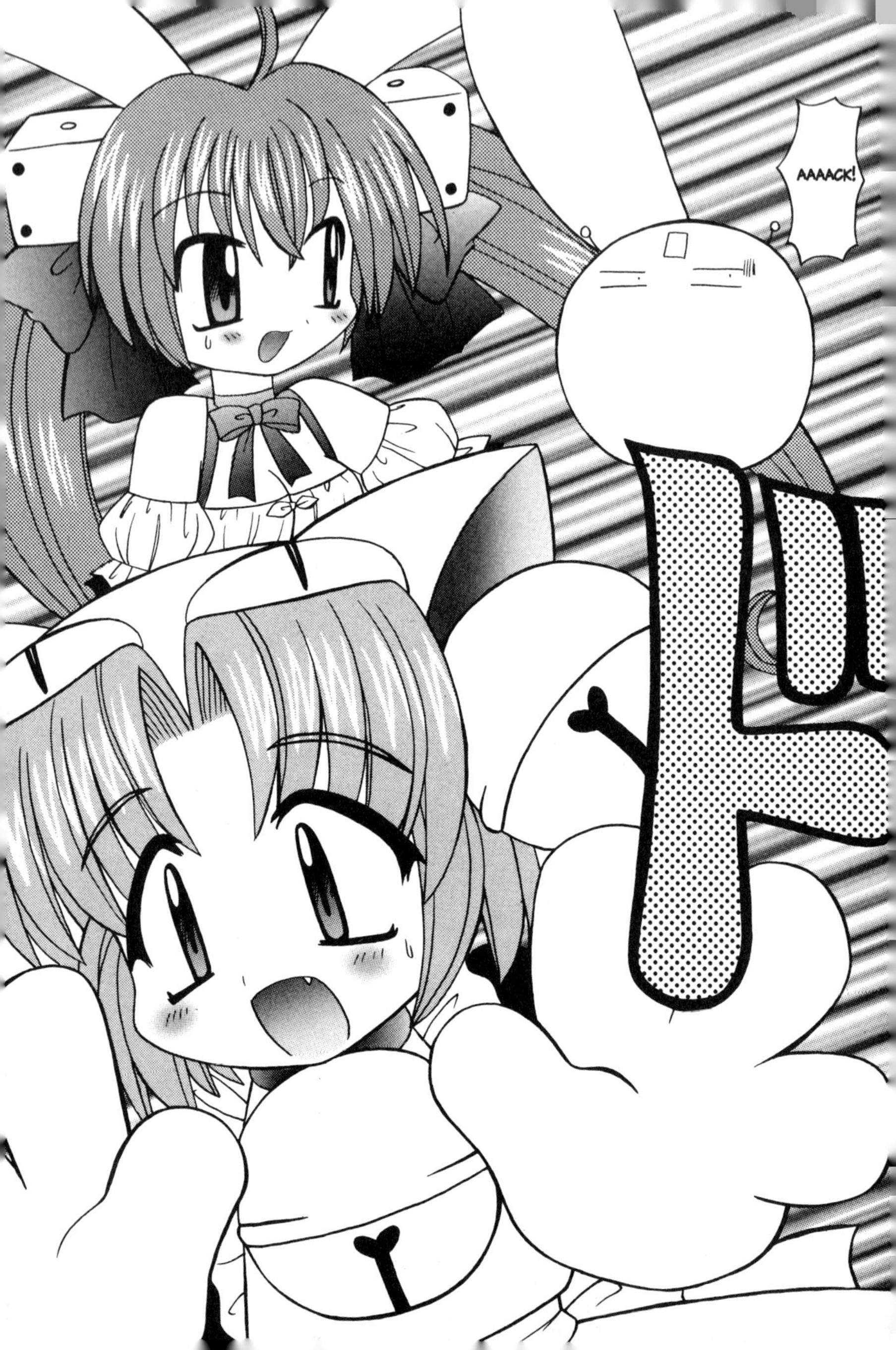
AAAACK!

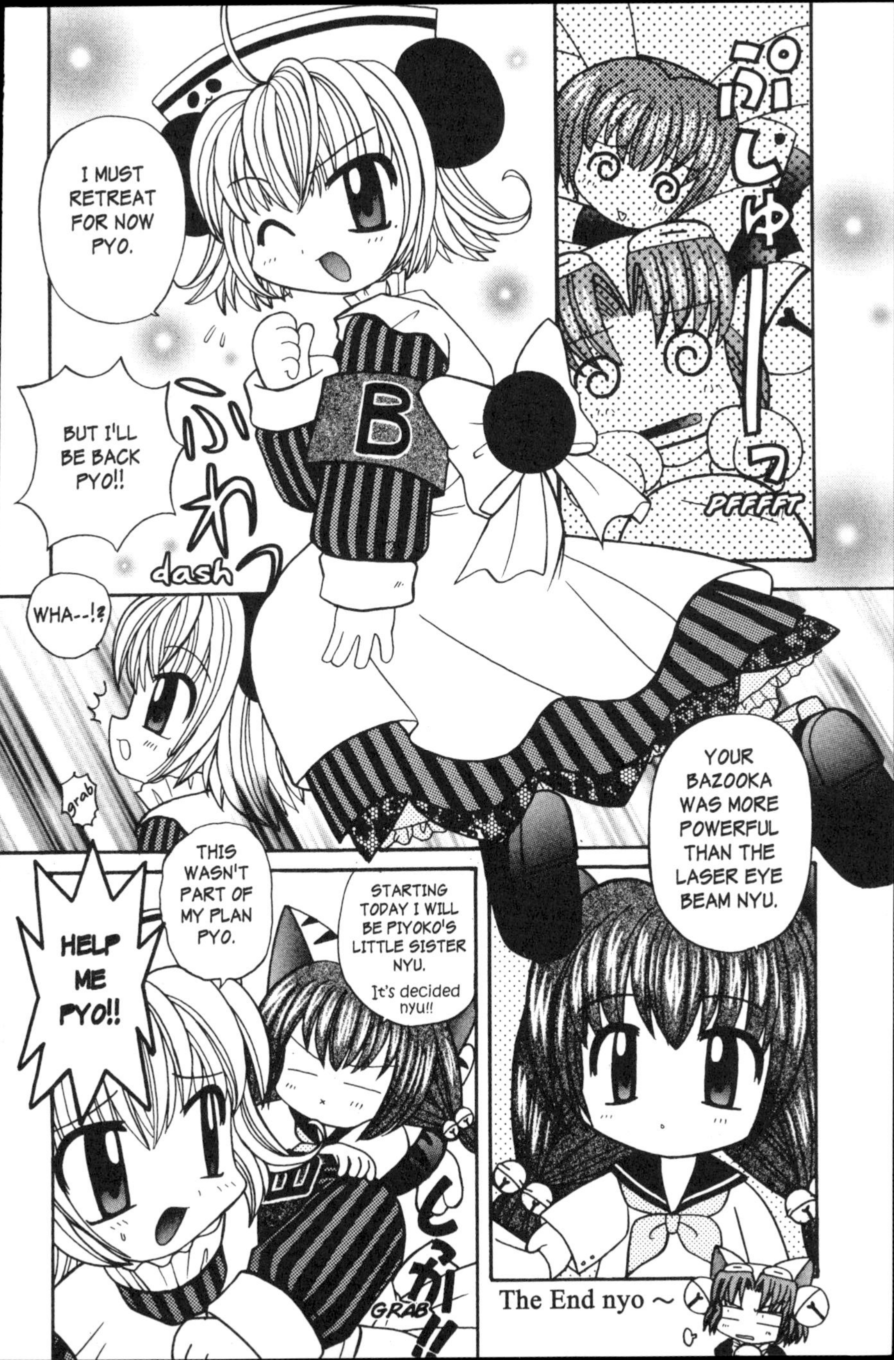
ぷしゅーっ
PFFFFT
I MUST RETREAT FOR NOW PYO.
BUT I'LL BE BACK PYO!!
ふわ
dash
WHA--!?
grab
YOUR BAZOOKA WAS MORE POWERFUL THAN THE LASER EYE BEAM NYU.
The End nyo ~
STARTING TODAY I WILL BE PIYOKO'S LITTLE SISTER NYU.
It's decided nyu!!
THIS WASN'T PART OF MY PLAN PYO.
HELP ME PYO!!
GRAB

Check-up

Kanan

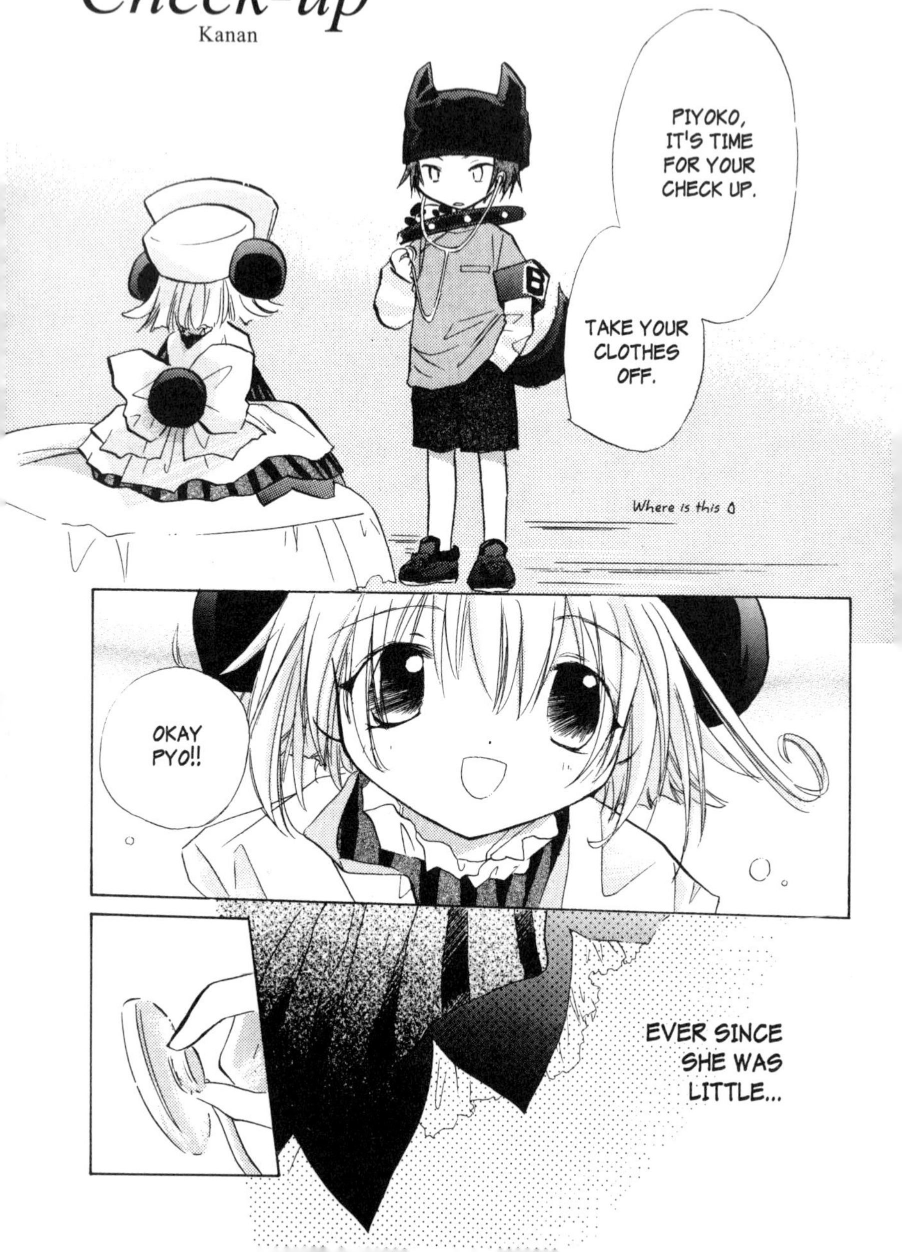
PIYOKO, IT'S TIME FOR YOUR CHECK UP.
TAKE YOUR CLOTHES OFF.
Where is this ◊
OKAY PYO!!
EVER SINCE SHE WAS LITTLE...

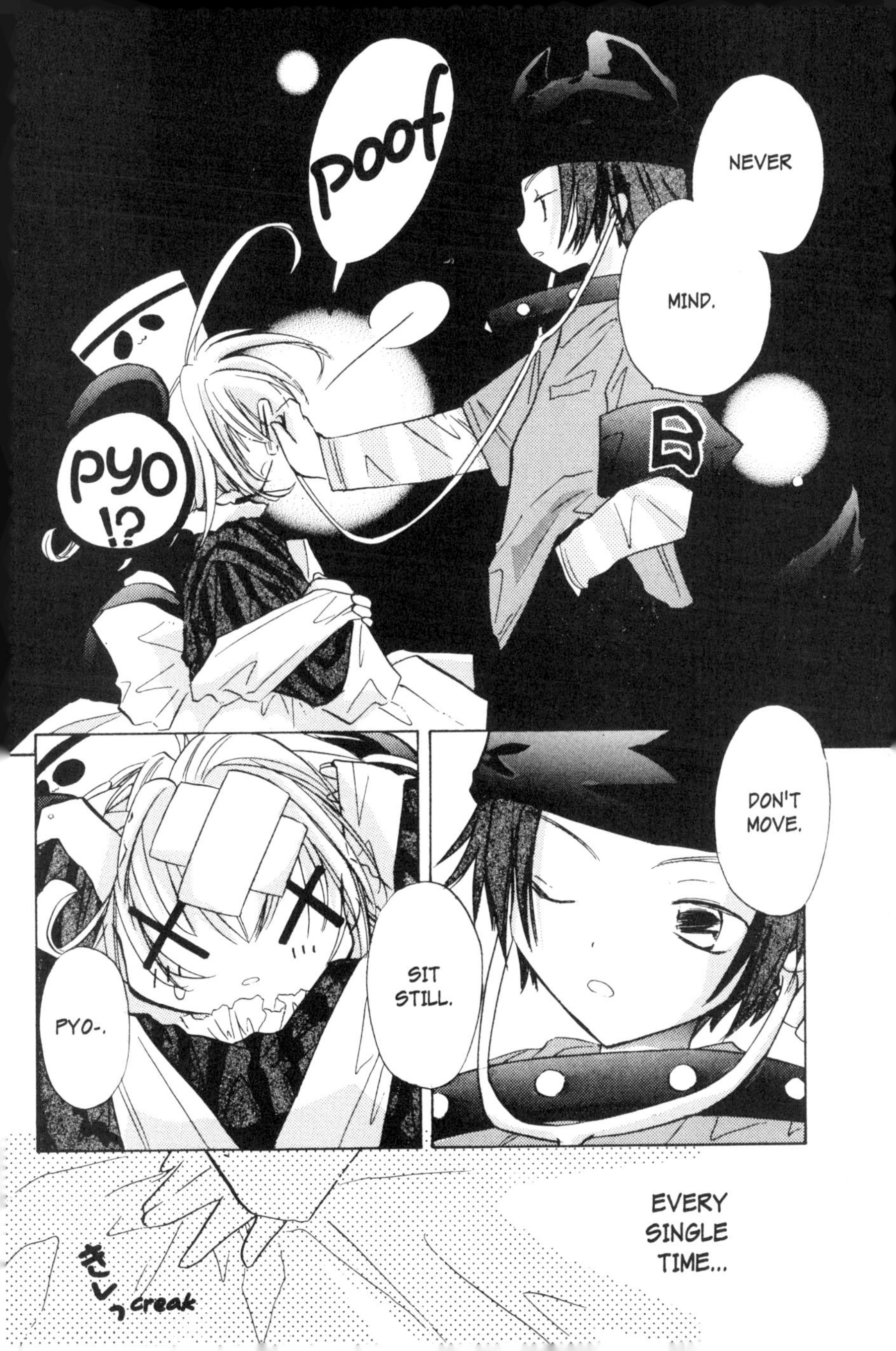
NEVER
MIND.
poof
PYO !?
DON'T MOVE.
SIT STILL.
PYO-.
EVERY SINGLE TIME...
きしっ
creak

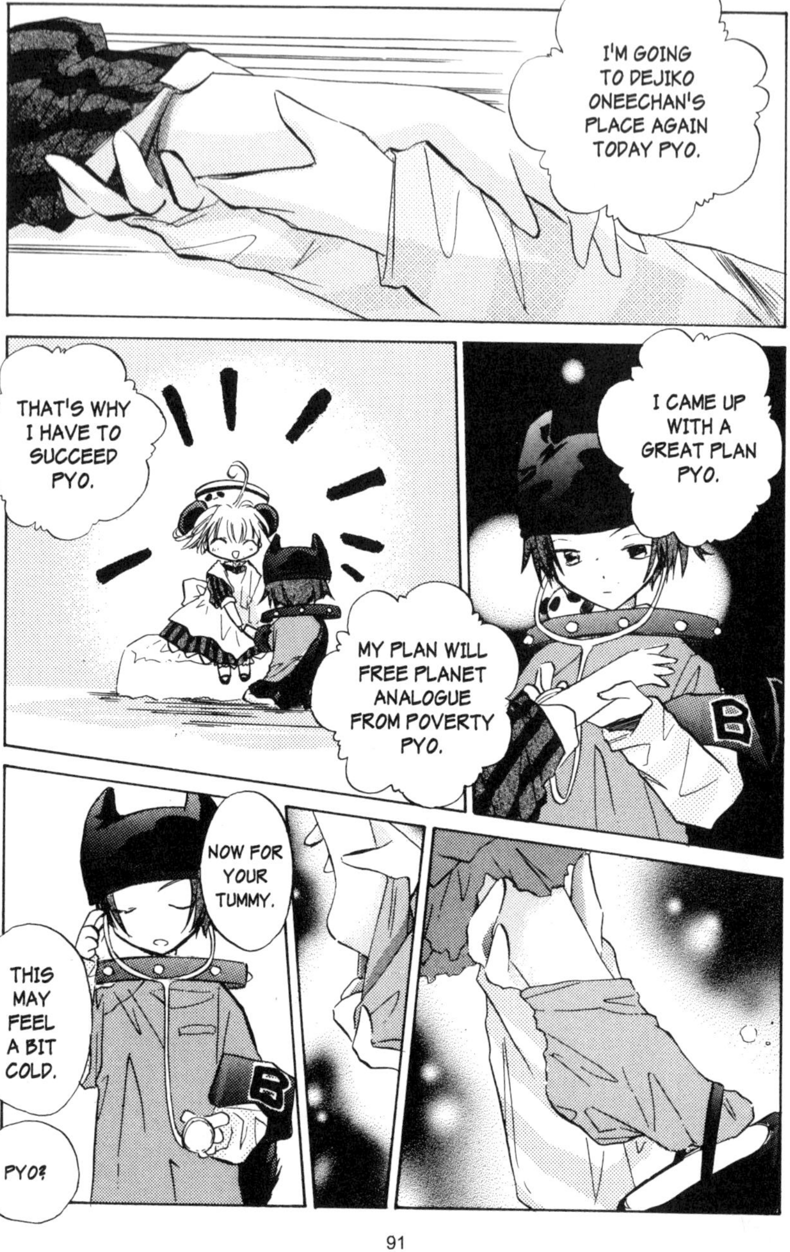
I'M GOING TO DEJIKO ONEECHAN'S PLACE AGAIN TODAY PYO.
I CAME UP WITH A GREAT PLAN PYO.
MY PLAN WILL FREE PLANET ANALOGUE FROM POVERTY PYO.
THAT'S WHY I HAVE TO SUCCEED PYO.
NOW FOR YOUR TUMMY.
THIS MAY FEEL A BIT COLD.
PYO?

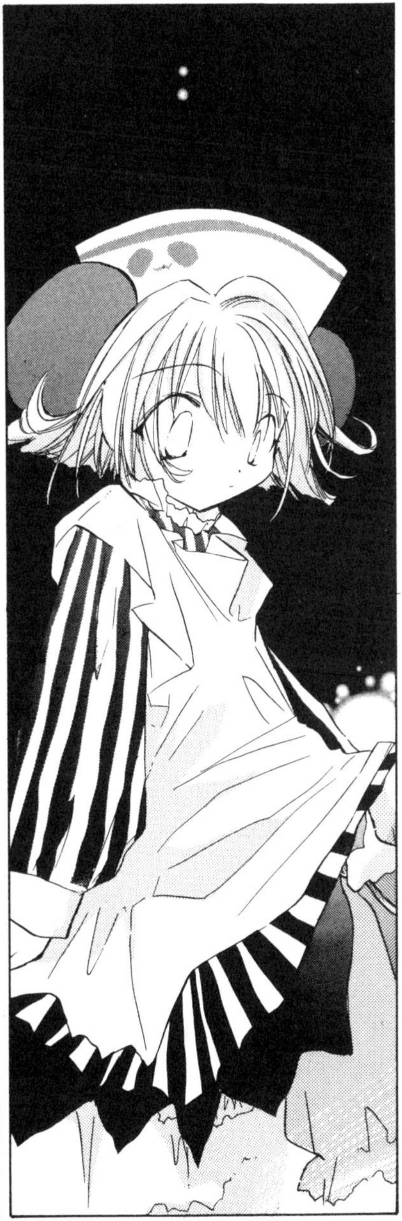

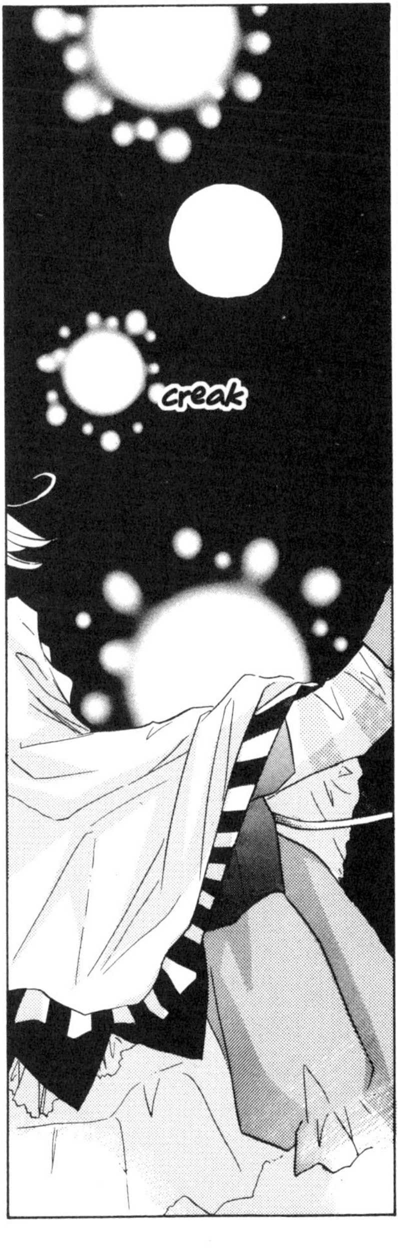
creak

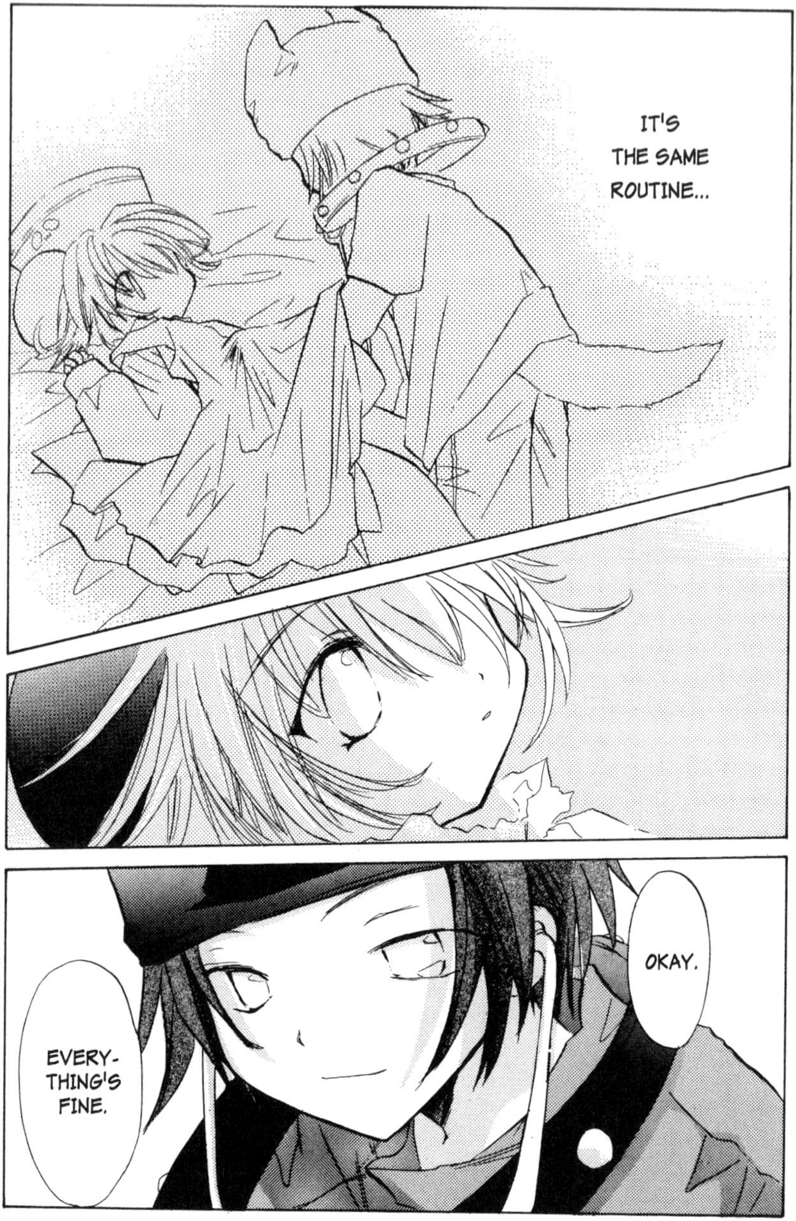
IT'S THE SAME ROUTINE...
OKAY.
EVERY-THING'S FINE.

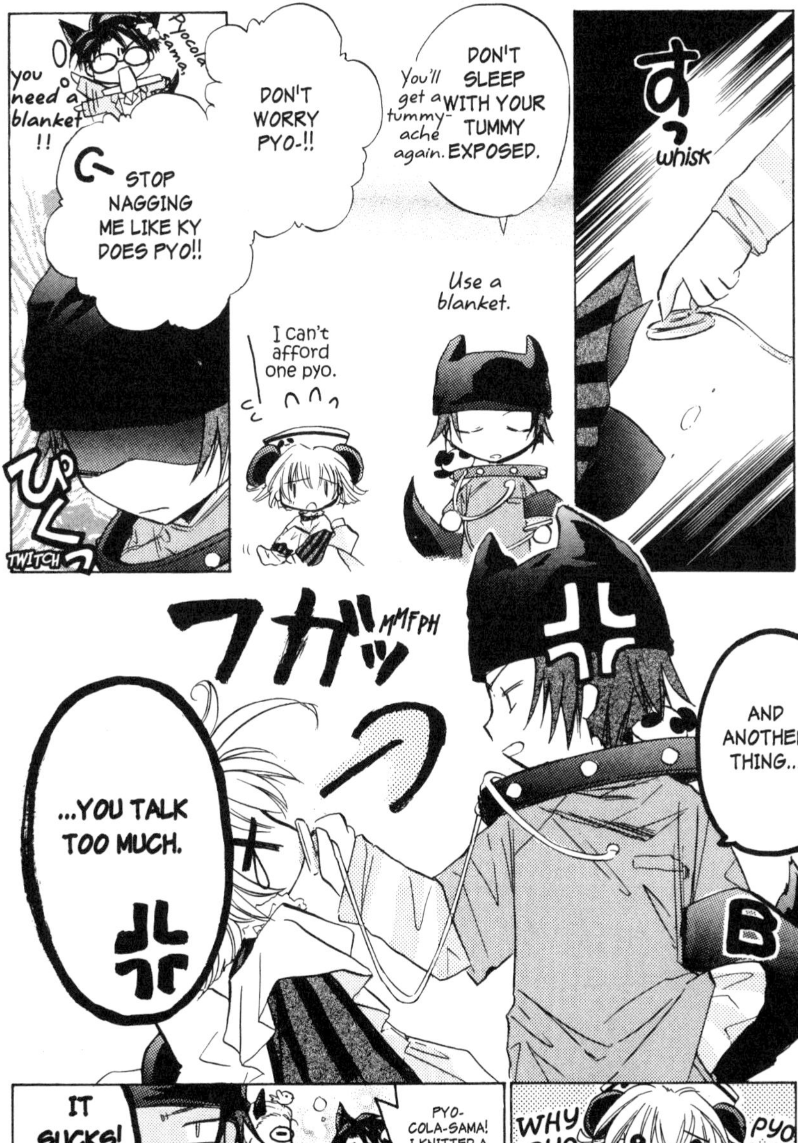
すっ
whisk
DON'T SLEEP WITH YOUR TUMMY EXPOSED.
You'll get a tummy-ache again.
Use a blanket.
I can't afford one pyo.
DON'T WORRY PYO-!!
STOP NAGGING ME LIKE KY DOES PYO!!
Pyocola-sama, you need a blanket!!
ぴくっ
TWITCH
AND ANOTHER THING...
フガッ
MMFPH
...YOU TALK TOO MUCH.
WHY PYO?
PYO~?
PYO-COLA-SAMA! I KNITTED A BLANKET FOR YOU!!
IT SUCKS!

END

A Message to Piyoko-sama!

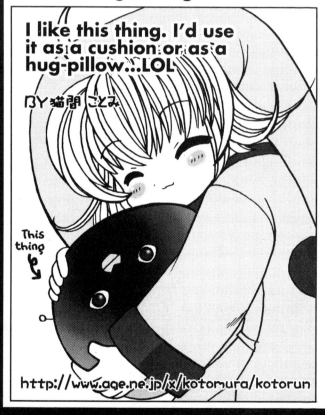

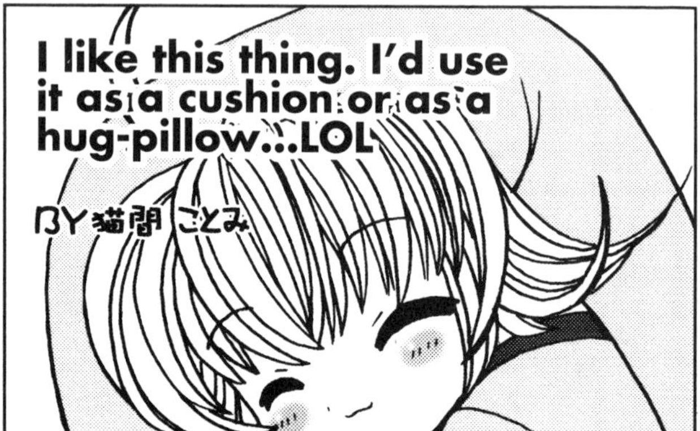
I like this thing. I'd use it as a cushion or as a hug-pillow...LOL
BY猫間ことみ
This thing
http://www.age.ne.jp/x/kotomura/kotorun

B Kotomi Nekoma

A Message to Piyoko-sama!

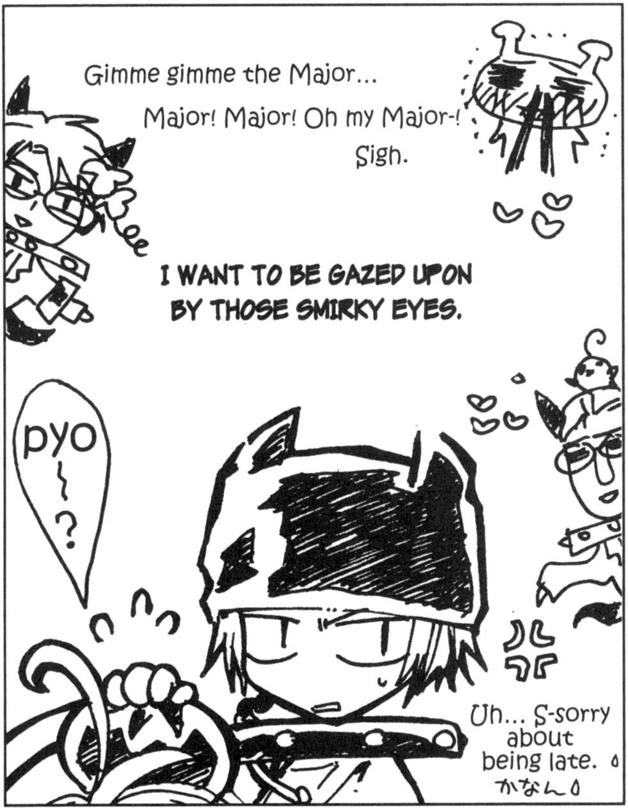

Gimme gimme the Major...
Major! Major! Oh my Major-!
Sigh.
I WANT TO BE GAZED UPON BY THOSE SMIRKY EYES.
pyo ~ ?
Uh... S-sorry about being late.
かなん

Kanan

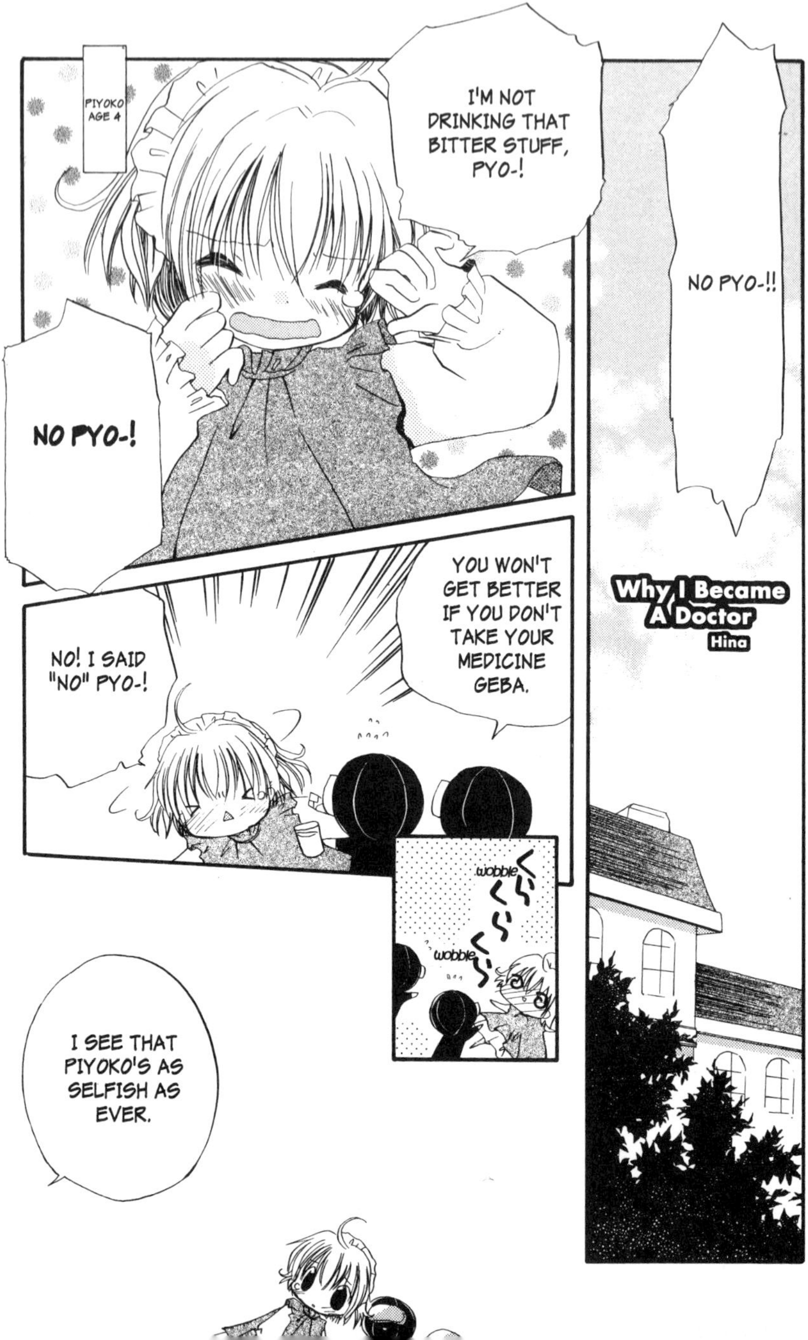
NO PYO-!!
Why I Became A Doctor
Hina
PIYOKO AGE 4
I'M NOT DRINKING THAT BITTER STUFF, PYO-!
NO PYO-!
YOU WON'T GET BETTER IF YOU DON'T TAKE YOUR MEDICINE GEBA.
NO! I SAID "NO" PYO-!
wobble
wobble
I SEE THAT PIYOKO'S AS SELFISH AS EVER.

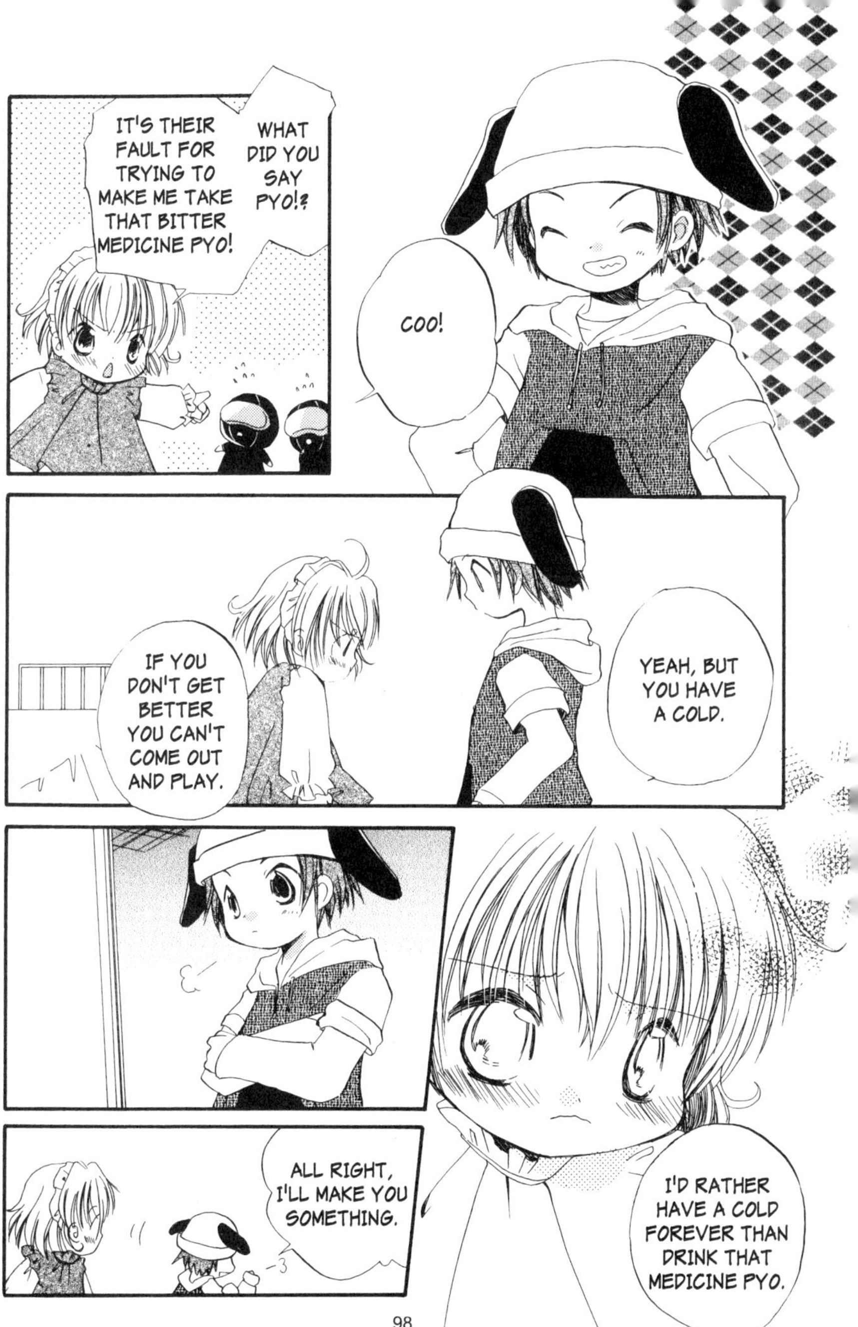
COO!
IT'S THEIR FAULT FOR TRYING TO MAKE ME TAKE THAT BITTER MEDICINE PYO!
WHAT DID YOU SAY PYO!?
YEAH, BUT YOU HAVE A COLD.
IF YOU DON'T GET BETTER YOU CAN'T COME OUT AND PLAY.
I'D RATHER HAVE A COLD FOREVER THAN DRINK THAT MEDICINE PYO.
ALL RIGHT, I'LL MAKE YOU SOMETHING.

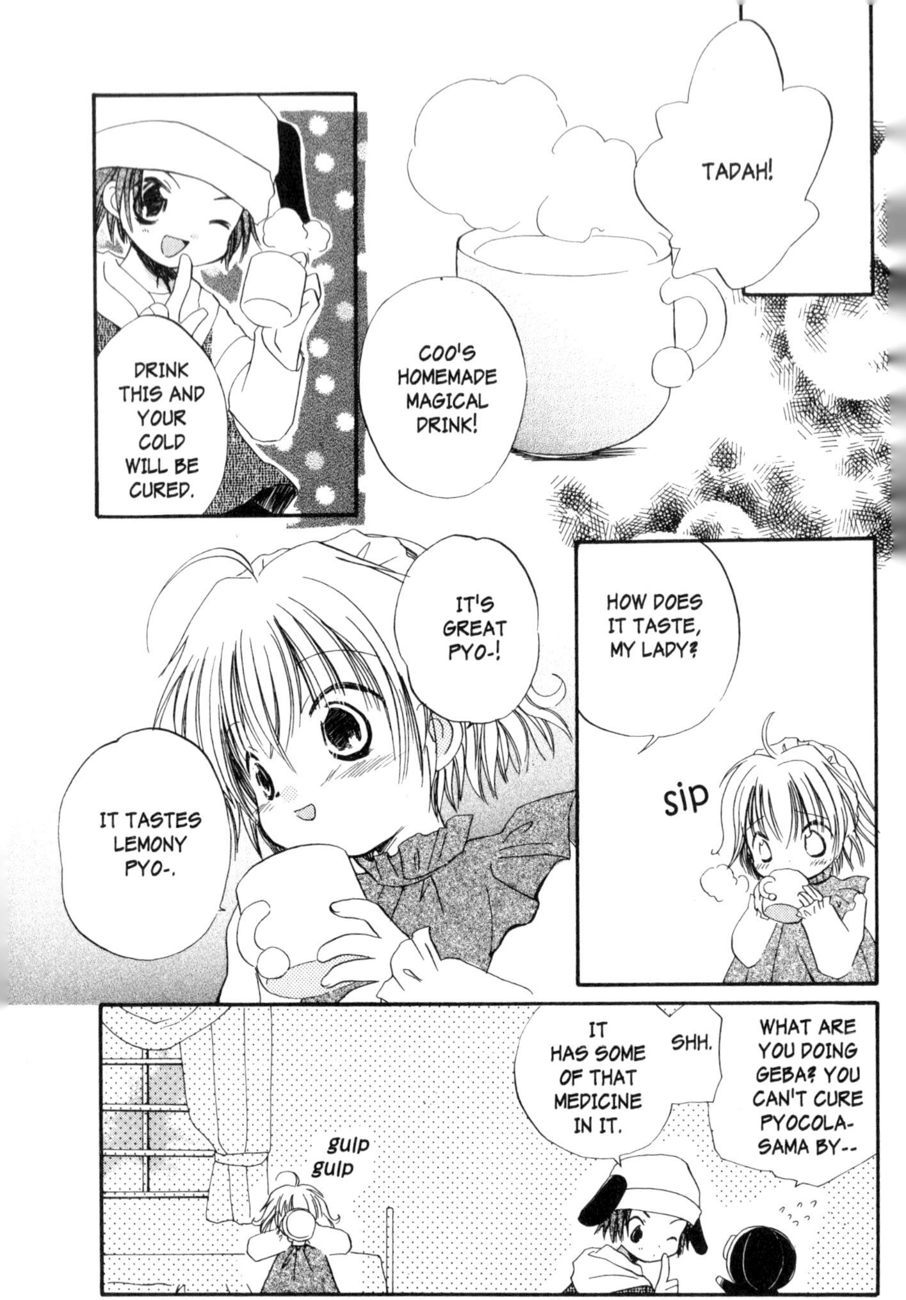
TADAH!
COO'S HOMEMADE MAGICAL DRINK!
DRINK THIS AND YOUR COLD WILL BE CURED.
HOW DOES IT TASTE, MY LADY?
sip
IT'S GREAT PYO-!
IT TASTES LEMONY PYO-.
WHAT ARE YOU DOING GEBA? YOU CAN'T CURE PYOCOLA-SAMA BY--
SHH.
IT HAS SOME OF THAT MEDICINE IN IT.
gulp gulp

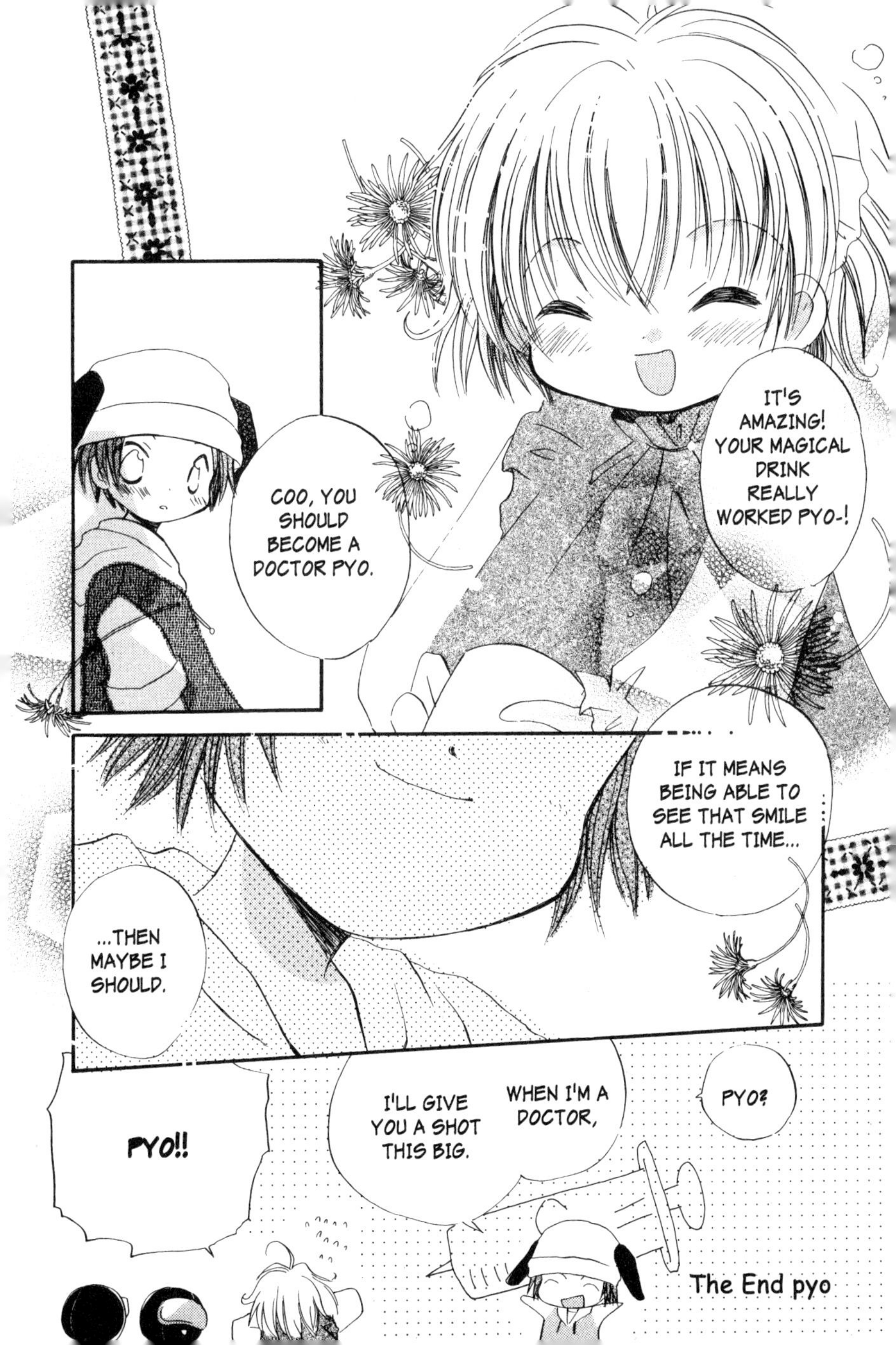
IT'S AMAZING! YOUR MAGICAL DRINK REALLY WORKED PYO-!
COO, YOU SHOULD BECOME A DOCTOR PYO.
IF IT MEANS BEING ABLE TO SEE THAT SMILE ALL THE TIME...
...THEN MAYBE I SHOULD.
PYO?
WHEN I'M A DOCTOR,
I'LL GIVE YOU A SHOT THIS BIG.
PYO!!
The End pyo

A Message to Piyoko-sama!

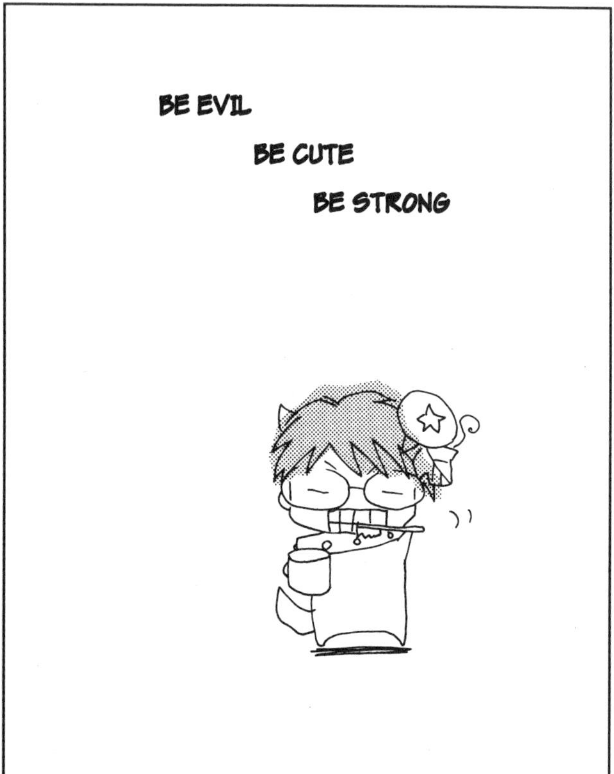
BE EVIL
BE CUTE
BE STRONG

B

Hina.

A Message from Clim

This is the second Broccoli Books release of the Di Gi Charat Theater series. For those of you who don't know the other books, please get a chance to read them.

By the way, Majin Gappa is a Kappa (although he doesn't really look like one). As a kappa, one of his special moves is water tricks. I don't know if that is useful at all, but I hope you can love him still.

-Clim

A Message from the CEO

The Black Gema Gema Gang take over!

Hello, this is Takaaki Kidani, CEO of Broccoli.

When we first introduced Piyoko and the Black Gema Gema Gang, we held many related events in Japan. We had the Black Gema Gema Gang take over a store in Akihabara, take over the Broccoli website, and even take over a concert.

In this version of the Di Gi Charat Theater - Piyoko is Number One!, we hope that Piyoko can have a chance at taking over the U.S. fans of Di Gi Charat. Whether she succeeds or fails is up to you, the reader. Please enjoy Piyoko's adventures.

Sincerely,
Takaaki Kidani
CEO, Broccoli Co., Ltd.

Profile
Takaaki Kidani founded Broccoli Co., Ltd in 1994. Since then, he has been one of the major players responsible for creating media such as *Di Gi Charat*, *Galaxy Angel*, *Aquarian Age*, and *Neppu Kairiku Bushi Lord*.

What is Gema Gema?

Gema Gema is the title of a 4-panel comic series featured in the monthly informational magazine *From Gamers*. While only Dejiko and Gema appeared at first, Gema Gema eventually became the springboard for other *Di Gi Charat* characters like Rabi~en~Rose and Piyoko.

Gema Gema is still currently featured in *From Gamers*, and Koge-Donbo hand draws and colors them each month. The hardcore industry jokes and random announcements make Gema Gema a very popular section of the magazine.

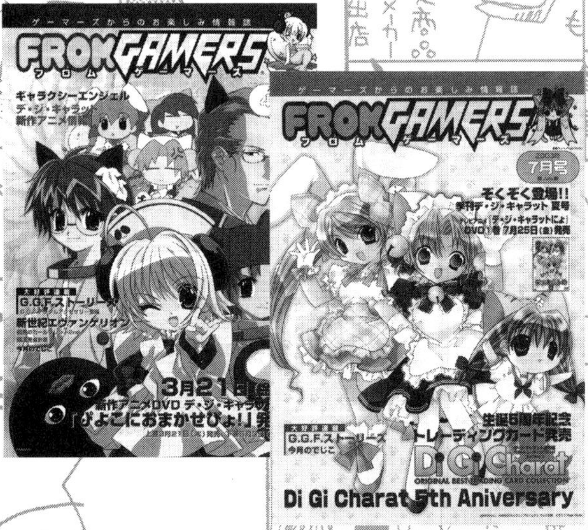
ゲーマーズからのお楽しみ情報誌
FROMGAMERS
フロムゲーマーズ
ギャラクシーエンジェル
G.G.F.ストーリーズ
新世紀エヴァンゲリオン
「ぴよこにおまかせぴょ!」
ゲーマーズからのお楽しみ情報誌
FROMGAMERS
フロムゲーマーズ
7月号
ぞくぞく登場!!
季刊デ・ジ・キャラット 夏号
「デ・ジ・キャラットにょ」
G.G.F.ストーリーズ
今月のでじこ
トレーディングカード発売
Di Gi Charat
Di Gi Charat 5th Aniversary

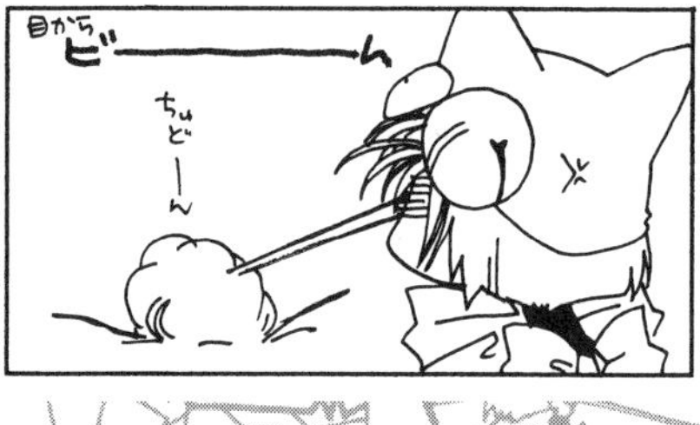
目から ビーーーーーーん
ちゅどーーん

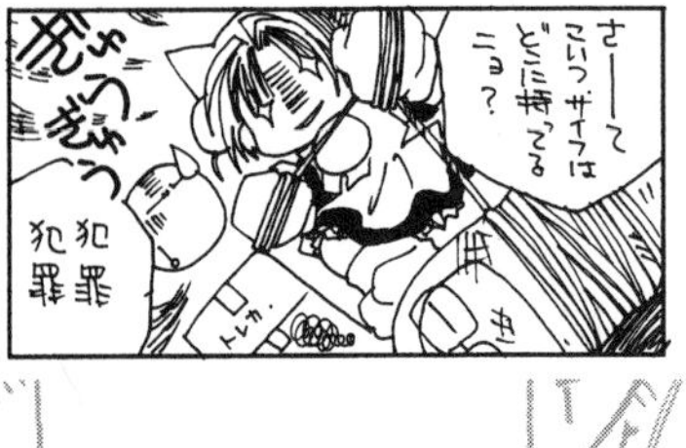
さーーて こいつサイフは どこに持ってる ニョ?
犯罪 犯罪

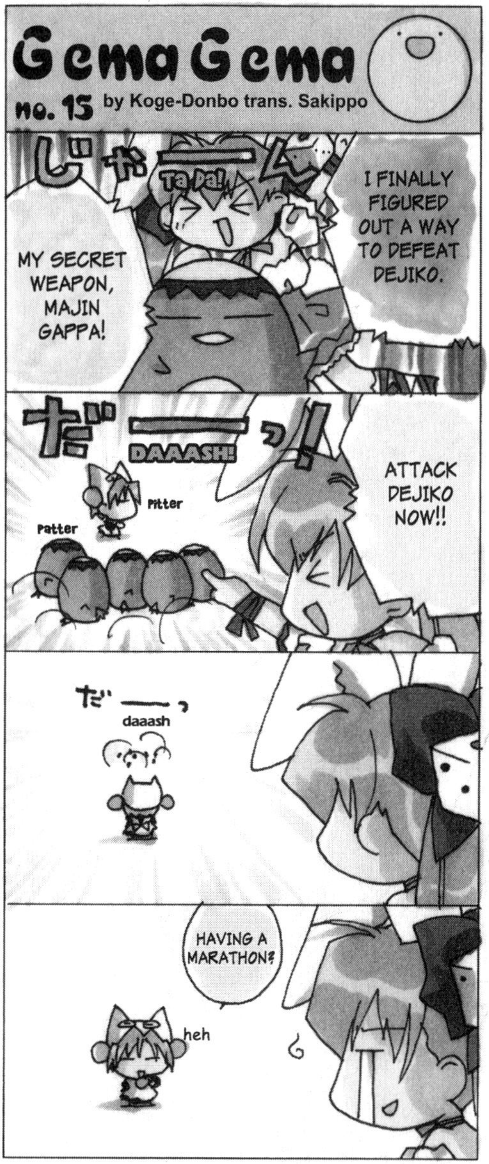
Gema Gema
no. 15 by Koge-Donbo trans. Sakippo
I FINALLY FIGURED OUT A WAY TO DEFEAT DEJIKO.
じゃーーん
Ta Da!
MY SECRET WEAPON, MAJIN GAPPA!
ATTACK DEJIKO NOW!!
だーーーっ!
DAAASH!
Pitter
Patter
だーーっ
daaash
HAVING A MARATHON?
heh

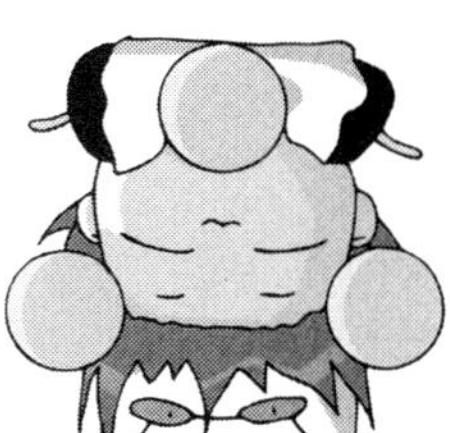

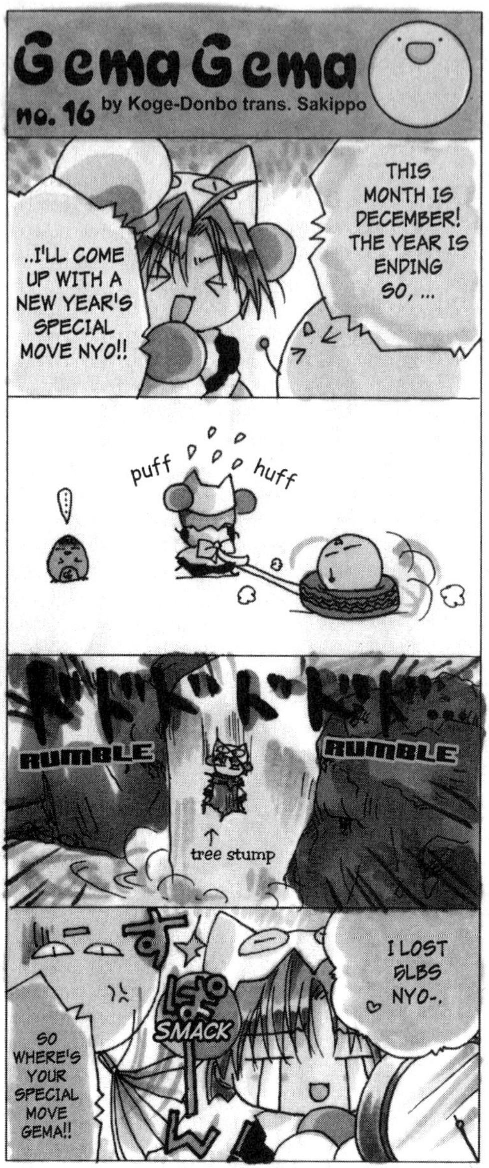
Gema Gema
no. 16 by Koge-Donbo trans. Sakippo
THIS MONTH IS DECEMBER! THE YEAR IS ENDING SO, ...
..I'LL COME UP WITH A NEW YEAR'S SPECIAL MOVE NYO!!
puff
huff
RUMBLE
RUMBLE
tree stump
I LOST 5LBS NYO-.
SMACK
SO WHERE'S YOUR SPECIAL MOVE GEMA!!

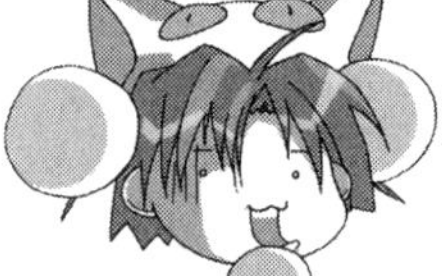

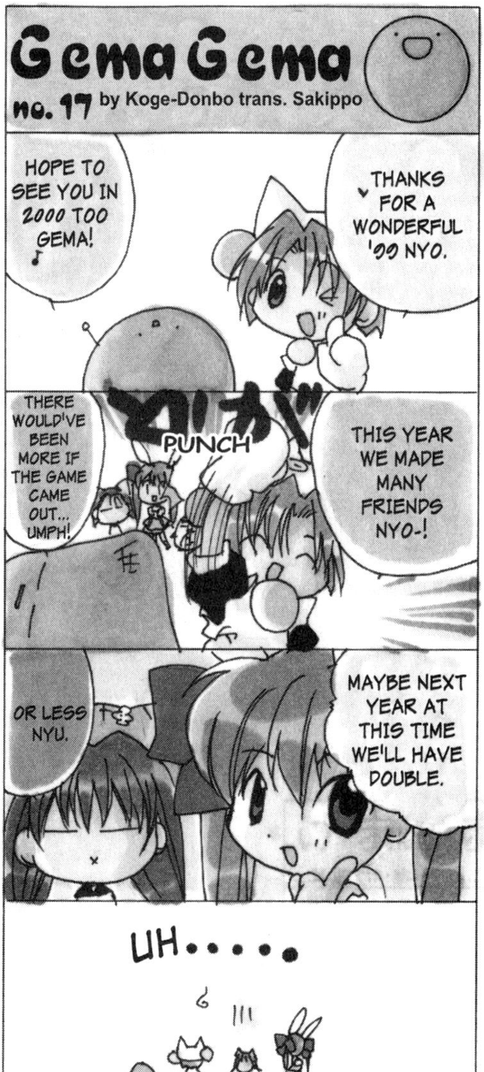
Gema Gema
no. 17 by Koge-Donbo trans. Sakippo
THANKS FOR A WONDERFUL '99 NYO.
HOPE TO SEE YOU IN 2000 TOO GEMA!
THIS YEAR WE MADE MANY FRIENDS NYO-!
PUNCH
THERE WOULD'VE BEEN MORE IF THE GAME CAME OUT... UMPH!
MAYBE NEXT YEAR AT THIS TIME WE'LL HAVE DOUBLE.
OR LESS NYU.
UH.....

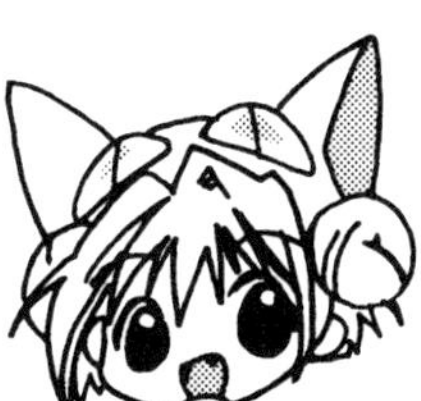

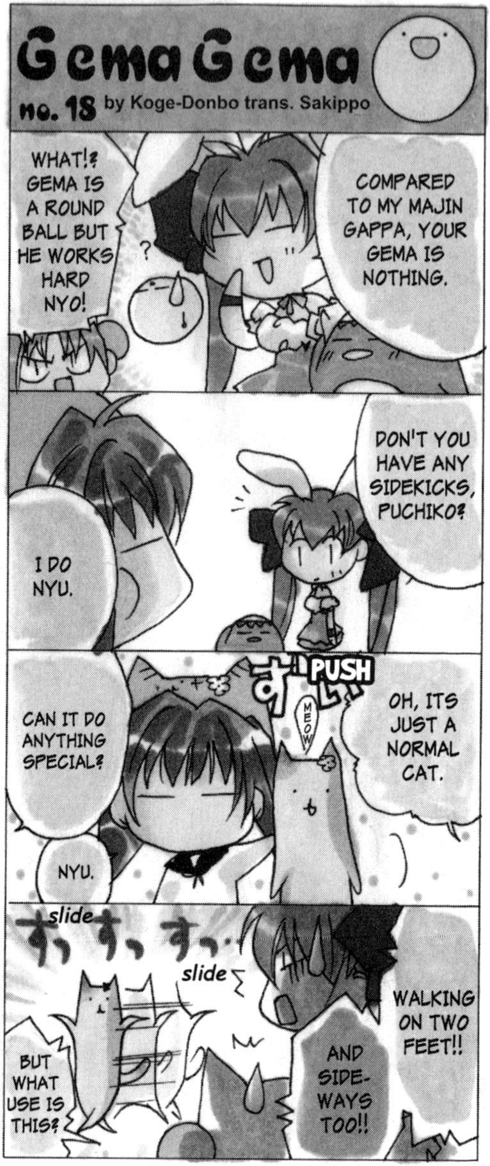
Gema Gema
no. 18 by Koge-Donbo trans. Sakippo
COMPARED TO MY MAJIN GAPPA, YOUR GEMA IS NOTHING.
WHAT!? GEMA IS A ROUND BALL BUT HE WORKS HARD NYO!
DON'T YOU HAVE ANY SIDEKICKS, PUCHIKO?
I DO NYU.
PUSH
OH, ITS JUST A NORMAL CAT.
MEOW
CAN IT DO ANYTHING SPECIAL?
NYU.
slide
WALKING ON TWO FEET!!
slide
AND SIDE-WAYS TOO!!
BUT WHAT USE IS THIS?

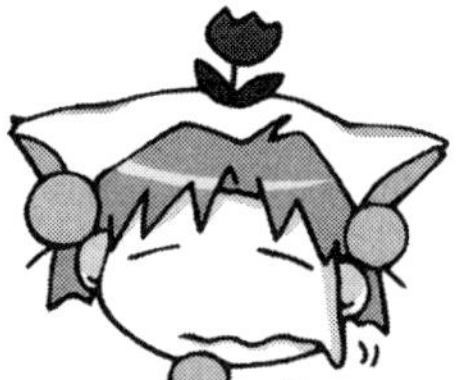

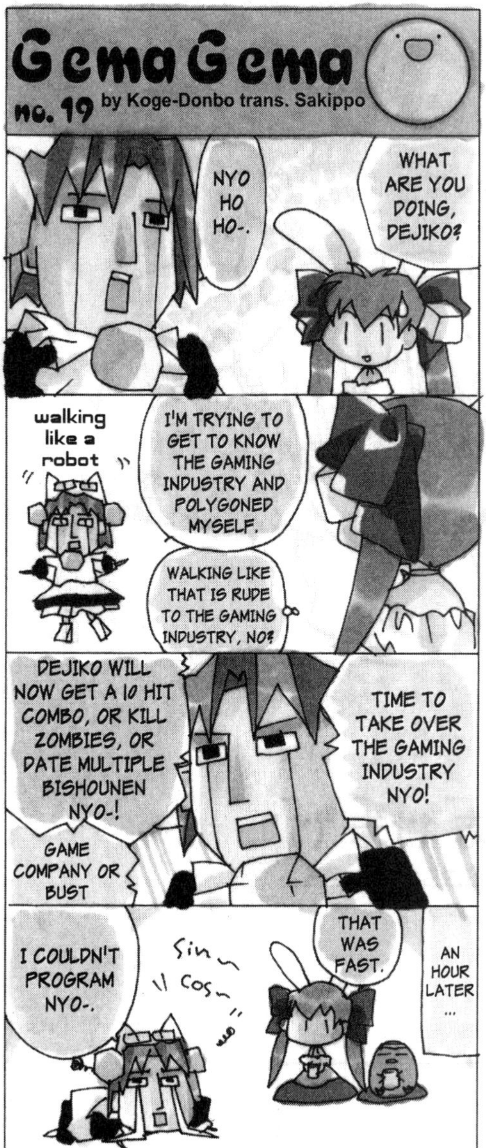
Gema Gema
no. 19 by Koge-Donbo trans. Sakippo
WHAT ARE YOU DOING, DEJIKO?
NYO HO HO-.
I'M TRYING TO GET TO KNOW THE GAMING INDUSTRY AND POLYGONED MYSELF.
walking like a robot
WALKING LIKE THAT IS RUDE TO THE GAMING INDUSTRY, NO?
TIME TO TAKE OVER THE GAMING INDUSTRY NYO!
DEJIKO WILL NOW GET A 10 HIT COMBO, OR KILL ZOMBIES, OR DATE MULTIPLE BISHOUNEN NYO-!
GAME COMPANY OR BUST
AN HOUR LATER ...
THAT WAS FAST.
Sin
Cos
I COULDN'T PROGRAM NYO-.

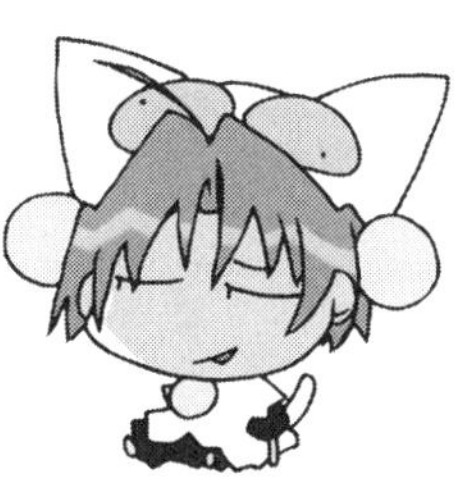

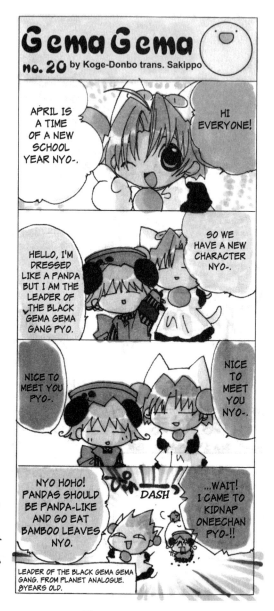

Gema Gema

no. 20 by Koge-Donbo trans. Sakippo

HI EVERYONE!
APRIL IS A TIME OF A NEW SCHOOL YEAR NYO-.
SO WE HAVE A NEW CHARACTER NYO-.
HELLO, I'M DRESSED LIKE A PANDA BUT I AM THE LEADER OF THE BLACK GEMA GEMA GANG PYO.
NICE TO MEET YOU NYO-.
NICE TO MEET YOU PYO-.
...WAIT! I CAME TO KIDNAP ONEECHAN PYO-!!
DASH
NYO HOHO! PANDAS SHOULD BE PANDA-LIKE AND GO EAT BAMBOO LEAVES NYO.
LEADER OF THE BLACK GEMA GEMA GANG. FROM PLANET ANALOGUE. 8YEARS OLD.

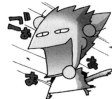

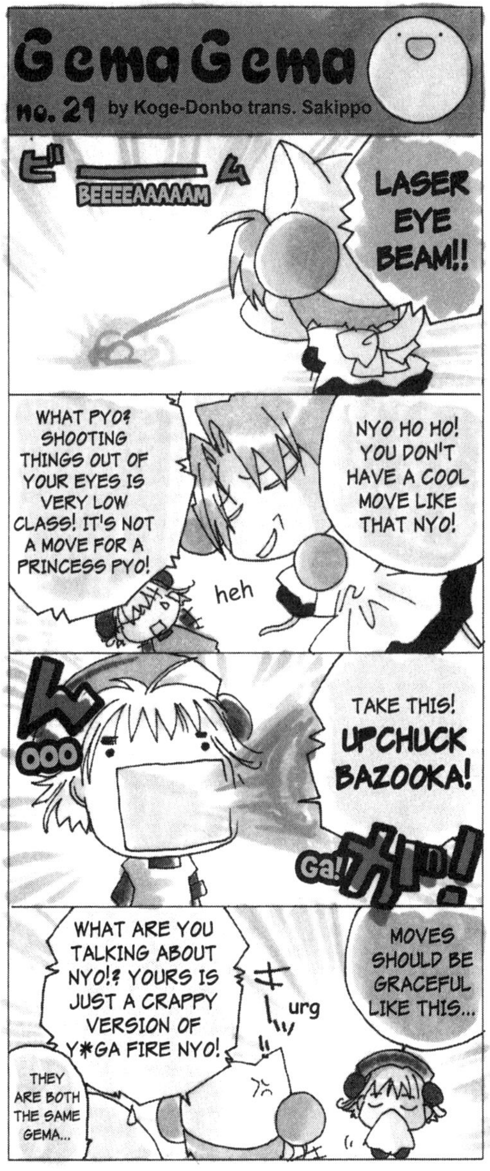
Gema Gema
no. 21 by Koge-Donbo trans. Sakippo
LASER EYE BEAM!!
ビーム
BEEEEAAAAAM
NYO HO HO! YOU DON'T HAVE A COOL MOVE LIKE THAT NYO!
WHAT PYO? SHOOTING THINGS OUT OF YOUR EYES IS VERY LOW CLASS! IT'S NOT A MOVE FOR A PRINCESS PYO!
heh
TAKE THIS! UPCHUCK BAZOOKA!
Ga!
ooo
MOVES SHOULD BE GRACEFUL LIKE THIS...
WHAT ARE YOU TALKING ABOUT NYO!? YOURS IS JUST A CRAPPY VERSION OF Y*GA FIRE NYO!
urg
THEY ARE BOTH THE SAME GEMA...

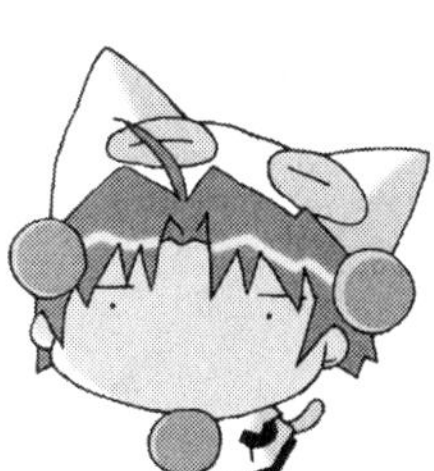

Gema Gema
no. 22 by Koge-Donbo trans. Sakippo
DEJIKO ONEECHAN HAS NO GRACE LIKE A PRINCESS SHOULD PYO!
WHAT NYO-!?
BUT LATELY, I HAVE BEEN TOO PEAS-ANT-LIKE AND VULGAR NYO!
FROM NOW ON DEJIKO WILL BECOME MORE GRACEFUL THAN WILL AND GRACE NYO.
YAY GEMA.
PHEWW!
ぷは EXHALE
huff
puff
AND THE TIME IS?
I MINUTE 12 SECONDS GEMA.
WHAT GRACE..

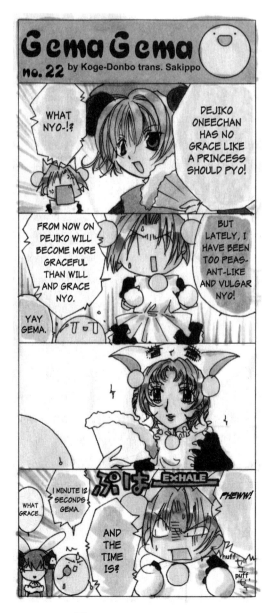

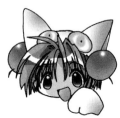

Gema Gema 23
by Koge-Donbo trans. Sakippo
MY NAME WAS DECIDED PYO.
YOU CAN CALL ME PYOCOLA ANALOGUE III PYO. NICE TO MEET YOU.
GODFATHER TAKASHI-SAN (14)
STOP TAKING THE SPOT-LIGHT NYO!
YOU'RE TICKING ME OFF NYO! I'LL GIVE YOU A NAME NYO!
HAVE YOUR CLASS-MATES MAKE FUN OF YOU NYO!!
WHA?
HIS CLASS-MATES AREN'T THAT MEAN PYO...
shock
WELL, SINCE YOU'RE TAKASHI...
"TAKA-PON."
WHAT A COOL NAME PYO-!!
HOW LAME
SHOCK
URG! I HATE YOU BOTH NYO!!
BOOM!
YOU'RE MAKING NO SENSE GEMA...

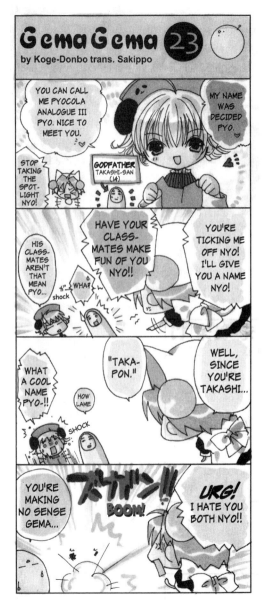

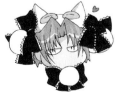

Gema Gema 24

by Koge-Donbo trans. Sakippo

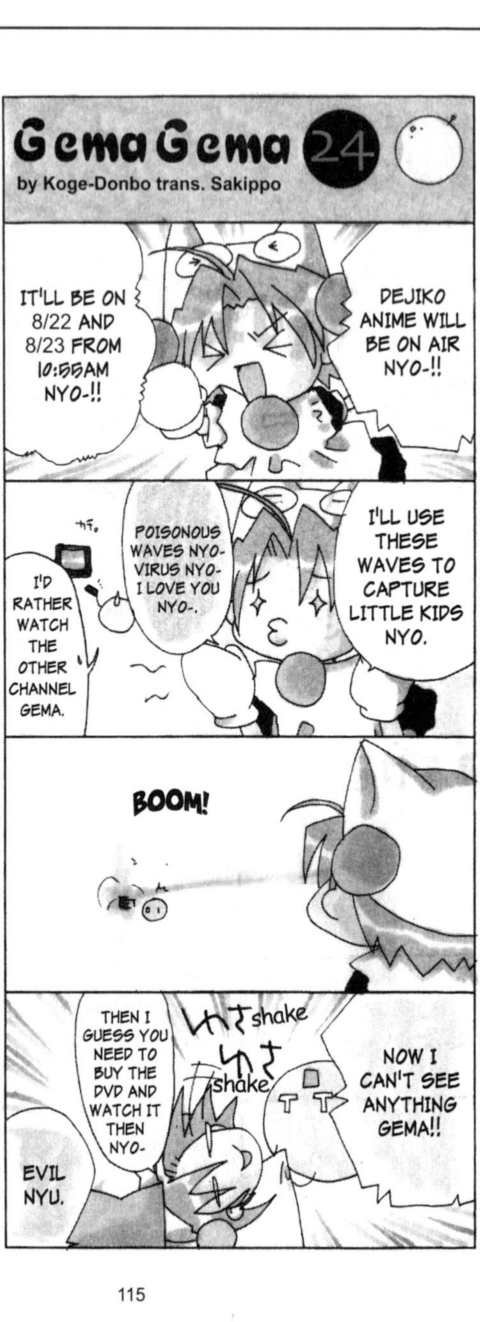
DEJIKO ANIME WILL BE ON AIR NYO-!!
IT'LL BE ON 8/22 AND 8/23 FROM 10:55AM NYO-!!
I'LL USE THESE WAVES TO CAPTURE LITTLE KIDS NYO.
POISONOUS WAVES NYO- VIRUS NYO- I LOVE YOU NYO-.
カチ。
I'D RATHER WATCH THE OTHER CHANNEL GEMA.
BOOM!
NOW I CAN'T SEE ANYTHING GEMA!!
ゆさ shake
ゆさ shake
THEN I GUESS YOU NEED TO BUY THE DVD AND WATCH IT THEN NYO-
EVIL NYU.

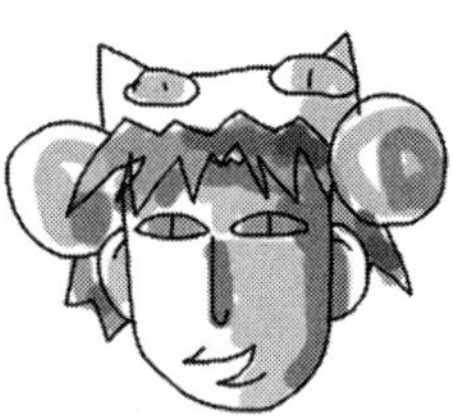

Gema Gema 25

by Koge-Donbo trans. Sakippo

ONEECHAN, I CAME TO TAKE OVER GEMA GEMA PYO!
baam
FOR INTER-VIEWS, YOU NEED TO GO THROUGH MY AGENT NYO.
...BUT SINCE I HAVE NOTHING TO FEATURE THIS MONTH, AND TIME IS RUNNING OUT, I'LL PLAY ALONG WITH YOU.
REALLY PYO!? VIVA DEAD-LINES PYO!
YES PYO! THE BLACK GEMA GEMA GANG TAKES OVER PYO-.
I CALL IT THE BLACK GEMA GEMA PYO!
AND NOW I WILL...
click
OK, TIME'S UP.
... ALREADY PYO-!?

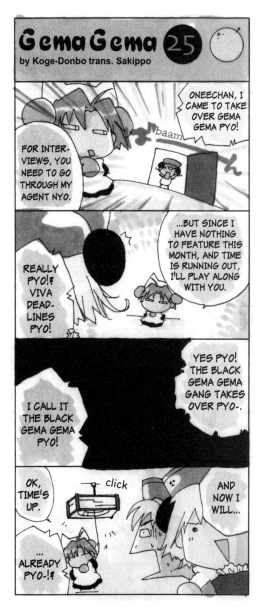

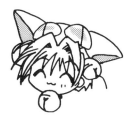

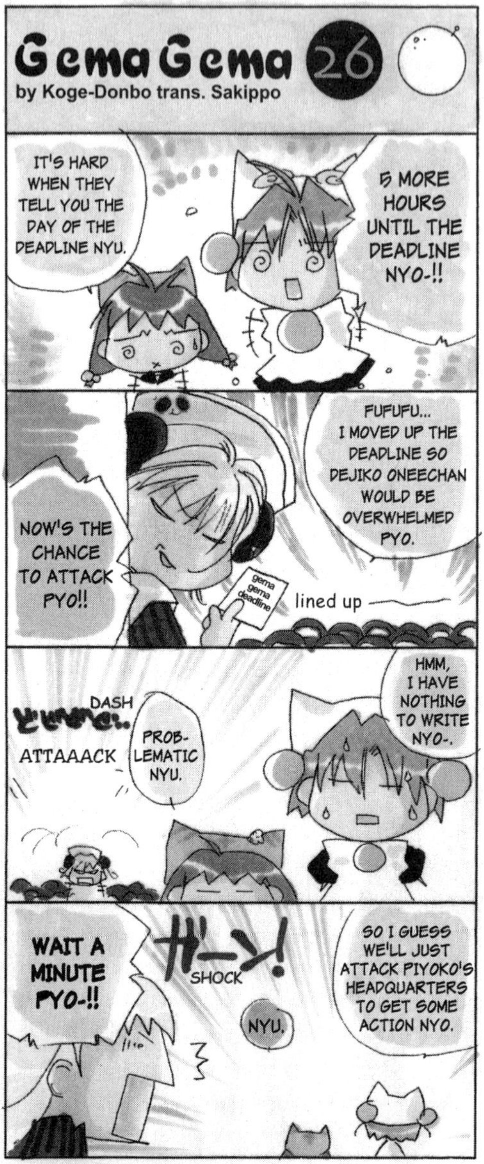
Gema Gema 26
by Koge-Donbo trans. Sakippo
5 MORE HOURS UNTIL THE DEADLINE NYO-!!
IT'S HARD WHEN THEY TELL YOU THE DAY OF THE DEADLINE NYU.
FUFUFU... I MOVED UP THE DEADLINE SO DEJIKO ONEECHAN WOULD BE OVERWHELMED PYO.
NOW'S THE CHANCE TO ATTACK PYO!!
gema gema deadline
lined up
HMM, I HAVE NOTHING TO WRITE NYO-.
PROB-LEMATIC NYU.
DASH
ATTAAACK
SO I GUESS WE'LL JUST ATTACK PIYOKO'S HEADQUARTERS TO GET SOME ACTION NYO.
SHOCK
WAIT A MINUTE PYO-!!
NYU.

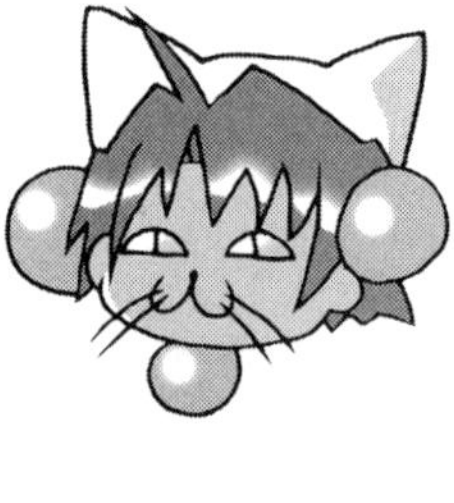

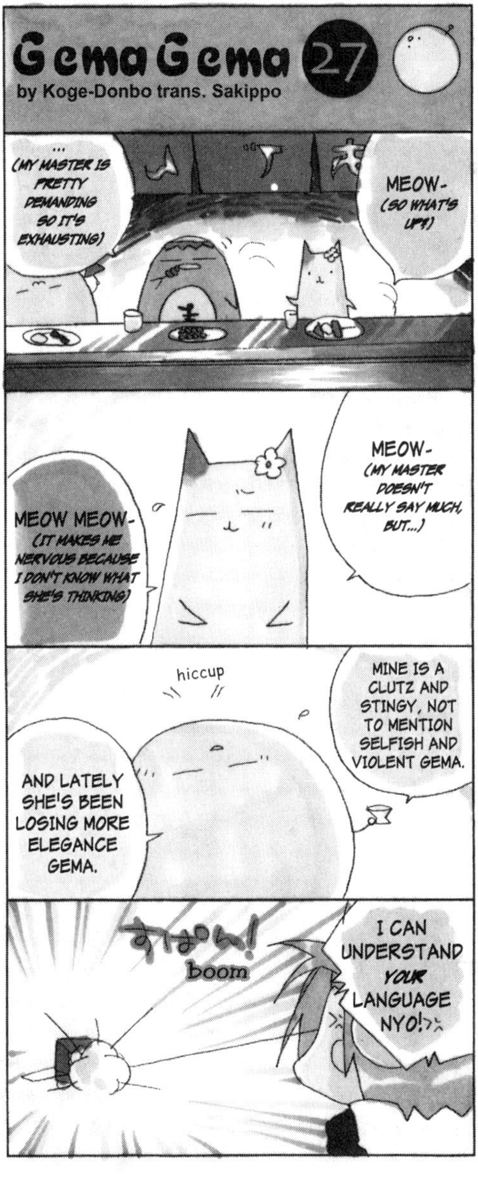
Gema Gema 27
by Koge-Donbo trans. Sakippo
MEOW- (SO WHAT'S UP?)
... (MY MASTER IS PRETTY DEMANDING SO IT'S EXHAUSTING)
MEOW- (MY MASTER DOESN'T REALLY SAY MUCH, BUT...)
MEOW MEOW- (IT MAKES ME NERVOUS BECAUSE I DON'T KNOW WHAT SHE'S THINKING)
MINE IS A CLUTZ AND STINGY, NOT TO MENTION SELFISH AND VIOLENT GEMA.
hiccup
AND LATELY SHE'S BEEN LOSING MORE ELEGANCE GEMA.
I CAN UNDERSTAND YOUR LANGUAGE NYO!
すぱん!
boom

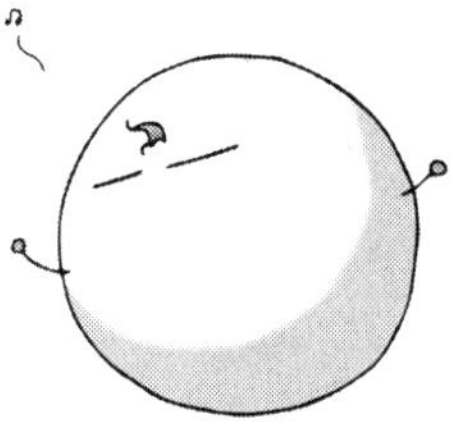

Gema Gema 28
by Koge-Donbo trans. Sakippo
I'M RIK HEISENBERG.
I'M KY SCHWEITZER.
COO ERHARD.
THESE ARE THE LOVELY LADIES WHO CAME UP WITH OUR NAMES.
AKIKO-SAN
ITSUKI-SAN
DA
TA
HEY, COOL. GOOD WORK.
AMAZING PYO-! AMAZING PYO-! ♡ NAMING EXPERTS PYO-!
THAT'S RIGHT PYOCOLA-SAMA. NOW YOU CAN CALL US BY OUR NAMES.
SO NOW, PLEASE NAME THE REST OF THE BLACK GEMA GEMA GANG MEMBERS.
HUH!?
GEBA
I HAD A HARD TIME CALLING THEM PYO-...

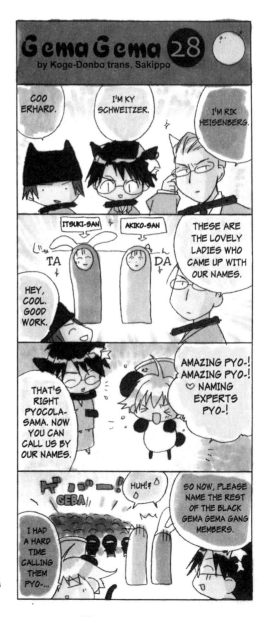

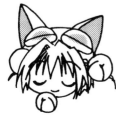

Gema Gema 29
by Koge-Donbo trans. Sakippo
THE DI GI CHARAT FANTASY GAME IS RELEASED, SO TIME FOR SOME FAN SERVICE NYO. ♪
ALL THE CHARAC- TERS FROM THE GAME...
...WILL GUEST APPEAR...
THUD
NYO-!!
TOO MANY PEOPLE NYO!!
CRASH
WHAT SERVICE WAS THIS?
ACTION NYU.
NO NYO!!

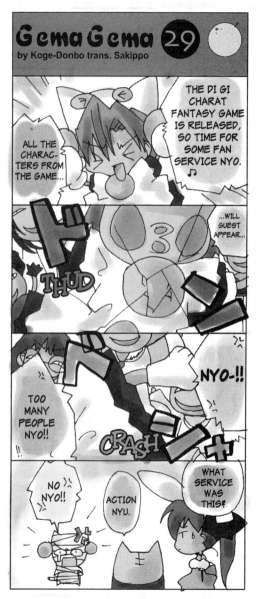

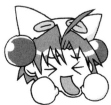

Gema Gema 30
by Koge-Donbo trans. Sakippo
PUCHIKO, YOU'RE SO SMALL NYO. IS THERE ANY WORK THAT YOU CAN DO?
THERE IS NYU!! I WORK HARD TO BRING IN CUS-TOMERS NYU!
I SEE... I WONDER HOW NYO?
heh heh
I DO A LOT NYU!
DEJIKO, DON'T PICK ON HER SO MUCH...
curses and incantations
I'M WORKING HARD WHERE PEOPLE CAN'T SEE NYU!
YEAH, RIGHT.
WHAT THE...

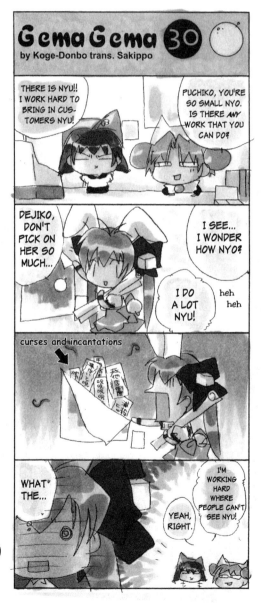

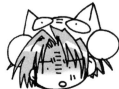

ema Gema Gang
de of Conduct

law 1
Members must always put "geba" at the end of their sentence.

Members must be wearing black at all times.
law 2

law 3
One evil a day.

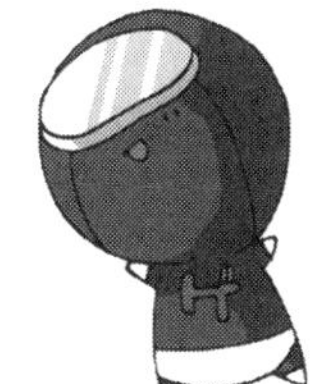

Black

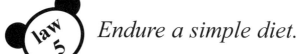

Prioritize health and well-being.

law 4

law 5
Endure a simple diet.

A History of the Black Gema Gema Gang
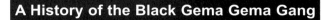

The Black Gema Gema Gang's executives, Rik, Ky, and Coo came from Planet Analogue to take care of Piyoko and assist in her objective to kidnap Dejiko for ransom.

September 2000 Like Rabi~en~Rose and Piyoko, Rik, Ky, and Coo are featured in *From Gamers* without names. A contest to decide their names follows after. The contest is limited to girls, and they each get to turn in a postcard featuring one of the three guys.

Two entries are chosen, and the winners are featured in the *Gema Gema* comic.

October 2000 The Gamers Square Store is taken over by the Black Gema Gema Gang, and renamed as "Black Gamers."

November 2000 *Di Gi Charat - Piyoko is Number One!* is released in Japan.

December 2000 Rik, Ky, and Coo hold a mini-concert, "Black Gema Gema Gang Special X'mas Party" at the Kagurazaka Twin Star.

Rik, Ky, and Coo are featured in the *Di Gi Charat* Christmas Special anime.

February 2001 Rik, Ky, and Coo's first Mini-album, "We are THE ONE!" is released.

"Black Valentine Party" is held at the Kagurazaka Twin Star.

March 2001 The Black Gema Gema Gang take over part of the "Di Gi Charat Concert in Yokohama Arena."

May 2001 Rik, Ky, and Coo get a group name, "Pyocola Keeping Operations (PKO)," which is decided by the general public.

July 2001 The mini-album "P.K.O." is released.

August 2001 The Di Gi Charat Concert Climax featuring PKO is held at the Roppongi Velfarre.

February 2002 The Di Gi Charat Valentine Concert "Happy!" featuring PKO is held at the Roppongi Velfarre.

June 2002 The PKO Live Tour starts; it continues for four days. All days are sold out.

July 2002 The mini-album "Black Generation" is released.

October 2003 The PKO Live Tour "Caution" starts; it continues for four days in 4 major cities.

Pyocola Analogue III

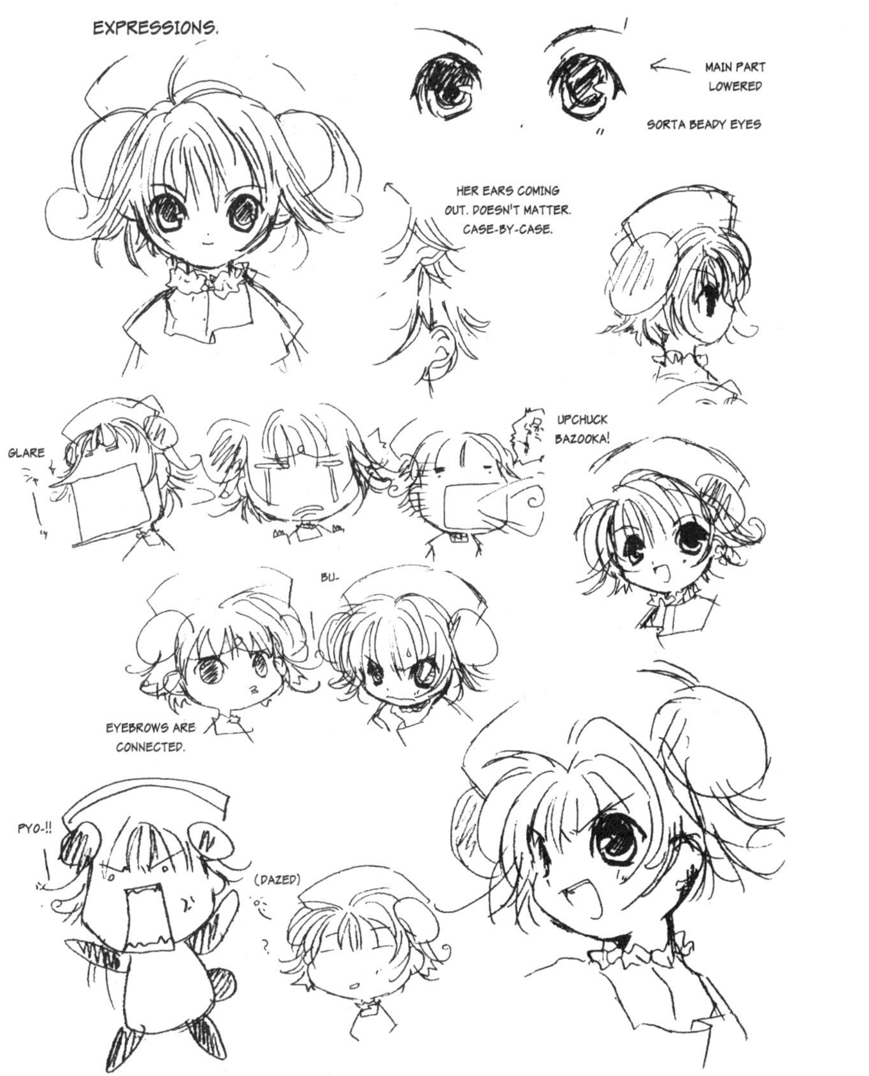
EXPRESSIONS.
MAIN PART LOWERED
SORTA BEADY EYES
HER EARS COMING OUT. DOESN'T MATTER. CASE-BY-CASE.
GLARE
UPCHUCK BAZOOKA!
BU-
EYEBROWS ARE CONNECTED.
PYO-!!
(DAZED)

Black Gema Gema Gang

Coo Erhard

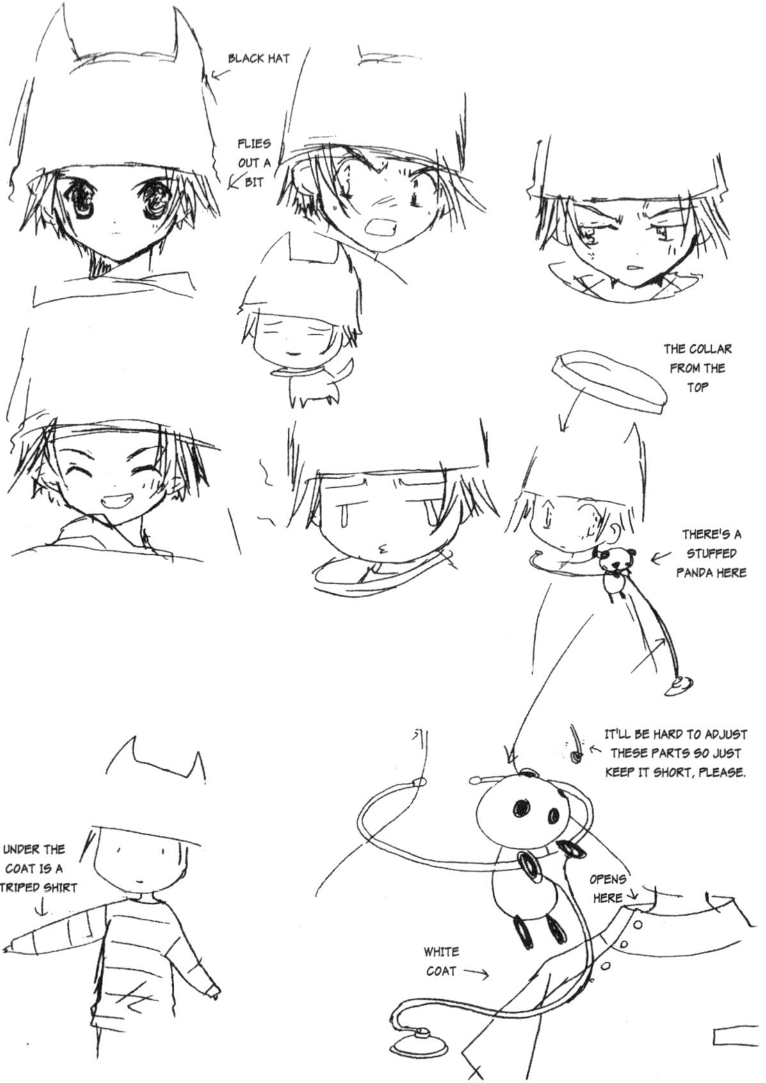
BLACK HAT
FLIES OUT A BIT
THE COLLAR FROM THE TOP
THERE'S A STUFFED PANDA HERE
IT'LL BE HARD TO ADJUST THESE PARTS SO JUST KEEP IT SHORT, PLEASE.
UNDER THE COAT IS A STRIPED SHIRT
OPENS HERE
WHITE COAT

Black Gema Gema Gang

Ky Schweitzer

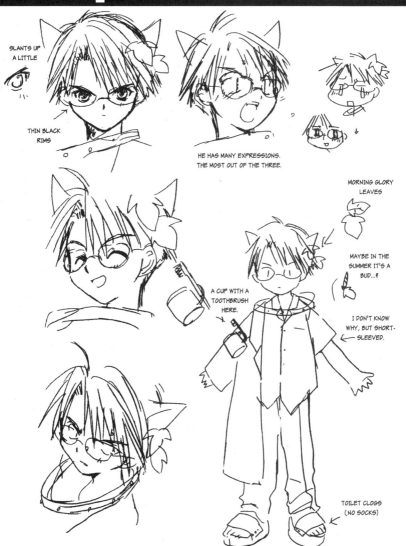

SLANTS UP A LITTLE

THIN BLACK RIMS

HE HAS MANY EXPRESSIONS. THE MOST OUT OF THE THREE.

MORNING GLORY LEAVES

MAYBE IN THE SUMMER IT'S A BUD...?

A CUP WITH A TOOTHBRUSH HERE.

I DON'T KNOW WHY, BUT SHORT-SLEEVED.

TOILET CLOGS (NO SOCKS)

Rik Heisenberg

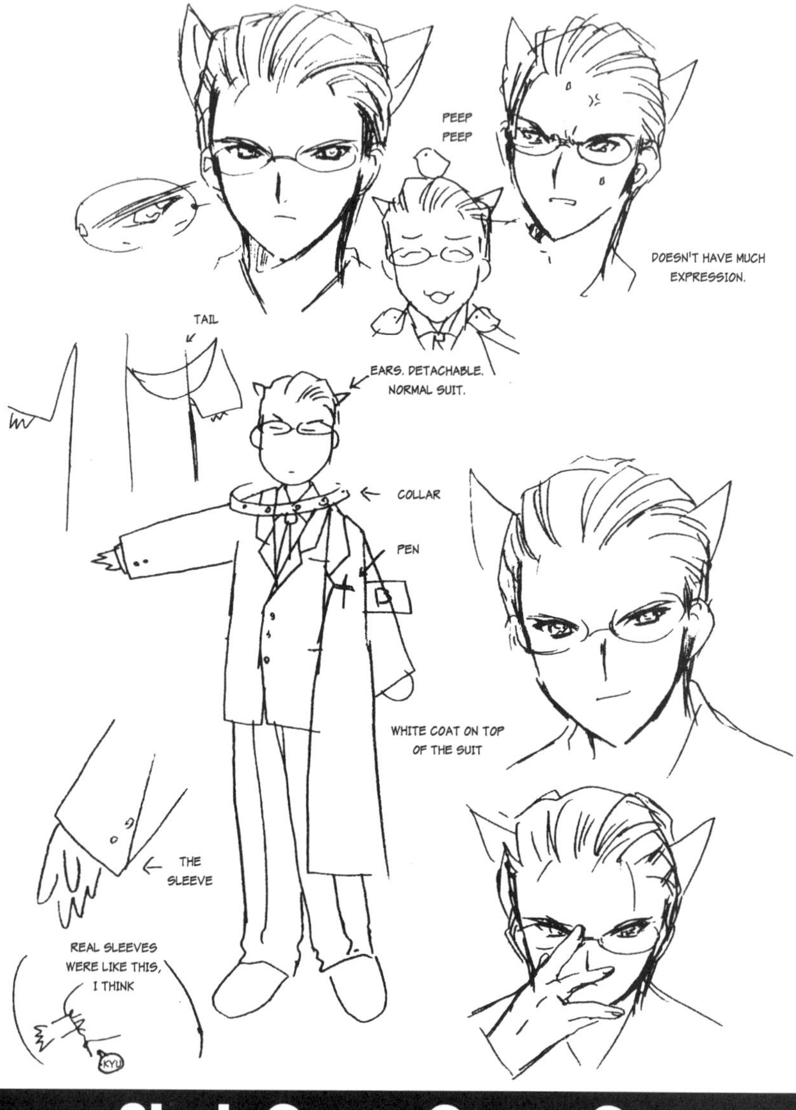
PEEP
PEEP
DOESN'T HAVE MUCH EXPRESSION.
TAIL
EARS. DETACHABLE.
NORMAL SUIT.
COLLAR
PEN
WHITE COAT ON TOP OF THE SUIT
THE SLEEVE
REAL SLEEVES WERE LIKE THIS, I THINK
KYU

Black Gema Gema Gang

Interview with Koge-Donbo

When did you start drawing comics? Where did you learn how to draw/illustrate?
If "drawing comics" means drawing in actual panels, I started at 5 years old. I learned how to draw on my own.

What is the best part and worst part about becoming a manga artist/illustrator?
The best part would be that my work could be shown to a lot of different people.

The worst part...hmm. I guess when I realize that what I just drew/wrote isn't that interesting.

Do you have any friends who are manga artists?
I actually went to the same Junior High as Kanan, who draws Galaxy Angel.

You have gotten quite famous not only in Japan but also worldwide, but how do the people around you react to your success?
My parents and my grandmother are very happy for me. As for my friends, they don't act any different.

What did you think of the United States?
Everything is huge! It surprises me.

Black Gema Gema Gallery

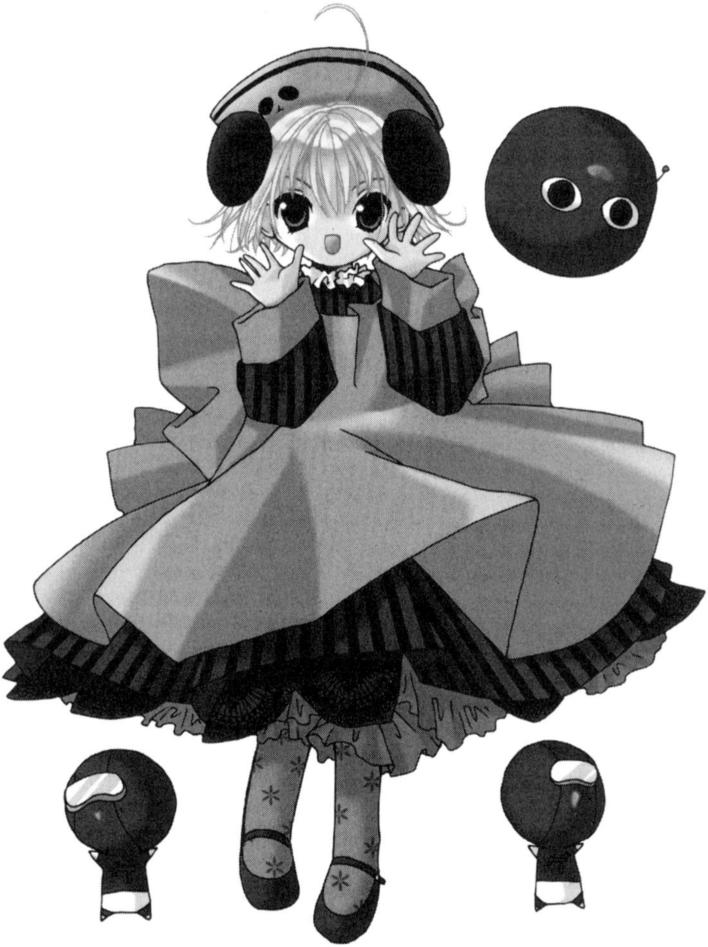

From *Dragon Jr.* promotional card
(Fujimi Shobou)

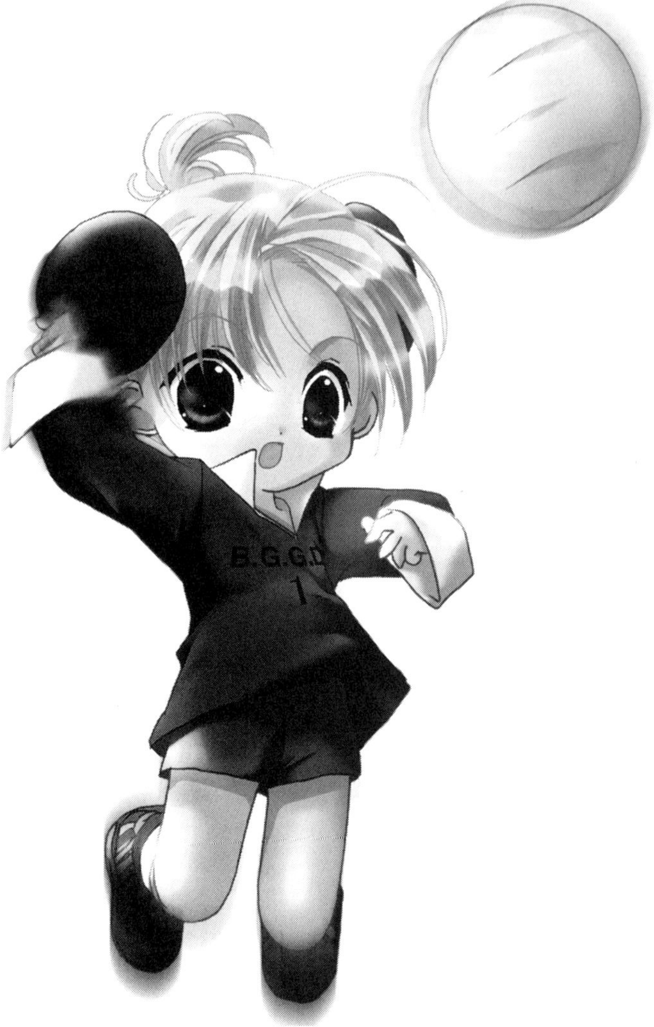
B.G.G.D
1

From *Di Gi Charat Character Card Game pt. 2*

From *From Gamers*

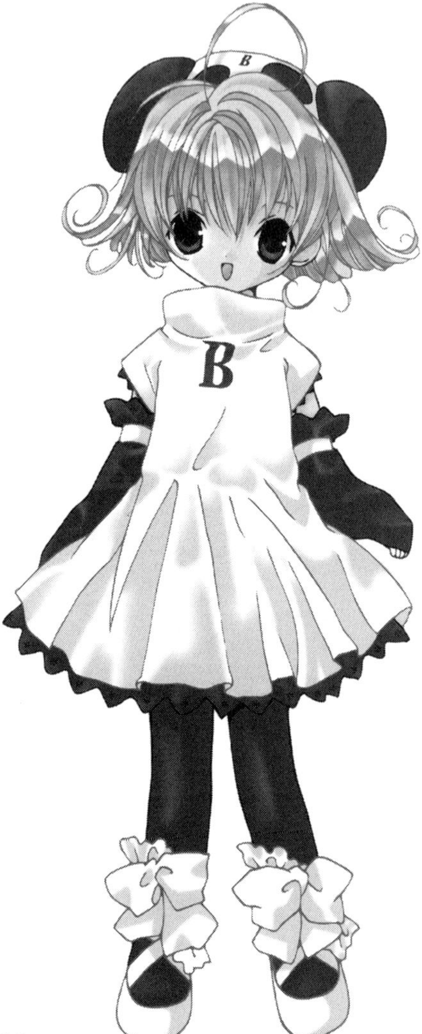
B
B

From *Dejiko's Party pt. 1* card series

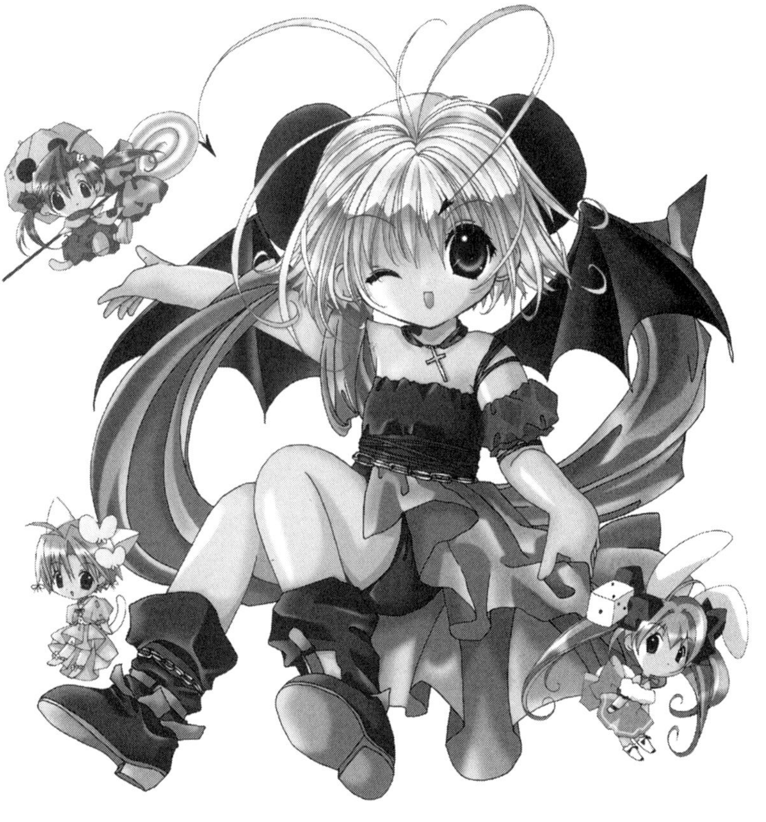

From *Dengenki Animation Magazine*
(Media Works)

Di Gi Charat Theater

★

Leave it to Piyoko!

Enjoy Piyoko and the Black Gema Gema Gang's adventures?

Well, there's more coming up from Broccoli Books!

Di Gi Charat Theater: Leave it to Piyoko!
will be coming out this Summer.

The following pages will give you a sneak peek in Piyoko's life!

For more information, visit **broccolibooks.com**!!

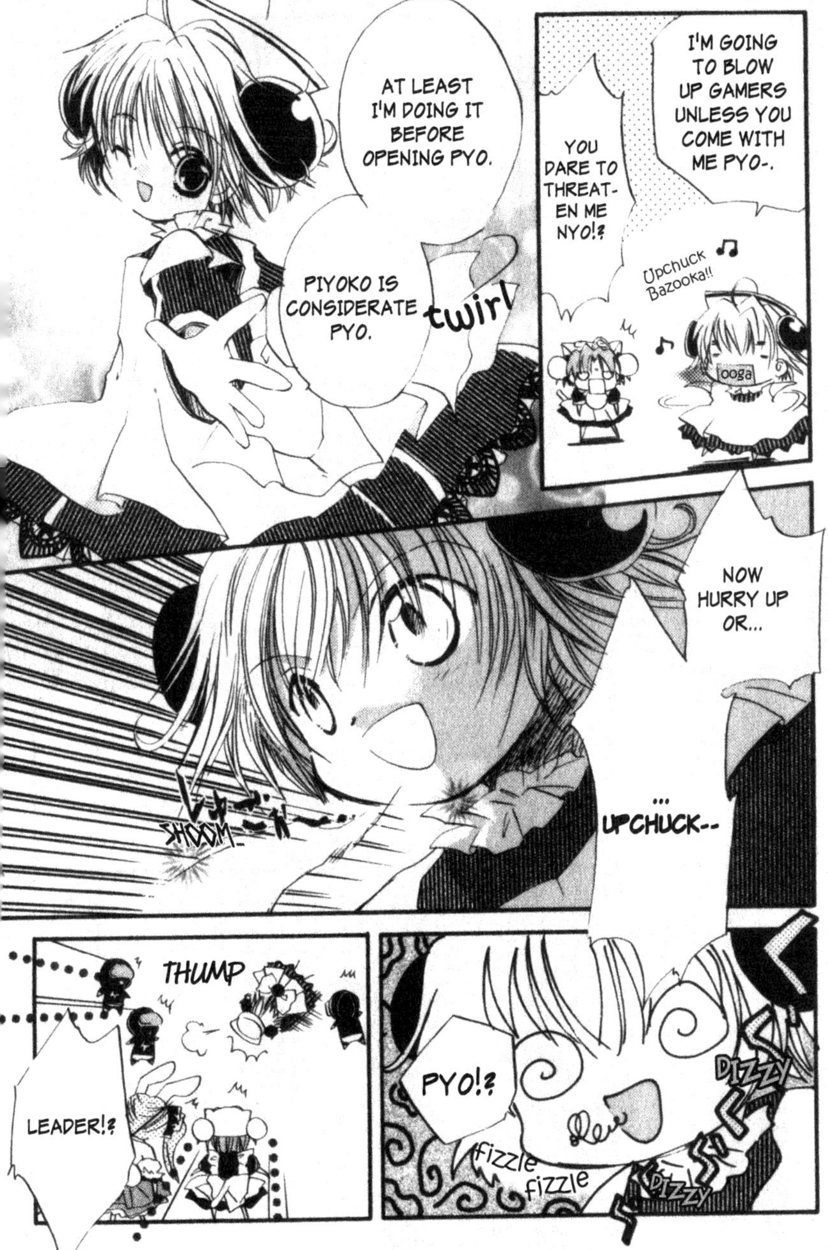
I'M GOING TO BLOW UP GAMERS UNLESS YOU COME WITH ME PYO-.
YOU DARE TO THREAT-EN ME NYO!?
Upchuck Bazooka!!
ooga
AT LEAST I'M DOING IT BEFORE OPENING PYO.
PIYOKO IS CONSIDERATE PYO.
twirl
NOW HURRY UP OR...
... UPCHUCK--
SHOOM
PYO!?
DIZZY
fizzle fizzle
DIZZY
THUMP
LEADER!?

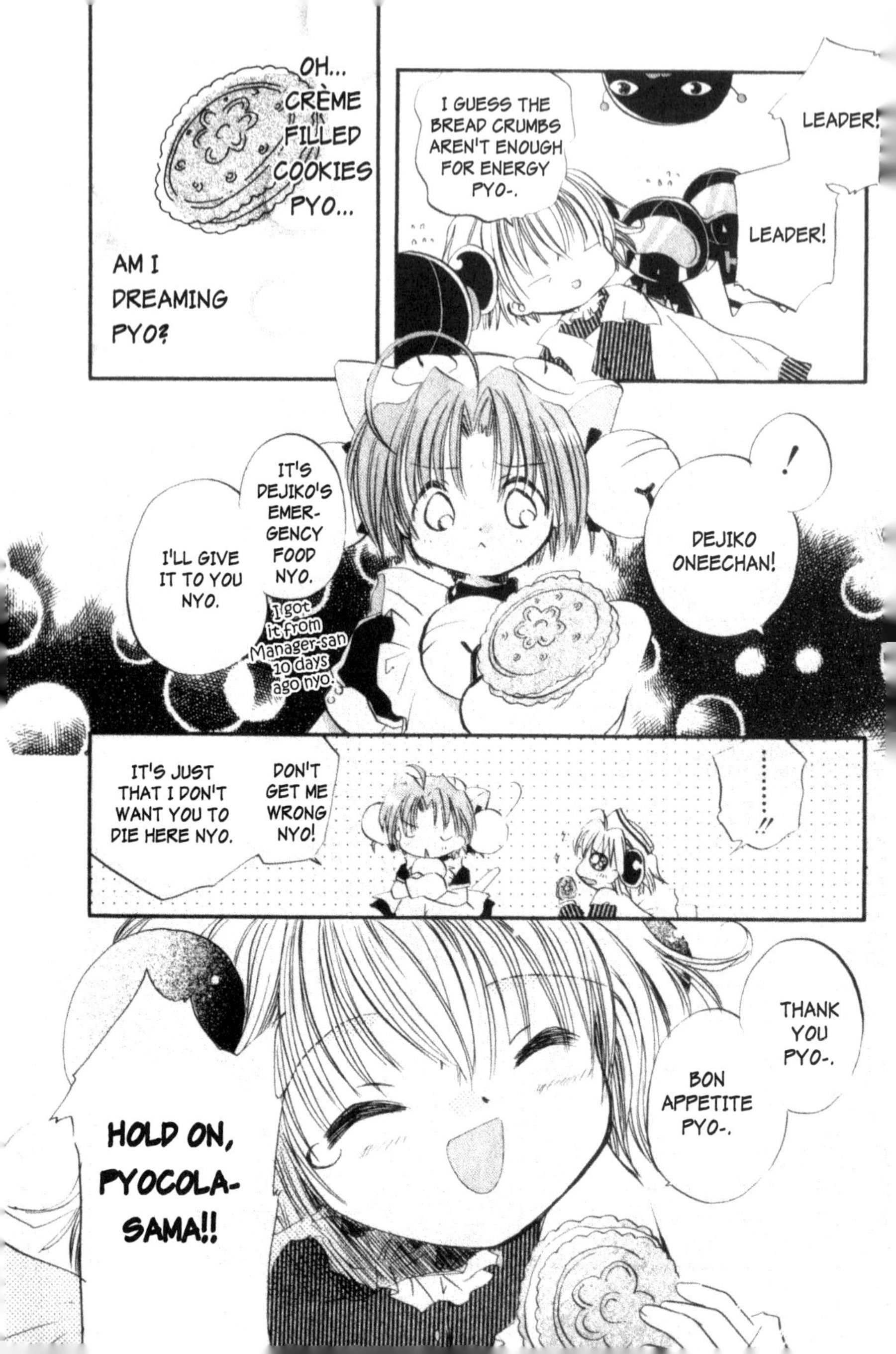
LEADER!
LEADER!
I GUESS THE BREAD CRUMBS AREN'T ENOUGH FOR ENERGY PYO-.
OH... CRÈME FILLED COOKIES PYO...
AM I DREAMING PYO?
!
DEJIKO ONEECHAN!
IT'S DEJIKO'S EMERGENCY FOOD NYO.
I got it from Manager-san 10 days ago nyo.
I'LL GIVE IT TO YOU NYO.
......!!
DON'T GET ME WRONG NYO!
IT'S JUST THAT I DON'T WANT YOU TO DIE HERE NYO.
THANK YOU PYO-.
BON APPETITE PYO-.
HOLD ON, PYOCOLA-SAMA!!

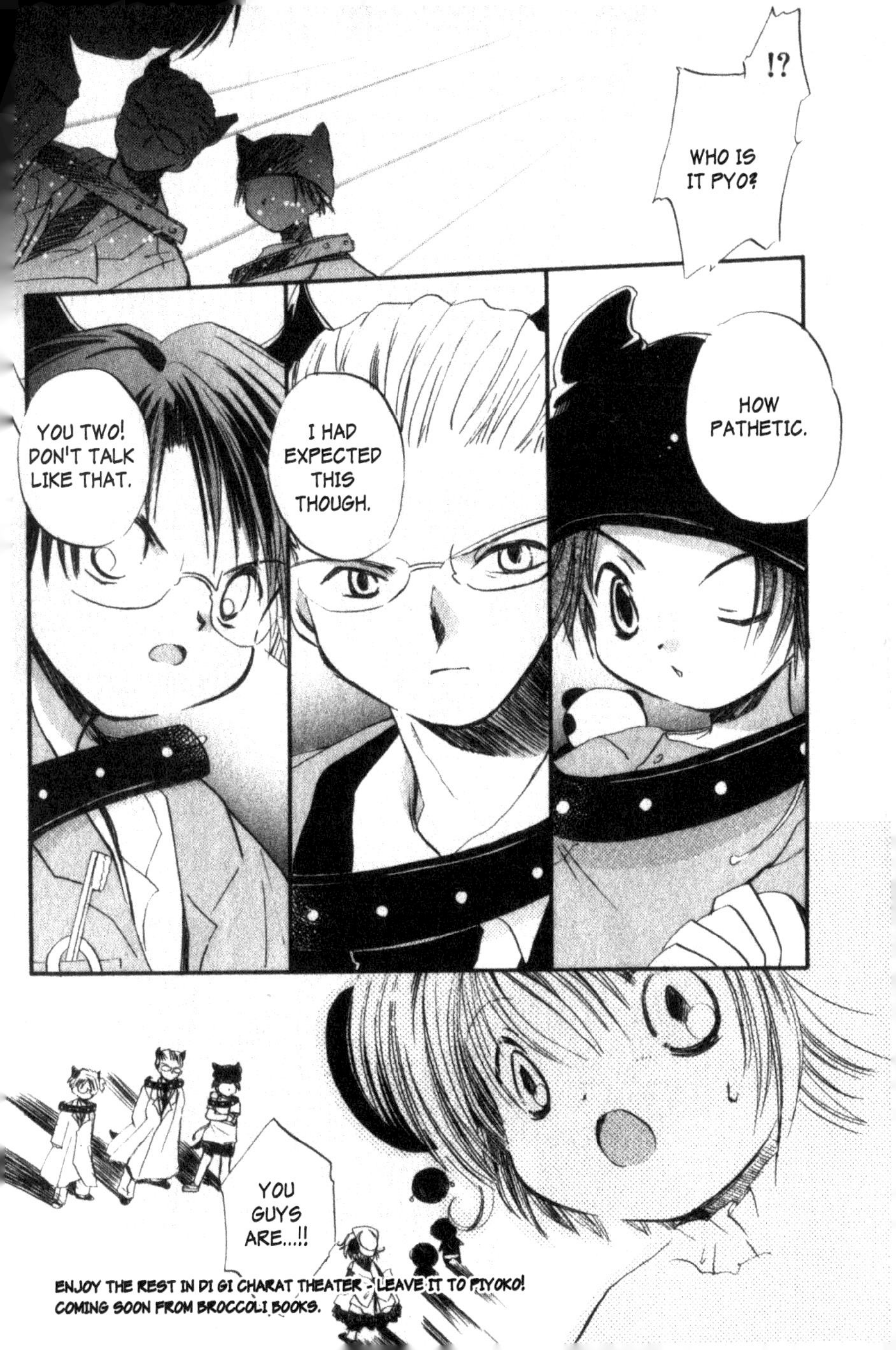
!?
WHO IS IT PYO?
HOW PATHETIC.
I HAD EXPECTED THIS THOUGH.
YOU TWO! DON'T TALK LIKE THAT.
YOU GUYS ARE...!!
ENJOY THE REST IN DI GI CHARAT THEATER - LEAVE IT TO PIYOKO! COMING SOON FROM BROCCOLI BOOKS.

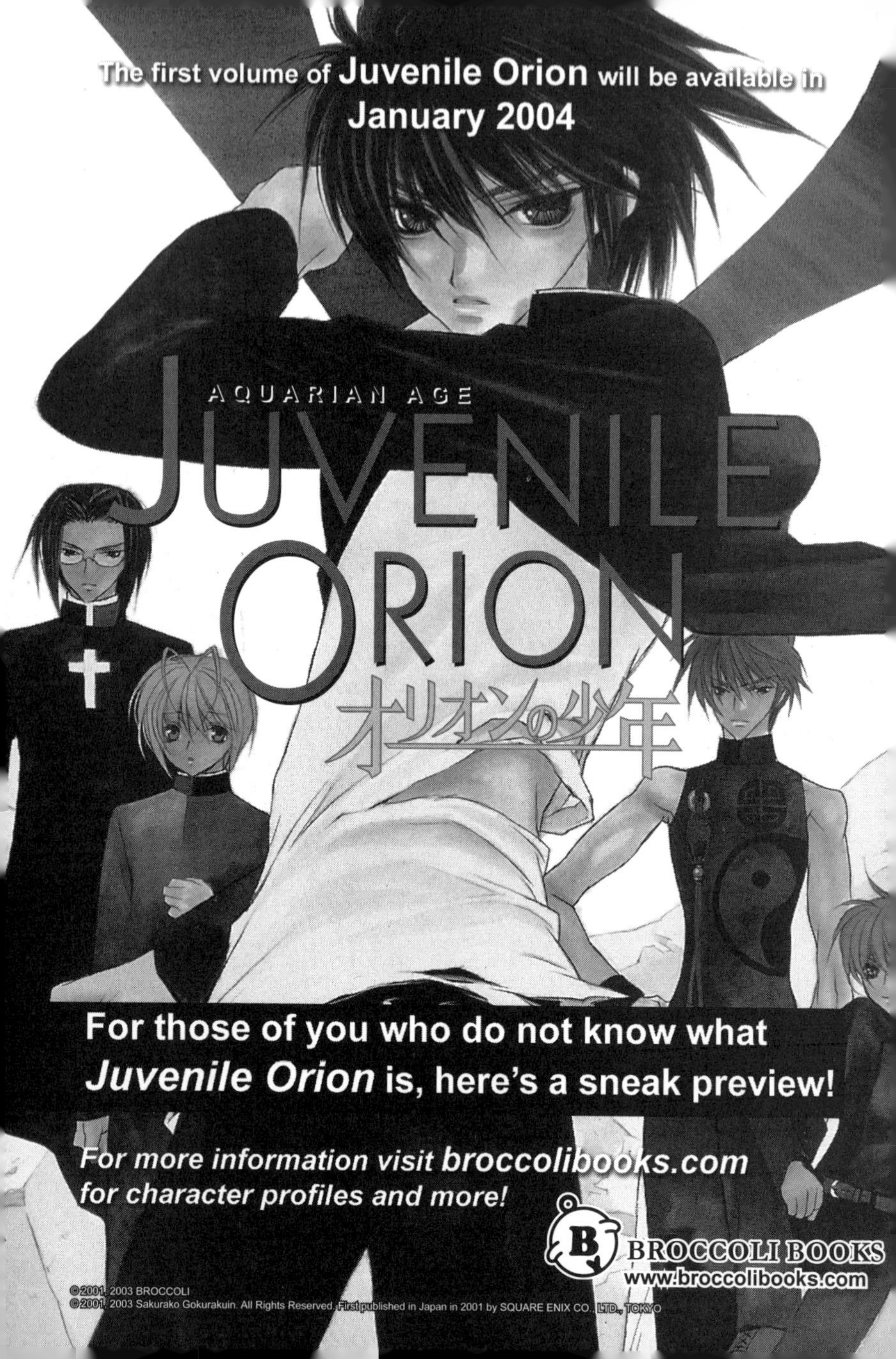
The first volume of Juvenile Orion will be available in
January 2004
AQUARIAN AGE
JUVENILE
ORION
オリオンの少年
For those of you who do not know what Juvenile Orion is, here's a sneak preview!
For more information visit broccolibooks.com for character profiles and more!
BROCCOLI BOOKS
www.broccolibooks.com
© 2001, 2003 BROCCOLI
© 2001, 2003 Sakurako Gokurakuin. All Rights Reserved. First published in Japan in 2001 by SQUARE ENIX CO., LTD., TOKYO

AQUARIAN AGE
JUVENILE ORION

Mana returns to Tokyo and reunites with her childhood friend Kaname after seven years. But he seems to have changed in their years apart...

Mana's presence triggers numerous events that changes the lives of Kaname and his best friend Naoya forever. Their classmates Isshin and Tsukasa, and their teacher Tomonori are affected as well.

They soon discover that they are part of the Aquarian Age - a secret war raging for thousands of years.

Now the fate of the world hangs in balance as one girl meets her destiny.

Naoya

Tsukasa

Kaname

Isshin

Mana

Tomonori

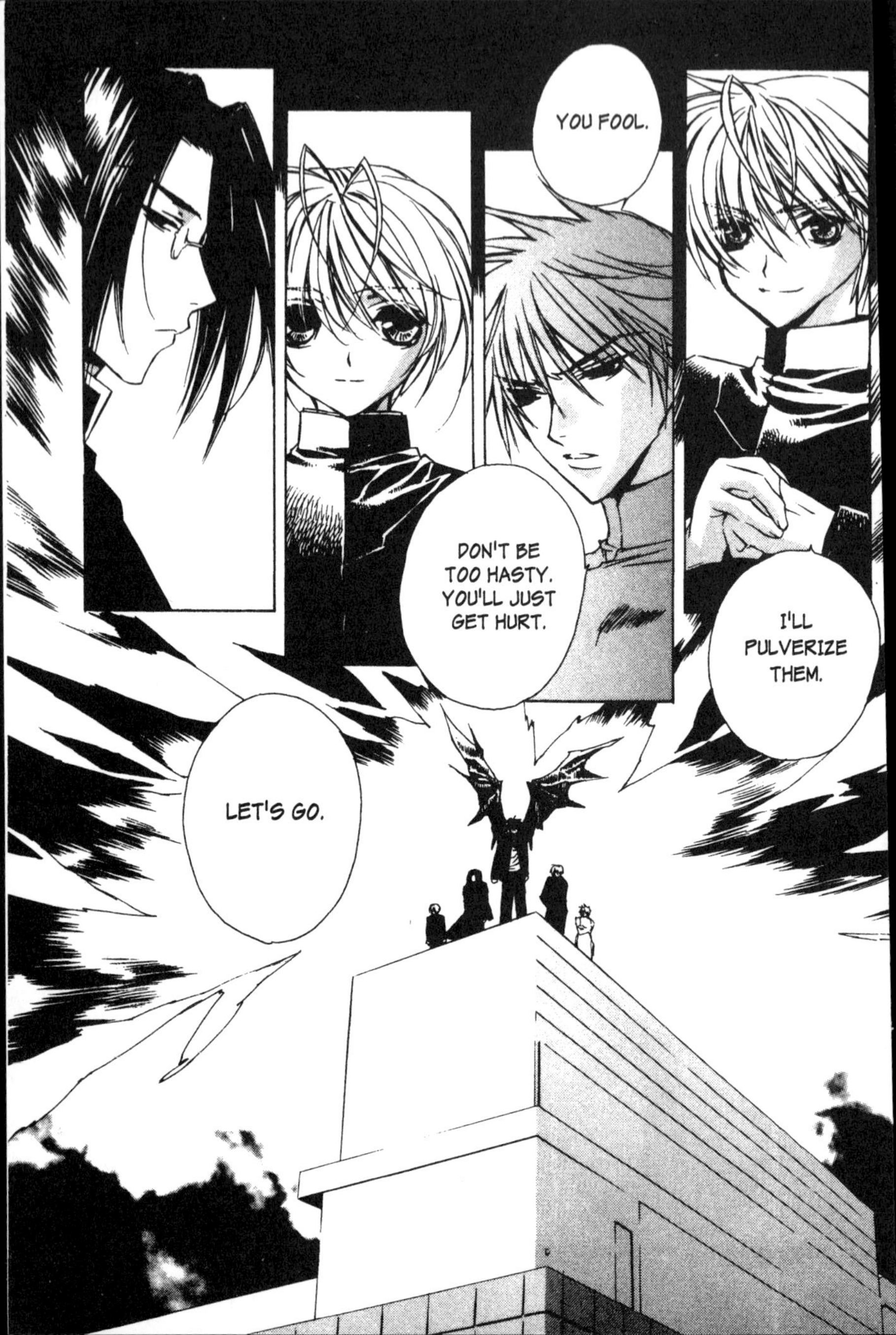
I'LL PULVERIZE THEM.
YOU FOOL.
DON'T BE TOO HASTY. YOU'LL JUST GET HURT.
LET'S GO.

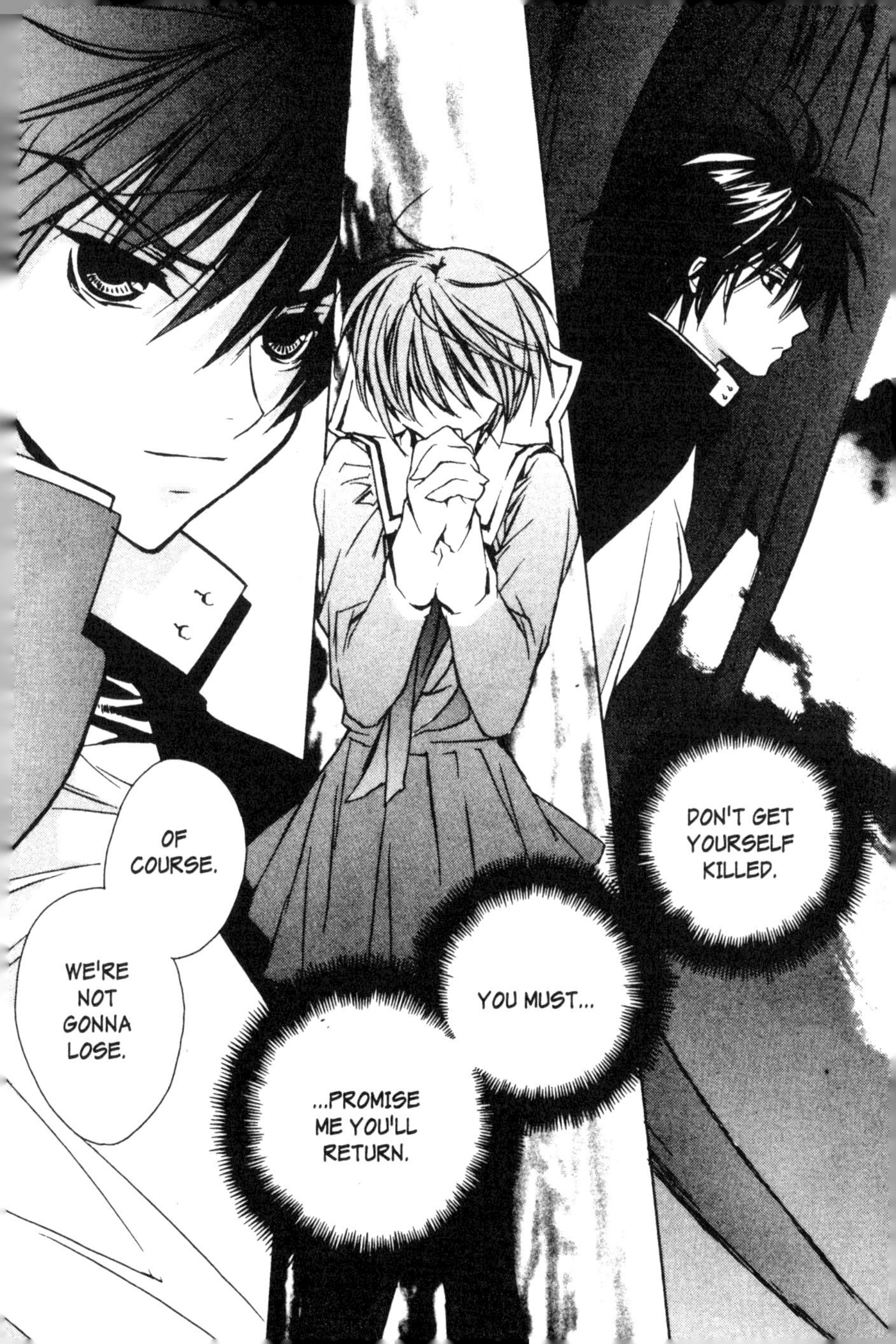
DON'T GET YOURSELF KILLED.
YOU MUST...
...PROMISE ME YOU'LL RETURN.
OF COURSE.
WE'RE NOT GONNA LOSE.

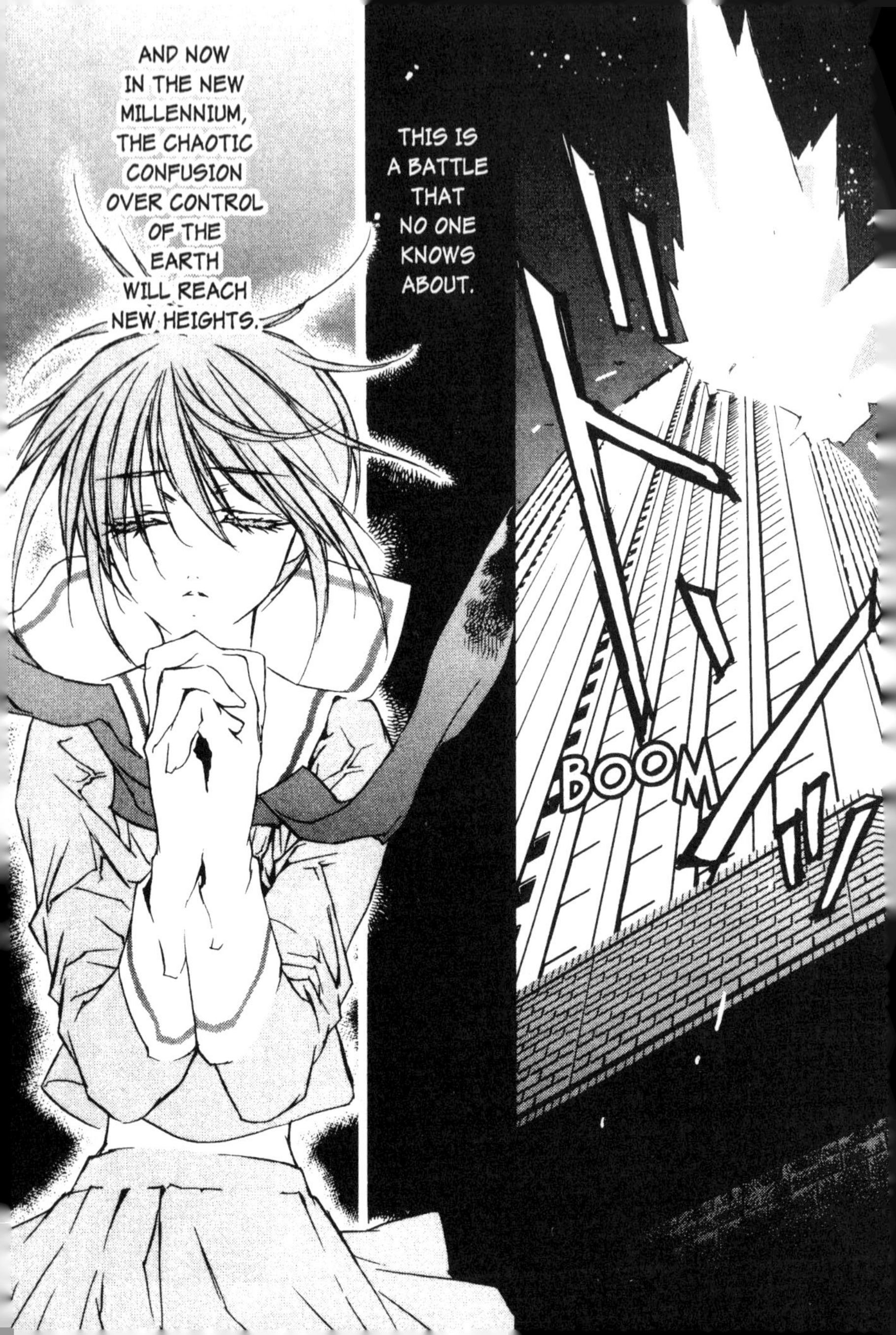
THIS IS A BATTLE THAT NO ONE KNOWS ABOUT.
BOOM
AND NOW IN THE NEW MILLENNIUM, THE CHAOTIC CONFUSION OVER CONTROL OF THE EARTH WILL REACH NEW HEIGHTS.

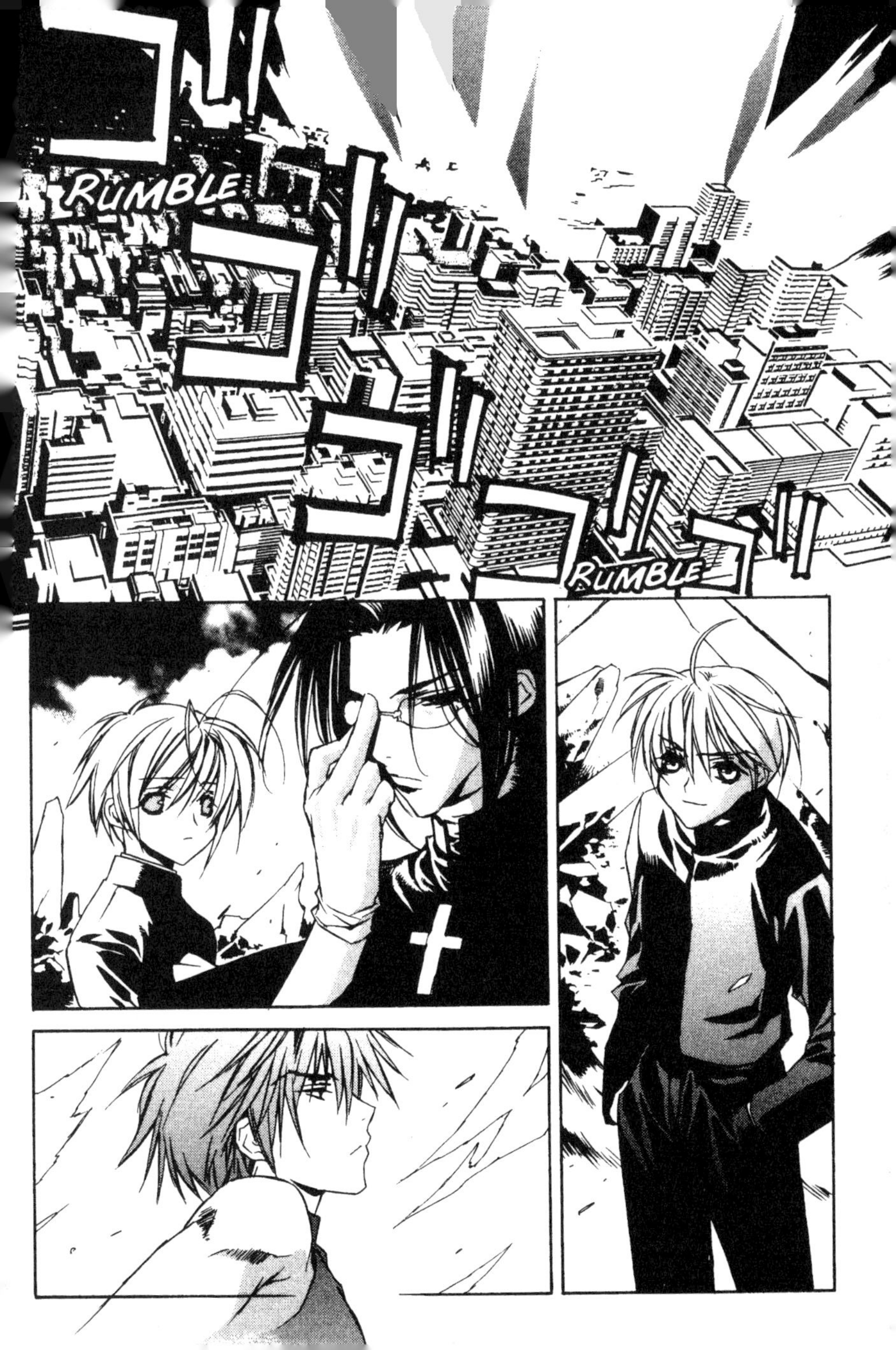
RUMBLE
RUMBLE

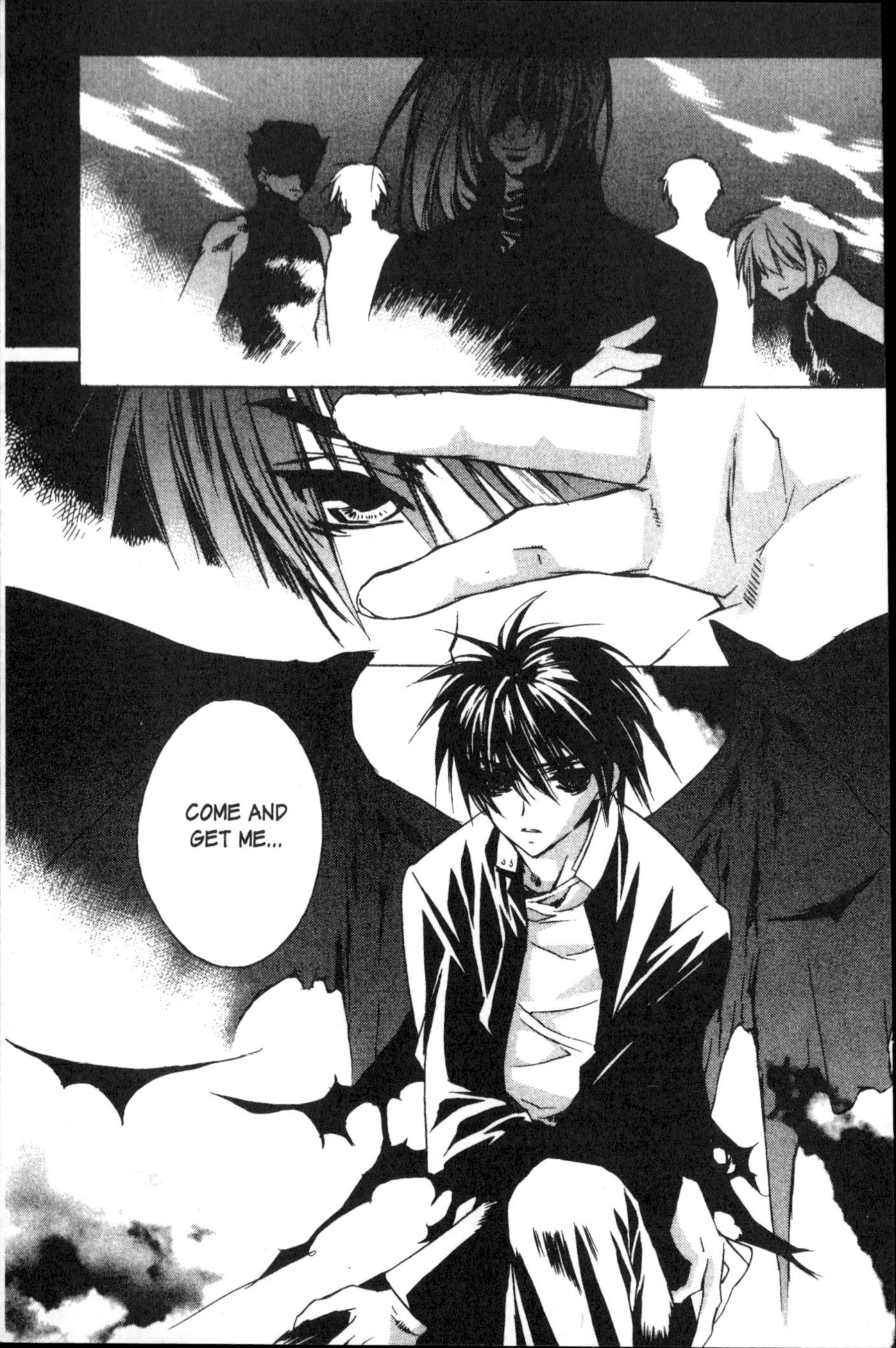
COME AND GET ME...

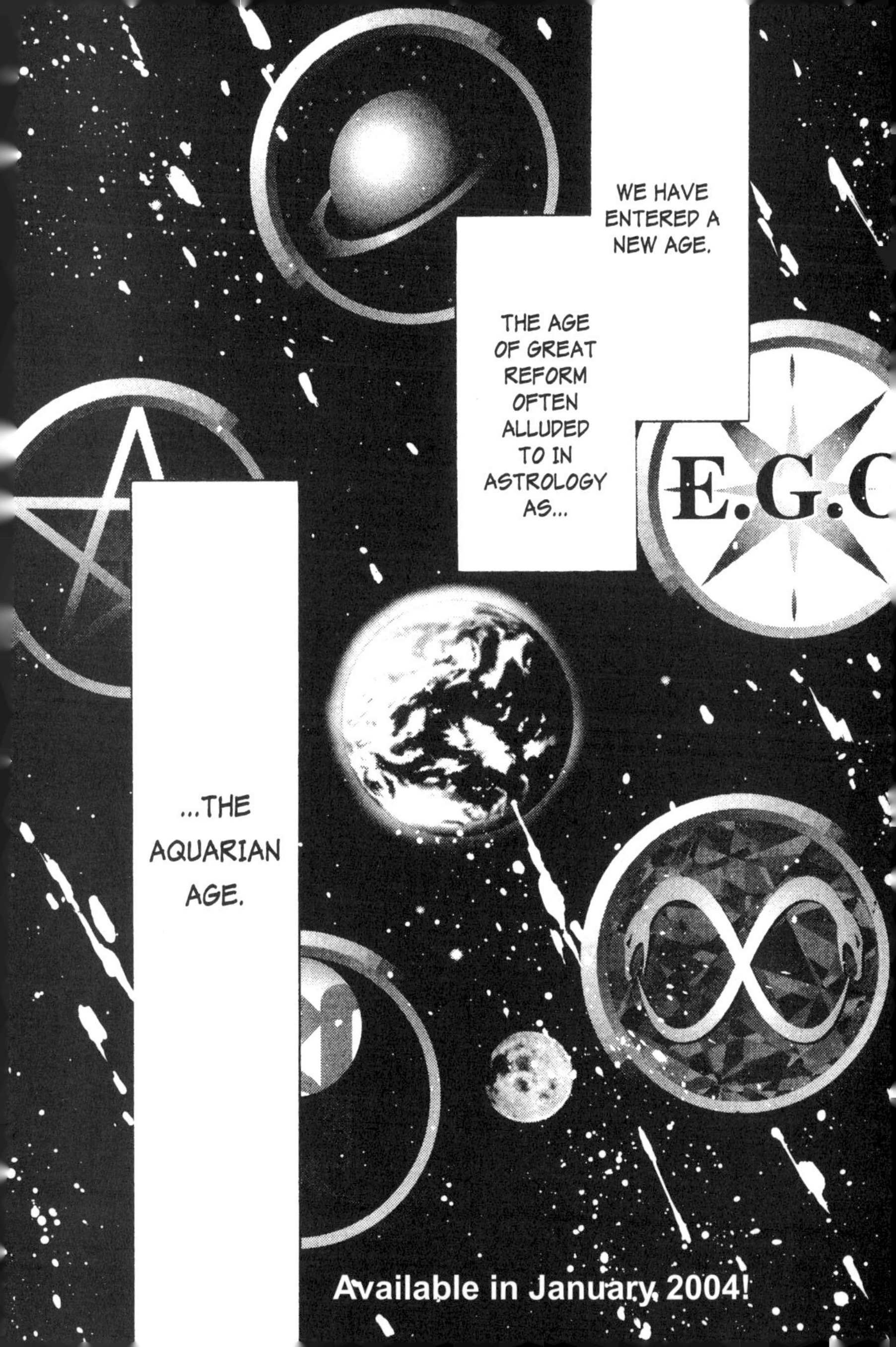
WE HAVE ENTERED A NEW AGE.
THE AGE OF GREAT REFORM OFTEN ALLUDED TO IN ASTROLOGY AS...
...THE AQUARIAN AGE.
Available in January 2004!

PLEASE SUPPORT THE BLACK GEMA GEMA GANG!

CONTINUED ON
NEXT PAGE

THE BLACK GEMA GEMA GANG SUPPORT FUND

In order to continue with their plans to save Planet Analogue, the poor Black Gema Gema Gang first needs food in their tummies! How can an evil organization survive without money?

That's why they need your help. Buying Black Gema Gema Gang merchandise from Anime Gamers supports the troops that have worked so hard at capturing Princess Di Gi Charat. Maybe one day, with your help, they can succeed!

Coo's fleece cap

normal - $16.95

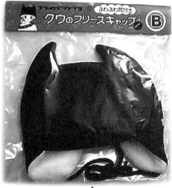

fluffy - $24.95

B.G.G.G. arm band

In small or large - $9.95

Piyoko's nurse cap

$32.50

PKO wrist band and finger wrap

In black or red - $11.95 each

zipper holders

ファスナーマスコット
P·K·O
Pyocola Keeping Operations

PKO
$4.95

Pyocola Analogue III
Di Gi Charat with Her Friends
ファスナーホルダー

Piyoko
mascot
$4.50

cellphone straps

Di Gi Charat

Piyoko
charm
$7.95

Pyocola
Analogue III
Pyocola Analogue III

Piyoko mascot
$11.95

P·K·O
Pyocola Keeping Operations
STRAP

PKO (in red or black)
$6.50 each

HMMM... THEY
EVEN HAVE
KEYCHAINS.

There's even more accessories on the website!

Get your ~~Di Gi Charat~~ Black Gema Gema Gang merchandise at:

www.animegamers.com

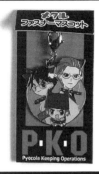

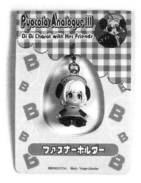

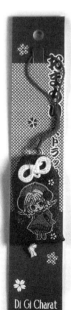

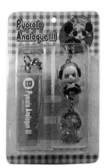

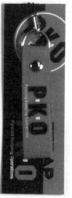

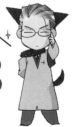

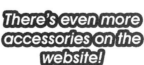

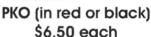

B.G.G.G. bags

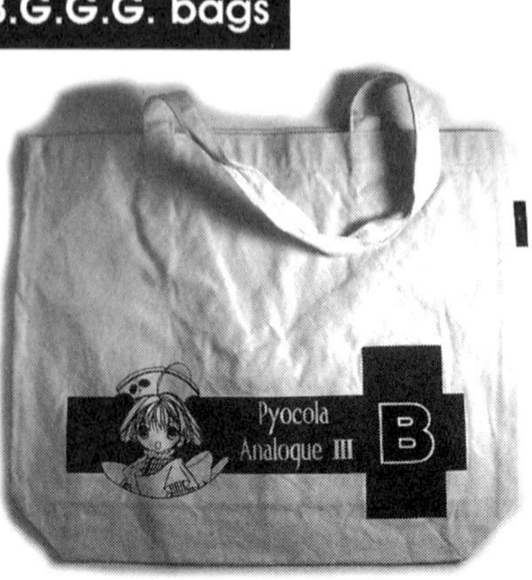
Pyocola
Analoque III
B

Piyoko tote
$19.95

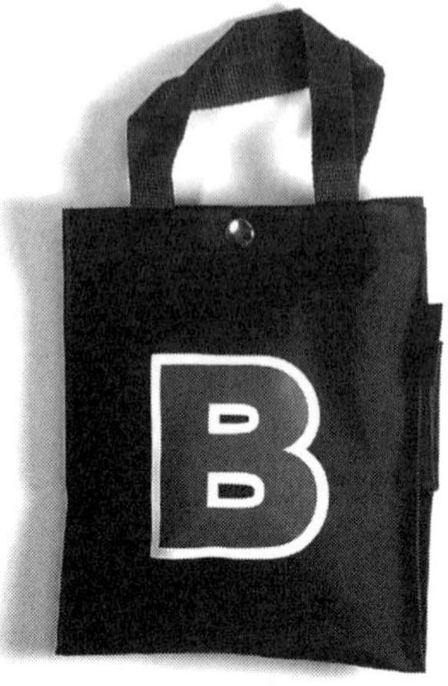
B

Mini tote $24.95

pillows

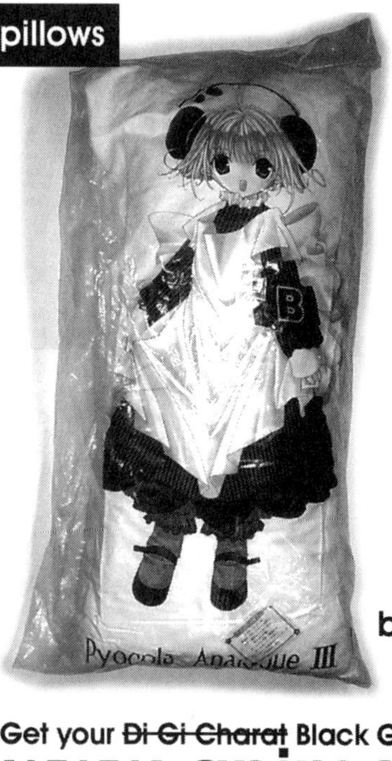
B
Pyocola Analoque III

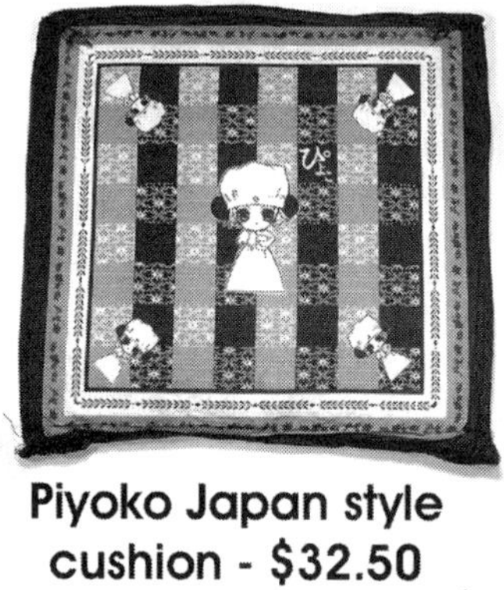

Piyoko Japan style
cushion - $32.50

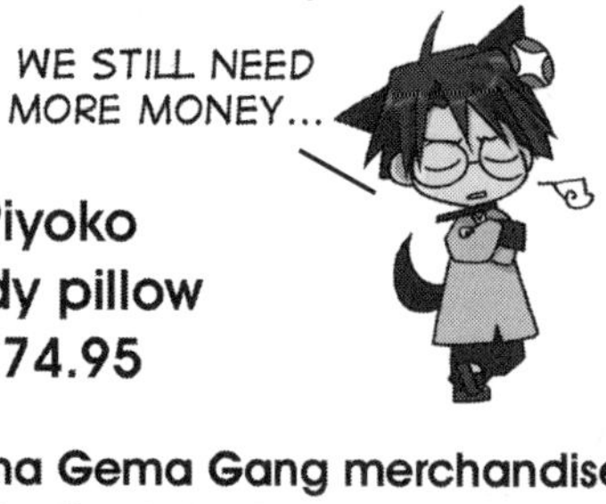
WE STILL NEED
MORE MONEY...

Piyoko
body pillow
$74.95

Get your ~~Di Gi Charat~~ Black Gema Gema Gang merchandise at:

www.animegamers.com

Leave it to Piyoko!

Join the celebration!

Di Gi Charat Theater - Leave it to Piyoko!, starring none other than Pyocola-sama, is coming out!

Support us, the Black Gema Gema Gang and our mission to save Planet Analogue by buying the manga!!

Coming soon to your local bookstores!

© HINA. 2002
© BROCCOLI 2002

© 2004 BROCCOLI
First published in 2002 by Media Works Inc., Tokyo, Japan. English
translation rights arranged with Media Works Inc. through BROCCOLI Co., Ltd

brought to you by
BROCCOLI BOOKS
www.broccolibooks.com

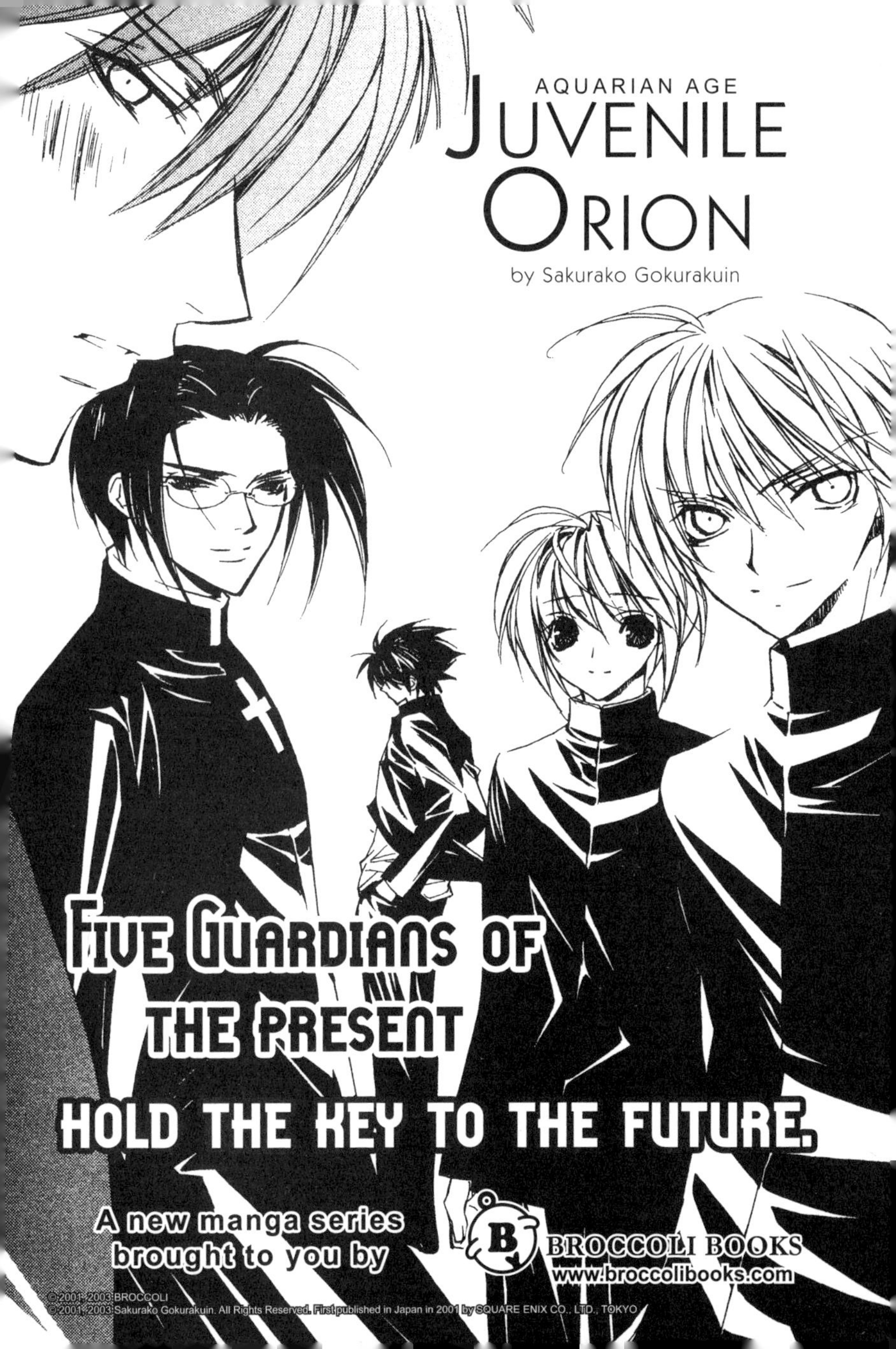

AQUARIAN AGE

JUVENILE ORION

by Sakurako Gokurakuin

FIVE GUARDIANS OF THE PRESENT

HOLD THE KEY TO THE FUTURE.

A new manga series
brought to you by

BROCCOLI BOOKS
www.broccolibooks.com

FIVE ANGELS

AT YOUR SERVICE!

When the going gets tough...
the tough get Angels!

Galaxy Angel
by Kanan

It's up to five lovely females, each possessing a unique specialty, to protect the young Prince Shiva and save the universe!

A new manga series brought to you by

B BROCCOLI BOOKS
www.broccolibooks.com

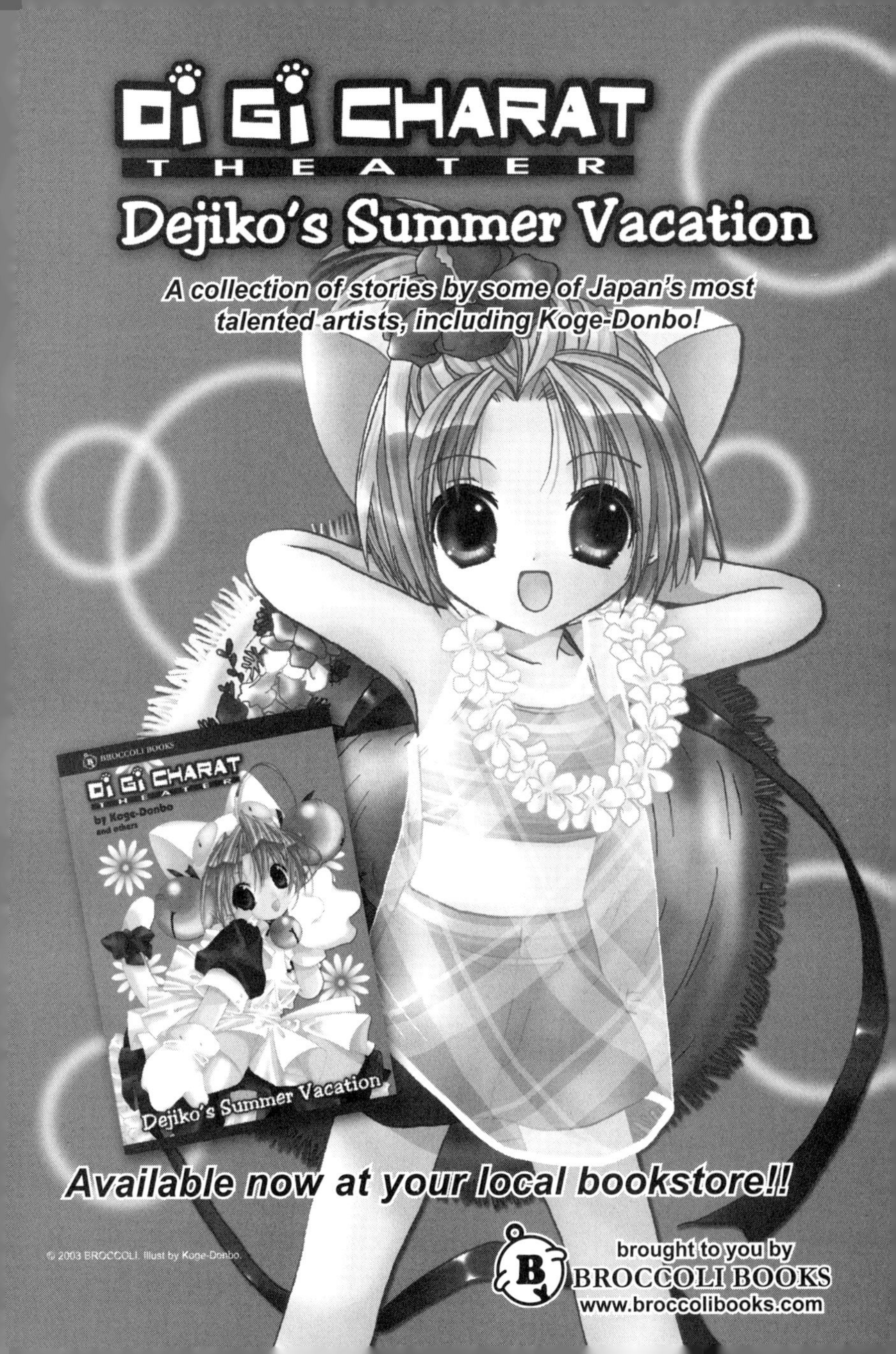
DI GI CHARAT
THEATER
Dejiko's Summer Vacation
A collection of stories by some of Japan's most talented artists, including Koge-Donbo!
BROCCOLI BOOKS
DI GI CHARAT
THEATER
by Koge-Donbo
and others
Dejiko's Summer Vacation
Available now at your local bookstore!!
© 2003 BROCCOLI. Illust by Koge-Donbo.
brought to you by
BROCCOLI BOOKS
www.broccolibooks.com

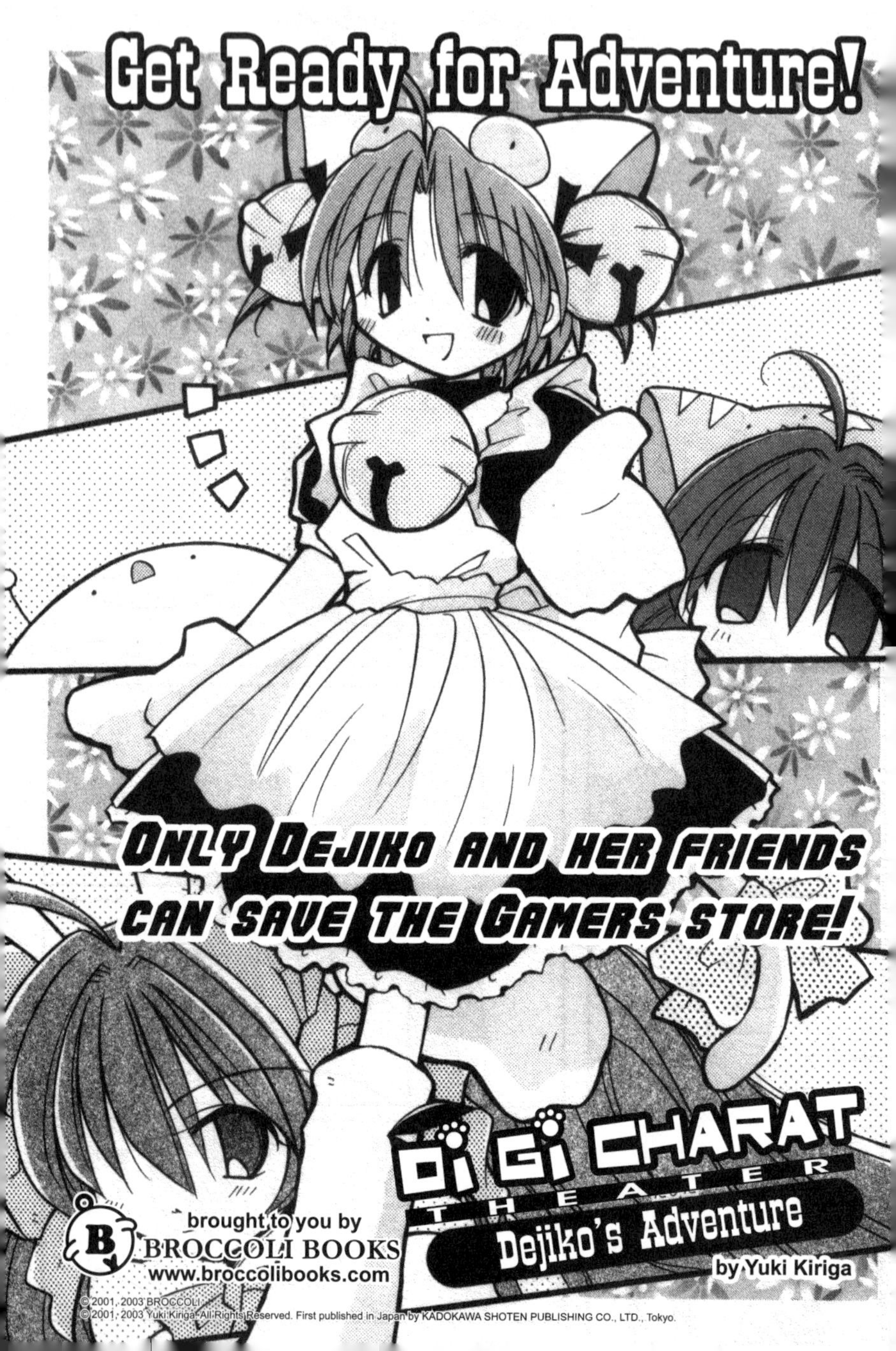
Get Ready for Adventure!
ONLY DEJIKO AND HER FRIENDS CAN SAVE THE GAMERS STORE!
DI GI CHARAT THEATER
Dejiko's Adventure
by Yuki Kiriga
brought to you by
BROCCOLI BOOKS
www.broccolibooks.com
© 2001, 2003 BROCCOLI
© 2001, 2003 Yuki Kiriga. All Rights Reserved. First published in Japan by KADOKAWA SHOTEN PUBLISHING CO., LTD., Tokyo.

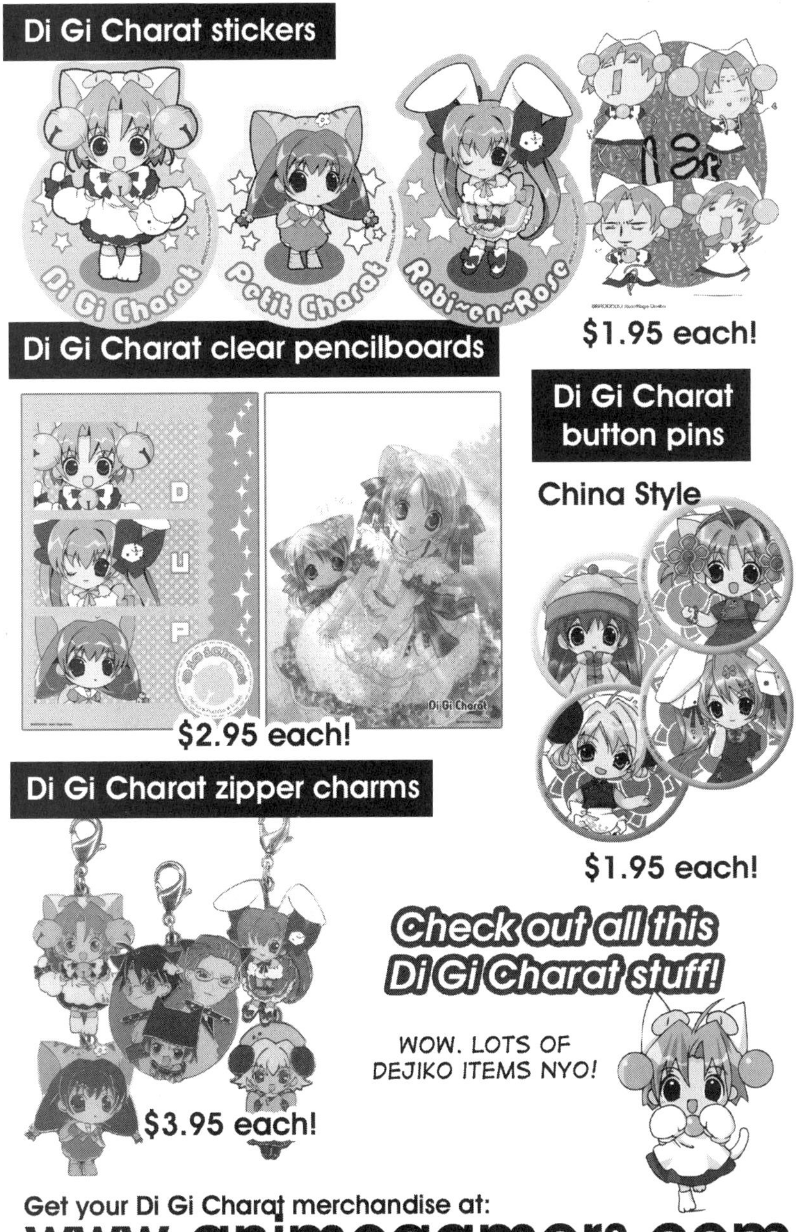
Di Gi Charat stickers
Di Gi Charat
Petit Charat
Rabi~en~Rose
$1.95 each!
Di Gi Charat clear pencilboards
D
U
P
Di Gi Charat
$2.95 each!
Di Gi Charat button pins
China Style
$1.95 each!
Di Gi Charat zipper charms
$3.95 each!
Check out all this Di Gi Charat stuff!
WOW. LOTS OF DEJIKO ITEMS NYO!
Get your Di Gi Charat merchandise at:
www.animegamers.com

READ:: POINT:: CLICK.::

broccolibooks.com

After reading some Broccoli Books manga, why not look for more on the web?
Discuss with other fans in the forums, check the production staff blog and MORE!

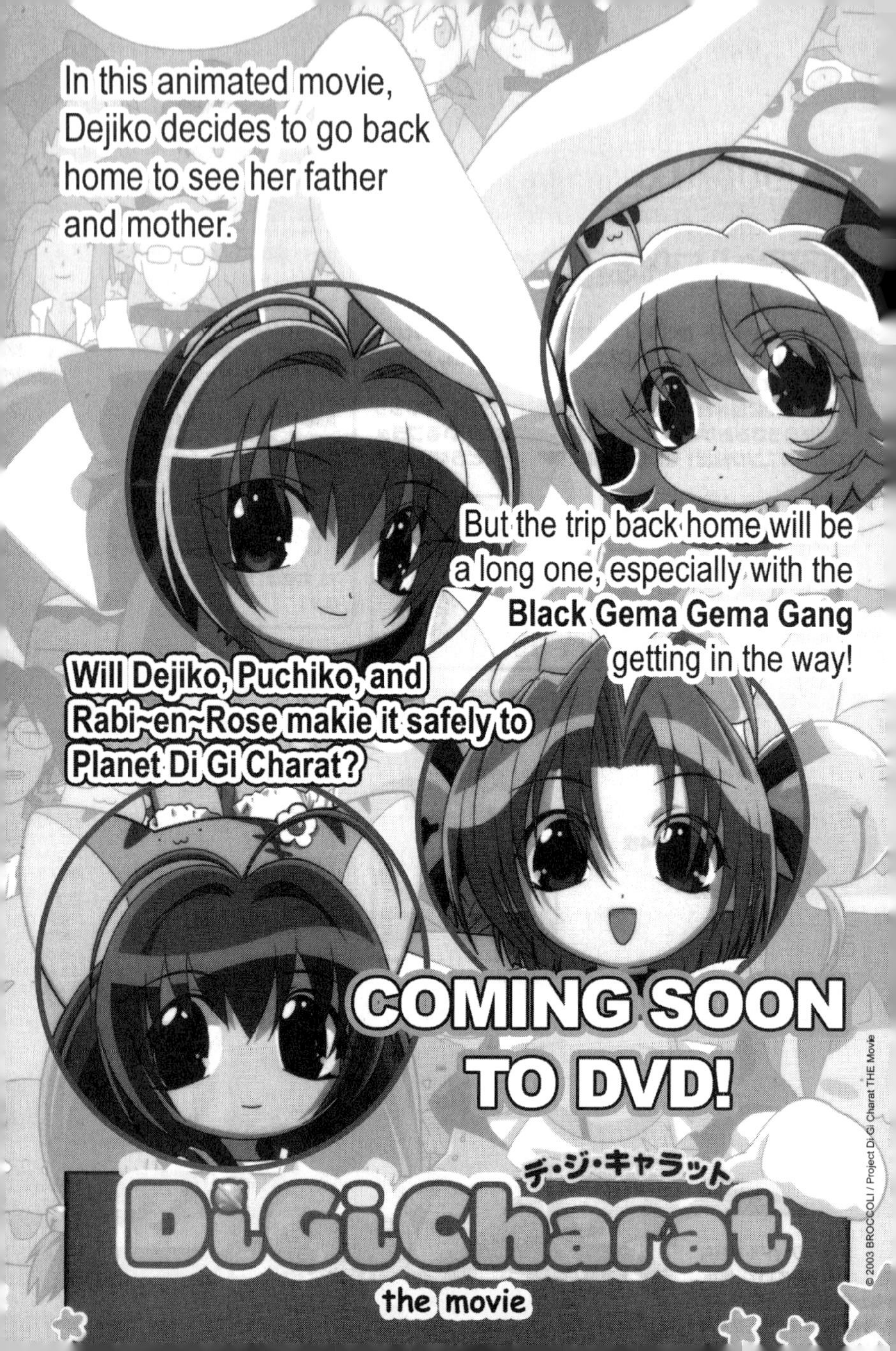
In this animated movie, Dejiko decides to go back home to see her father and mother.
But the trip back home will be a long one, especially with the Black Gema Gema Gang getting in the way!
Will Dejiko, Puchiko, and Rabi~en~Rose makie it safely to Planet Di Gi Charat?
COMING SOON TO DVD!
デ・ジ・キャラット
Di Gi Charat
the movie
© 2003 BROCCOLI / Project Di Gi Charat THE Movie

THIS IS COOL.

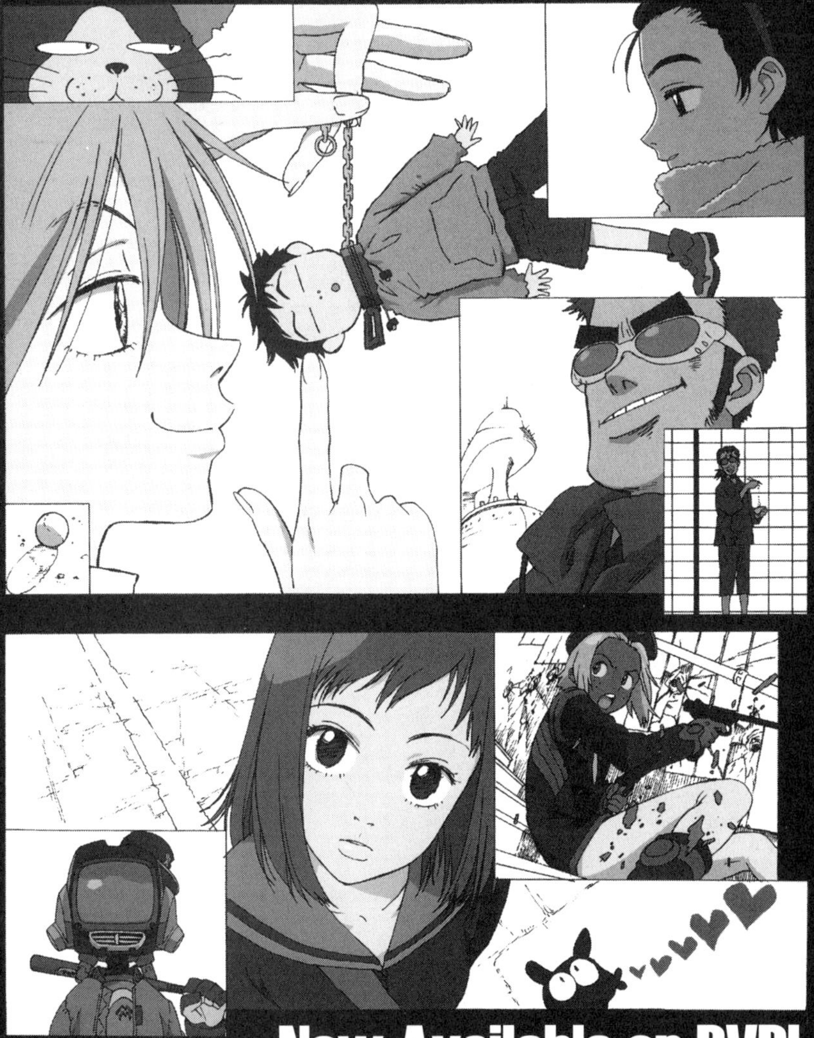

FLCL © GAINAX/KGI.

Now Available on DVD!

STOP!
YOU'RE READING THE WRONG WAY!

This is the end of the book! In Japan, manga is generally read from right to left. All reading starts on the upper right corner, and ends on the lower left. American comics are generally read from left to right, starting on the upper left of each page. In order to preserve the true nature of the work, we printed this book in a right to left fashion. Those who are unfamiliar with manga may find this confusing at first, but once you start getting into the story, you will wonder how you ever read manga any other way!